THE YOGASŪTRAS OF PATAÑJALI
On Concentration of Mind

The Yogasūtras of Patañjali

ON CONCENTRATION OF MIND

FERNANDO TOLA
CARMEN DRAGONETTI

Translated into English from the revised Original Spanish by
K.D. PRITHIPAUL

MOTILAL BANARSIDASS PUBLISHERS
PRIVATE LIMITED • DELLHI

First Edition: Delhi, 1987
Reprint: Delhi, 1991, 1995, 2001

ISBN: 81-208-0258-6 (Cloth)
ISBN: 81-208-0259-4 (Paper)

Also available at:
MOTILAL BANARSIDASS
41 U.A. Bungalow Road, Jawahar Nagar, Delhi 110 007
8 Mahalaxmi Chamber, Warden Road, Mumbai 400 026
120 Royapettah High Road, Mylapore, Chennai 600 004
236, 9th Main III Block, Jayanagar, Bangalore 560 011
Sanas Plaza, 1302 Baji Rao Road, Pune 411 002
8 Camac Street, Kolkata 700 017
Ashok Rajpath, Patna 800 004
Chowk, Varanasi 221 001

Printed in India
BY JAINENDRA PRAKASH JAIN AT SHRI JAINENDRA PRESS,
A-45 NARAINA, PHASE-I, NEW DELHI 110 028 AND
PUBLISHED BY NARENDRA PRAKASH JAIN FOR
MOTILAL BANARSIDASS PUBLISHERS PRIVATE LIMITED,
BUNGALOW ROAD, DELHI 110 007

For our beloved daughters and sons

FERNANDO

JOSE MIGUEL

FRANCISCO

SHRUTI ELENA

ELEONORA

FLORENCIA CARMEN

CONTENTS

INTRODUCTION

The Philosophical Systems (darśana) of India

In India one comes across six *darśanas* or orthodox systems of philosophy : *Vedānta* or *Uttara-Mīmāṃsā*, *Pūrva Mīmāṃsā*, *Sāṃkhya*, *Yoga*, *Nyāya* and *Vaiśeṣika*. These systems recognize the brahminical or priestly tradition and are recognized by it.

Besides these orthodox systems, there are others, which are heterodox, such as the system of the *cārvākas*, that of the Buddhists, etc. These systems do not recognize the brahminical or priestly tradition, and are rejected by it.[1]

Each of the systems mentioned owns a basic text. There are commentaries and commentaries of commentaries or sub-commentaries for each of them. Generally, on account of its quality and ancientness, one of these commentaries succeeds in forming a unity with the text upon which it is commenting. It then acquires a great authority for interpretation of that text.

The Yogasūtras

The *Yogasūtras*, the authorship of which is unanimously attributed by Indian tradition to Patañjali, constitute the basic text of the orthodox philosophical system of *Yoga*.[2]

1. For the systems referred to in this section consult the works of S. N. Dasgupta, S. Radhakrishnan, J. Sinha, C. D. Sharma, Max Müller, Masson-Oursel, von Glasenapp, mentioned in the bibliography.

2. *Rāja Yoga* and *Haṭha Yoga* are the two main schools of Yoga. The basic texts of *Rāja Yoga* are the *Yogasūtras* of Patañjali, the *Yoga-bhāṣya* of Vyāsa, the *Tattvavaiśāradī* of Vācaspati Miśra, to which reference will be made in this work. The *Haṭha Yoga* is the Yoga formulated by the famous yogin Gorakṣanātha who lived *circa* 1200 A.D. He is the founder of the *Śaiva* sect of the *Gorakṣanāthīs*. The basic texts of this school are the *Gorakṣa-śataka* or *Gorakṣapaddhati* of this yogin; the *Haṭhayogapradīpikā* of Svātmā-rāma Yogīndra of the 15th century and the later *Gheraṇḍasaṃhitā* and the *Śivasaṃhitā*. *Rāja Yoga* is fundamentally concerned with mental control, while *Haṭha Yoga* lays greater emphasis on the discipline of the body.

The *Yogasūtras* are one of the most important works of Indian culture. This is so partly on account of their intrinsic worth as a masterly analysis of trance and as an equally masterly description of the method by which it is reached. Its importance derives also from its being the foundational text of *Yoga*, the system which plays a basic role in the culture of India. Indeed a knowledge of this system is necessary to understand the highly varied expressions of Indian culture, including those which like Buddhism, reject the orthodox brahminical tradition.[3]

The *Yogasūtras* do not give the impression of being a unitary text. Contradictions are found among different parts, and often the union of several sections seems contrived so that one may be inclined to think either that the *Yogasūtras* are not an original work and are actually composed in their entirety of texts derived from a plurality of sources, texts juxtaposed and unified, in some way, by the compiler of the work, in the form in which we have them today, or that the original work was an object of more or less extensive interpolations, more or less in contradiction with the doctrine of the original. Unfortunately, it is impossible to express a firmly established opinion with regard to the form of the composition of the *Yogasūtras*.[4]

Patañjali

According to Indian tradition, Patañjali, the author of the great commentary of the grammatical aphorisms of *Pāṇini* (4th century B.C.) who lived in the second century B.C., would also be the author of the *Yogasūtras*.

But the more widely held view nowadays is that there are two Patañjalis—one the grammarian and the other the yogin,

3. As a matter of fact the influence of Yoga in Buddhism does not stem from the *Yogasūtras* but from the pre-Pātañjala form of yoga. In relation to the importance which Yoga has for Buddhism, see É. Sénart, "Bouddhisme *et Yoga*", "*Origines Bouddhiques*"; Beckh, *Buddhismus*, II, pp. 10 and ff; Heiler, *Die Buddhistische Versenkung;* Masson-Oursel, *Esquisse*, p. 184; de la Vallée-Poussin, *Nirvāṇa*, p. 11.

4. Deussen, *Allgemeine Geschichte der Philosophie*, 3rd. edition I, pp. 507 and ff: Hauer, *Der Yoga*, pp. 223 and ff; von Glasenapp, *Die Philosophie*, p. 222. Bronkhorst, "Patañjali and the Yoga Sūtras", and *The Two Traditions of Meditation in Ancient India*, pp. 67-70; Feuerstein, *The Yoga Sūtra*, pp. 36-89.

author of the *Yogasūtras*—and that Patañjali the Yogin lived between 300 and 500 A.D.[5]

Indian as well as Western scholars generally consider that Patañjali was not the creator of *Yoga,* which had existed well before him. Patañjali had only restricted himself to writing a systematic exposition of it. Moreover, it is also considered that Patañjali was not the first author who wrote about *Yoga.* Others did so before him. He used their works in the composition of his treatise. But, as it often happens, his text caused the others to be forgotten and became itself the classic and basic text of the system.[6]

It behoves us to make a few remarks regarding the opinions referred to in the preceding paragraphs.

In view of the results obtained by philological criticism, it seems that it is not possible to conclude that the *Yogasūtras* would have been written by Patañjali the Grammarian, as the Indian tradition would have it. But there exists a solid reason to think that the author of the *Yogasūtras,* in conformity with Western criticism, was another author also called Patañjali. Although it is certainly possible that the *Yogasūtras* would have been composed by a second Patañjali of the period between 300 and 500 A.D., and that subsequently the Indian tradition identified this second Patañjali with Patañjali the Grammarian of the second century B.C., in agreement with the opinions of the Western critics, likewise it is certainly equally possible that the *Yogasūtras* would have been composed by an author *whose name is not known* and they would have later been attributed, by Indian tradition, to Patañjali the Grammarian. There would be nothing strange in this view as in India the works of forgotten or second-rate authors are not infrequently attributed to

5. Jacboi, "*The dates of the philosophical Sūtras of the Brahmans*", pp. 583-584; Woods, *The Yoga System*, pp. xiii-xix; M. Eliade, *Yoga*, pp. 376-378; von Glasenapp, *Die Philosophie*, pp. 221-222; Keith, *Sāṃkhya*, pp. 69-70; Frauwallner, *Geschichte* I, p. 285; Hauer, *Der Yoga*, p. 223; Winternitz, *History* III, 2, p. 517. Renou, "On the Identity of the two Patañjalis"; Bhattacharya, *An Introduction to the Yogasūtra*, pp. 94-97.

6. Rāmaśaṅkarabhaṭṭācārya, *Pātañjalayogadarśanam*, p. 28; Hauer, *Der Yoga*, pp. 19-220; M. Eliade, *Yoga*, III-VIII.

authors of the first rank.

On the other hand, if the *Yogasūtras* are held to be works of compilation, then Patañjali (or the unknown author) would not be the author. He would only be the compiler of the *Yogasūtras*. And if we accept that the *Yogasūtras* contain many interpolations, then Patañjali (or the unknown author) would be the author of the central nucleus, to the exclusion of the interpolations or, it could be the opposite : Patañjali would be the author of the interpolations, with the corresponding central nucleus attributed to another equally anonymous author.

Nevertheless, without the prejudice of the faregoing and in the absence of elements of a judgment which can help elucidate with absolute certainty the questions raised in the preceding paragraphs, we shall continue to abide by the established practice and continue to call Patañjali the author of the *Yogasūtras* and we shall consider him as the author of the entire text.

The Contents of the Yogasūtras

The *Yogasūtras* comprise four books with the following titles :

1. *Of Samādhi* (concentration of mind); 2. *Of Sādhana* (method); 3. *Of the Siddhis* (magic powers); and 4. *Of Kaivalya* (isolation of the spirit). They consist of a totality of 195 *sūtras*, or brief aphorisms.

Three elements go into the constitution of the *Yogasūtras* :

1. An experiential element made up of (a) the method which produces the *samādhi*, by means of which the complete and absolute *cittavṛtti-nirodha* (cessation of thought process) will in its turn be attained, and (b) the process which occurs in the mind while this cessation is being produced.
2. A supernatural element made up of the *siddhis* acquired by the yogin in the course of his practices, but which do not constitute his ultimate goal.
3. A speculative element constituted by the *Sāṃkhya* doctrine, the philosophical foundation of the yoga of Patañjali and which comes through in many of the aphorisms of the *Yogasūtras*.

The Restraint of the Mental Process and the Method by which it is Attained

The total and absolute restraint of the mental functions constitutes the yogic trance. With this restraint the mind empties itself of all contents, it becomes still in a complete quietude. The senses then do not receive the messages coming from the external world, the faculties stop functioning, the conceptualizing activity comes to a halt.

The main aspects of the yogic method which produces the cessation of the mental functions or the trance are the following. At the outset the yogin must of necessity submit himself to an ascetic discipline (*tapas*) which weakens or annihilates his natural impulses; he must free himself from all attachment and destroy in himself all desire, all craving for and interest in things (*vairāgya*). Besides this, the yogin shall practise breath control (*prāṇāyāma*). With the exercise of breath control he determines the number of inhalings and exhaling, their duration as well as the duration of holding air in the lungs, the volume of air inhaled. All this is done for the purpose of reducing the function of breathing to the minimum possible. The reduction of air received by the organism will necessarily affect the brain and will result in the reduction of mental activity, both in volume and intensity, and also in the diminishing of the vital manifestations to the minimum (circulation of blood, sensibility etc.) leading the yogin into a cataleptic comatose state, close to extinction. It is a state which has been compared to the hibernation of certain animals. This enables the yogins to remain buried for many hours with a reduced volume of air.[7]

7. The physiological phenomena which accompany the yogic practices have been studied by Ch. Laubry and Th. Brosse, "Documents receuillis" and Th. Brosse, *Études Instrumentales.* The All India Institute of Medical Sciences also has studied these phenomena (see *Times of India* June 29/69). Moreover, more than twenty disciples of Mahesh Yogi have been examined for the same purpose by three researchers in New Delhi (see *Times of India* May 27/69). See also Evans-Wentz, *Tibetan Yoga*, p. 27 and M. Eliade, *Yoga*, p. 57. For other references see: *Altered States of Consciousness, Altered States of Awareness,* and the articles of B. K. Anand and others; B. Bagchi and M. Wenger; N. Das and H. Gastaut; A. Kasamatsu and T. Hirai; A. Kasamatsu

Finally, the yogin will concentrate his mind on a determined entity. For example, he will fix his sight and his attention on a luminous point.[8] The mental function or process made up of this intensified perception will eliminate little by little all the other processes. The more intense the concentration, the greater the restraint of the mental functions. When the concentration has reached its highest stage, the restraint would have equally attained its highest stage. Then the yogin enters what is called the trance. We believe that the yogic trance, as any other mystical trance, is a *sui generis* phenomenon, although similar and related in many of its aspects to hypnotism, to catalepsy, and to hysteria.

The Magic Powers

As an example of these powers we have : the knowledge of the previous existences, the knowledge of the thoughts of others, the invisibility of the body, the knowledge of the moment of death, the cessation of hunger and of thirst, and the "*perfections*" or faculties of the yogin who can reduce or increase his size, levitate, reach the moon with the hand, penetrate the earth and emerge from it as if it is water, master the elements, the vision of divine beings, etc.[9]

Naturally it is a matter of auto-suggestions and hallucinations on the part of the yogin and, in many cases, of sensations which

---

and others; R. K. Wallace and H. Benson; R. K. Wallace; R. K. Wallace and others; M. Wenger and others, mentioned all of them in *References*. For the corresponding phenomena in Christian mystics, see Underhill, *Mysticism*, pp. 329, 359, 360 and 377.

8. The object on which the yogin fixes his attention can be of a varied nature: the rhythmic noise like the ticking of a clock; the repetition of the sacred syllable *aum;* the image or the idea of a favourite divinity; a sentiment —such as love—for the divinity etc.

9. See Patañjali, *Yogasūtras* III.16-25 with the commentaries of Vyāsa and Vācaspati Miśra, and also J. Daniélou, *Yoga*, pp. 137-145; M. Eliade, *Yoga*, pp. 85-90; Śivānanda, *Kuṇḍalinī Yoga*, pp. 139-143. For a physiological explanation of the experience of levitation and of the variation of heat in the body as the effect of autogenous training (which has many points in common with Yoga), see Schultz, *El Entrenamiento Autógeno*, pp. 284 and 96-98 respectively.

are truly experienced by him and interpreted on a supernatural level.

The Speculative Element

The speculative element of the Yoga of Patañjali is constituted by the *Sāṃkhya* system. What follows is a summary of this doctrine.

According to *Sāṃkhya* there exists a primordial matter (*prakṛti*) from which originates the totality of the material reality. The mind is part of this material reality. Beside the matter (*prakṛti*) stands spirit (*puruṣa*) though in truth we should say the *puruṣas* as the *Sāṃkhya* maintains the existence of an infinite number of *puruṣas*, spirits, individual souls. The nature of *prakṛti* is absolutely different from that of *puruṣa*. *Prakṛti* is the first cause. *Puruṣa* is neither cause nor effect. *Prakṛti* is active; *puruṣa* is inactive. *Prakṛti* is devoid of consciousness; *puruṣa* is conscious. *Prakṛti* is in constant mutation; *puruṣa* is immutable. *Prakṛti* is the object of knowledge; *puruṣa* is the subject of knowledge. *Puruṣa*, the spirit, incarnate in an individual being, comes into contact with the external material world by means of the mind and of its functions or processes.

There exists, in the normal state of the individual, an identification between the embodied individual spirit and the mental processes. On one hand the embodied individual spirit appears as if it were the mental processes, and manifests itself in the from of the said processes. On the other hand, the spirit identifies itself with and thinks itself to be these said processes.

While this false identification persists, the individual embodied spirit remains in bondage to error and to ignorance. What follows from this identification and from the error that arises out of it are suffering and the realization of those actions which will bear the consequences or the fruit of maintaining the spirit shackled to matter. An expression of this enslavement to matter is the series of reincarnations to which the spirit is subjected.

To free itself from suffering and from the reincarnations the *puruṣa* must cease to identify itself with the mental processes, disentangle itself from them, return to its pristine and essential purity, isolate itself from matter and all its manifestations, among which are, as we have said, the mind and its functions. Its goal must be *kaivalya* or isolation.

Kaivalya can be attained only by the practice of Yoga[10] the culmination of which consists in the cessation of the thought processes. It is clear why Yoga lays so much emphasis on the restraint and elimination of the mental processes : *puruṣa* is mixed, confused with them. By eliminating these processes, one after the other, the *puruṣa* will stand out at the end, by the method of elimination, free and alone in its total and absolute purity.[11]

Yoga and Christian Mysticism

The yogic trance bears strong similarities to Christian mystical trance. We may even dare think that they are essentially the same, since both consist fundamentally of the cessation of the mental processes or the emptiness of consciousness. Moreover, the methods which produce both trances are equally similar. For this reason precisely we dare assert that they are fundamentally the same, since both have a purificative stage and a contemplative stage.[12] Finally, both yoga and Christian Mysticism admit

10. As Max Müller has so aptly observed, in *The Six Systems* (p. 309), the aim and end of Yoga is not to *unite*, as is generally believed, but to *dis-unite*, to separate, to isolate the *puruṣa* from *prakṛti*, giving back to him his essential and original purity. It is only in the other forms of mysticism (as referred to in note 11) which make use of Yoga, that the latter has *union* as its end.

11. In agreement with the *Sāṃkhya-Yoga*, the isolation of the spirit occurs in the state of trance. The other forms of Indian mysticism which have used the method to produce the trance described by Patañjali, have constructed for trance an interpretation which conforms to their philosophical postulates. Thus, according to the *Vedānta*, in trance, the individual soul, by freeing itself from the veil of ignorance, appears in its primal, authentic and pure state of identity with *Brahman*, the Absolute; for the schools which follow the *bhakti-mārga*, or the way of divine love, the mystical union of the individual soul with God is realized in trance.

12. As a technique of trance, Yoga can, in principle, be used by any mysticism, on account of its high level of theoretical and practical development, the transparence of its analysis, and the explanation of the path to

the belief in such supernatural phenomena, concomitant with trance, as levitation, the ability to transport oneself to great distances, visions etc.

On the one hand, all that precedes follows clearly from a comparative study of Patañjali's treatise, of its commentators, and of the descriptions made by the yogins of India of their own experiences. On the other hand, it comes from the treatises of Christian Mysticism and of the descriptions given by the Christian mystics of their respctive experiences.[13] In accord with the distinct, fundamental philosophical-religious presuppositions of Yoga and of Christian Mysticism, the difference lies in the interpretations of trance. In the Yogic trance, there occurs the separation of the spirit (*puruṣa*) from matter, the isolation (*kaivalya*) of the spirit. For Christian Mysticism, there occurs in trance the union of individual soul with God.

Yoga is a Mysticism

Patañjali's Yoga is a mysticism since, in conformity with the preceding explanations, we do find in it the essential elements constitutive of any mysticism: a) trance (*nirodha*), b) a method to produce the trance (*tapas, vairāgya, samādhi*), c) the conviction that in trance there occurs a transcendent experience (*kaivalya*). We have already referred to these elements.

---

follow to attain trance. Also on account of the independence which the yogic technique has with regard to its philosophical postulates, which precisely enables it to be adapted to any mystical system whatsoever. Of course every form of mysticism will give of trance an interpretation that fits in with its own philosophical or religious postulates.

13. For the trance and the method which produces it and for the belief in the supernatural phenomena in Christian Mysticism, see: Underhill, *Mysticism*, Part II, Ch. III: the Purification of the Self; Ch. IV: Voices and Visions; Ch. V: Introversion: Part I: Recollection and Quiet; Ch. VII, Introversion: Part II: Contemplation; and Ch. VIII: Ecstasy and Rapture; Arintero, *La Evolución mística*, pp. 598-602; and the studies of J. Bernhart, A. Cuvillier, J. M. Dechanet, E. Gilson, P. Humbertclaude, H. Hatzfeld, F. D. Joret, R. de Maumigny, A.-M. Meynard, S. Siddheswarananda, R. Thibaut, W. Völker, and the works of Bonaventura, L.de la Palma, Dionysius, Meister Eckhart, Saint Francois de Sales, San Juan de la Cruz. M.de Molinos, Santa Taresa de Jesús, all of which are included in our *References*.

Commentaries and Commentators of the Yogasūtras

The *Yogasūtras* of Patañjali have been commented upon[14] on many occasions.[15] The oldest and most important of the commentaries and commentators are the following :

1. The *Yogabhāṣya* of between 650 and 850 A.D., attributed to Vyāsa. It is the fundamental commentary of the *Yogasūtras.*
2. The *Rājamārtaṇḍa* of Bhoja, 11th century A.D.
3. The *Maṇiprabhā* of Rāmānanda Sarasvatī, 7th century A.D.
4. The *Vṛtti* of Nāgeśa or Nāgoji Bhaṭṭa, early 18th century A.D.
5. The *Candrikā* or *Vṛtti* of Nārāyaṇa Tīrtha, end of 18th century A.D.

The commentary of Vyāsa has in its turn various commentaries and commentators, the most ancient and important of which are the following :

A. Vācaspati Miśra, middle of the 9th century A.D. wrote a sub-commentary called *Tattvavaiśāradī,* which is as important as that of Vyāsa.

B. The sub-commentary *Pātañjalayogasūtrabhāṣyavivaraṇa* is attributed to Śaṅkara of the 8th century A.D. But there are reasons to doubt that Śaṅkara was actually the author of this sub-commentary.

C. Vijñānabhikṣu who lived at the beginning of the 12th century is the author of the sub-commentary called *Yogavārtika*. Vijñānabhikṣu is also the author of a small text,

14. Rāmaśaṅkarabhaṭṭācārya, *Pātañjalalayogadarśanam* pp. 45-76; Woods, *The Yoga System*, pp. xx-xxiii; Hauer, *Der Yoga,* pp. 265-268, 272; M. Eliade, *Yoga,* p. 372; Potter, *Bibliography,* pp. 17-22; Aufrecht, *Catalogus* I, p. 480; II, p. 219; III, p. 103.

15. In a general sense, a Sanskrit work usually has one or several commentaries which are edited jointly with it. These commentaries clarify the meaning of the words, give the direct order of the sentences, criticise the grammatical constructions, explain the doctrine, quote the parallel texts, establish each passage in its proper relation to the rest of the work, etc.

called *Yogasārasaṃgraha*, which expounds in a systematic way the teachings of Patañjali, according to the interpretation of Vyāsa.

In addition to the commentaries and commentators mentioned earlier, there exist others, ancient and modern, which in a general sense, follow the Vyāsa's line of interpretation.

Appreciation of the Commentaries

The commentaries and the commentators mentioned earlier explain the *Yogasūtras* on the basis of the *Sāṃkhya* doctrines. These doctrines constitute in the main a philosophical system constructed *a priori* in which speculation, not the observation of facts, occupies the greater part.

It is necessary to refer to the *Sāṃkhya* doctrine to understand a series of the aphorisms, where Patañjali has recourse to concepts, expressions or doctrines specific to the *Sāṃkhya*, as for example I.3 which says that "the seer establishes himself in his own nature" to describe the total restraint of the mental processes. This *sūtra* can be understood only in the light of the *Sāṃkhya* doctrines which have been described earlier. That is, there exists a matter (*prakṛti*) from which everything is derived, including the mind with its processes; that there exists, in contradistinction to matter, the spirit (*puruṣa*), which is totally different and separate from it; that spirit is bound to matter while identifying itself with it, above all, with the mental processes. The seer is the spirit which recovers its pristine and original purity when it isolates itself from the mental processes.

In these cases the commentaries and sub-commentaries are very useful for they constitute a constant source of information about the history of philosophy in India.

But there are other *sūtras* where Patañjali confines himself to describing and analyzing, in an objective and subtle way, facts of experience. Such *sūtras* are for example those which describe the different stages of the yogic process which lead to trance (*Yogasūtra* I. 17-22, 35-51). To understand these *sūtras* the explanations supplied by the commentators are not only of no great usefulness but often these very explanations, based on

Sāṃkhya speculations, turn out to be, in their turn, mere speculations. They do not elucidate the actual facts described and analyzed by Patañjali. On the contrary, they cloud them and constrain them to conform to the doctrines on which they are founded. Thus they contribute to the elimination of the worth which these descriptions and analyses of Patañjali have for the objectivity and the subtle observation of the facts to which they refer.

Criteria for an Interpretation of the Yogasūtras of Patañjali

The criteria to which we continually refer are those which we have applied in our translation and commentary of the first book of Patañjali's *Yogasūtras* which we now offer. These criteria were established gradually as we proceeded in our study of the *Yogasūtras* and after repeated attempts and exercises in interpretation. The application of these criteria explains the differences which exist between our interpretation and the traditional Indian and European interpretations and it enables, we think, to redeem the original meaning of the *Aphorisms* of Patañjali, from disfigurement under the layers of the later commentaries and of the interpretatians deriving more from these commentaries than from the very text of Patañjali.

In a general sense, in agreement with the contents of footnote 15th and with the preceding section, the interpretation of the *Yogasūtras* requires the use of the commentaries and sub-commentaries which we mentioned earlier, but without submitting oneself to them. They must be our auxiliaries, not our guides. Just as for the interpretation of the *Vedas* philological criticism makes use of the ancient commentaries, like that of *Sāyaṇa*, but without adhering blindly to what they affirm, in the same way we believe that it is necessary, for the interpretation of the *Yogasūtras*, to use the commentaries and sub-commentaries, but with prudence and freedom.

Moreover, in dealing with those *sūtras* in which Patañjali describes and analyzes real phenomena, it is necessary to interpret them not within the perspective of the *Sāṃkhya* speculation but as what they actually are: descriptions of facts of experience. To such an end it is necessary at the outset to have a clear idea of the phenomena to which Patañjali refers. In the pursuit of this task we do find it extremely useful to consider the descriptions which the yogis af India or the Christian mystics make of their experiences and the comparative study of these. Once we have succeeded in understanding the phenomena referred to by Patañjali we shall be able to explain the *sūtras* in which they are described and analyzed, in terms of the said phenomena. This mode of operation—from the phenomenon to the *sūtra*—becomes imperative on account of the *Yogasūtras* being a technical treatise on trance and not a work of a strict philosophical speculation. An explanation of the *sūtras* conforming to the reality of the facts will enable us to have a better understanding of the importance of Patañjali's work as a profound description and analysis of trance and of the method which leads to it.

On the other hand, we must adhere to a unitary and singular meaning for the technical terms of Patañjali, avoiding in this manner the translation of the same term in various ways in the different *aphorisms* in which it occurs. This principle can be rigorously applied within the scope of the First Book. That is to say, when a technical term appears once or several times in the First Book, then it can be attributed a single and unique meaning on all the occasions when it occurs in the First Book. This is so with the expressions *pratyaya*, *smṛti*, *bhāvana*. See our commentaries on *sūtras* I.10; I 11; I 28.[16]

In fine, when Patañjali proffers the definition of a term it is necessary to adhere to this definition in all the *sūtras* in which the term appears. See our commentary on *sūtras* I.11 (*smṛti*) and I.16 (*vairāgya*).

16. But if a technical expression is *further* used in one or several *sūtras* outside the First Book then it becomes difficult to give to this technical expression, outside the First Book, the same unitary and single meaning which can be attributed to it in the First Book. Thus it is with the word *vitarka* which has one single meaning in the *sūtras* 17 and 42 of the First Book, meaning which does not hold in *sūtras* 33 and 24 of the Second Book. The reason for this difference in the application of the principle earlier mentioned, is undoubtedly based on the form of the composition of the *Yogasūtras* and on the possible interpolations to which we have already referred.

The present work

In the *References* at the end of the book can be seen the Sanskrit texts that we have employed. The complete bibliographical information about the books quoted by us is also given in the *References*

We started this work in Delhi, October, 1968, and finished it in Buenos Aires, October, 1972. It was first published in Spanish, in Barcelona (Spain), 1972 by Barral Editores. This English translation now published by Motilal Banarsidass has been done by Prof. Prithipaul, of Alberta University (Canada), and revised by us. We have introduced some modifications in our original Spanish text.

This volume presents our commentary on the First Book of Patañjali's treatise, "On concentration of mind". The First Book constitutes a work complete in itself, and we consider it the most important of the whole treatise.

SYNOPSIS OF THE BOOK OF SAMĀDHI OR CONCENTRATION OF MIND

BOOK I

Sūtras

I.1 Beginning of book.

Yoga and its Effect

I.2 Definition of Yoga, as the total restraint of all mental processes.

I.3 State of the spirit at the moment of total restraint (isolation of the spirit).

I.4 State of the spirit outside the previous case.

The Mental Processes

I.5 Number of the mental processes.

I.6 Enumeration of the mental processes.

I.7 Perception, Inference, Testimony.

I.8 Definition of error.

I.9 Definition of *vikalpa*.

I.10 Definition of Deep Sleep (*nidrā*).

I.11 Definition of *smṛti* (attention, memory).

Means to produce the restraint of the mental processes

I.12 Means to produce restraint (*abhyāsa* and detachment).

I.13 Definition of *abhyāsa* as effort for stability.

I.14 Form of the affirmation of *abhyasa*.

I.15 Definition of detachment.

I.16 Metaphysical indifference.

Classes of Restraint

I.17 The restraint with knowledge.

I.18 Other type of restraint with knowledge.

I.19 Automatic restraint of the disembodied (ones) and of those who dissolve in primal matter.

I.20 The restraint of the yogins and its requisites.

Acceleration of Restraint

I.21 Fervour as accelerator of restraint.
I.22 Levels of fervour.
I.23 Surrender to the Lord as accelerator of restraint.
I.24 Definition of the Lord.
I.25 Omniscience of the Lord.
I.26 The Lord as master.
I.27 Form of designation of the Lord : *Aum.*
I.28 Yogic practices related to the mystical syllable *Aum.*
I.29 Effects of former practices : introversion of consciousness and disappearance of the obstacles of restraint.

Obstacles of Restraint

I.30 Enumeration of the obstacles of restraint and their condition of dispersions of the mind.
I.31 Concomitants of the dispersions of the mind.
I.32 Form of elimination of the obstacles : the stabilization of the mind in one single entity.

Means to obtain the Stability of the Mind

I.33 The serenity of the mind.
I.34 *Prāṇāyāma* (controlled breathing).
I.35 A continuous mental process with object.
I.36 A continuous mental process without pain, and luminous.
I.37 Mental fixation in a being lacking of passion.
I.38 Mental fixation in dream knowledge or in "nidric" knowledge (cf. *Sūtra* I·10).
I.39 Meditation on any object.
I.40 Limits of the ability of the mind to concentrate.

Concentration of the Mind

I.41 Definition of *Samāpatti* : concentration on an object and absorption in it.
I.42 *Samāpatti*, with analysis, on a gross object.
I 43 *Samāpatti*, without analysis, on a gross object.
I.44 Identification of the *Samāpattis*, with and without analysis,

on a gross object with the *Samāpattis*, with or without analysis, on a subtle object.

I.45 Extreme limit of the condition of the subtle object.

I.46 Identification of the *Samāpattis* earlier indicated with the concentration (*samādhi*) with "seed".

I.47 Emergence of inner quietude in the transparence of *samāpatti*, without analysis, on a subtle object.

I.48 Emergence of the intuitive yogic knowledge in the transparency mentioned earlier.

I.49 Difference between intuitive yogic knowledge and other types of intuitive knowledge.

I.50 The last subliminal impression, produced by the intuitive yogic knowledge, as a hindrance to the production of other subliminal impressions.

Last stage of the Mental Concentration.
Total Restraint. (period) Isolation of Spirit

I.51 Restraint of the last subliminal impression, which implies total and absolute restraint. It is *samādhi* without "seed", it is the isolation of spirit.

1

अथ योगानुशासनम् ॥

ATHA YOGĀNUŚĀSANAM.

Now, the exposition of Yoga (is to be initiated).

A. Now (atha)

Many treatises, particularly of aphorisms, begin with this word, such as, among others, the *Brahmasūtras* of Bādarāyaṇa, the *Vyākaraṇamahābhāṣya* of Patañjali the Grammarian, the *Dharmaśāstra* of Vasiṣṭha. This word indicates that a new theme is being introduced.

B. Yoga

This word derives from the root yuj which means : 1. "to yoke", 2. "to unite". It can be compared with the Greek *zygón, zeúgnymi, á-zyg*, and with the Latin *jugum, con-jug, ju-n-go.*

In the context of Patañjali's Yoga we must prefer the first meaning "to yoke" and its derived meanings "to master", "to control", "to subdue". Yoga is the fact of yoking, of placing under the yoke, of mastering, of subduing. For this reason the following *sūtra* defines yoga as the restraint of the mental processes. The yogin yokes, dominates, subdues the mental processes. The meaning "unite" is not proper for Patañjali's Yoga, the end of which is as Max Müller observes (*The Six Systems*, p. 309) far from uniting, indeed to dis-unite, to separate, to isolate the Spirit (*puruṣa*) from Matter (*prakṛti*), returning it to its essential and original purity, as we have indicated in Note 11 of the introduction.

In the context of Yoga used in the service of some particular current of religious devotion (*bhakti*) it is the second meaning "to unite" which predominates. For these forms of devotion the Yoga has for its purpose the union of the *soul* with God.

2

योगश्चित्तवृत्तिनिरोधः ॥

YOGAŚ CITTAVṚTTINIRODHAḤ.

Yoga is the restraint (nirodha) of the processes (vṛtti) of the mind (citta).

A The Mind (*citta*)

We have translated the expression *citta* by "mind", viewed as the seat, the organ, the aggregate of intellective (cognitive), volitive and emotional activities, functions and processes of the individual. Taimni, Purohit, H. Āranya and Bengali Baba translate the term, in the same way we do, by "mind". Woods and Vivekananda by "mind-stuff"; Ballantyne by "thinking principle"; Hauer (*Der Yoga*, p. 239) by "die innere Welt" and Jacobi (*über das*..., p. 587) by "Psyche".

B. The Mental Processes (*vṛtti*)

We have translated the term *vṛtti* by "processes". Others translate it by "fluctuations" (Woods), "modifications" (H. Āranya, Rama Prasada and Taimni), "Bewegungen" (Hauer, *Der Yoga*, p. 240), "acts" and "function" (Max Müller, *The Six Systems*, p. 337), "Funktionen" (Jacobi, *über das*..., p. 588), "activities" (Purohit).[17]

Whatever the translation adopted, we must understand by the *vṛtti* of the mind the mental processes which Patañjali mentions, defines or analyzes in *sūtras* I.6-11. These processes are : perception (*pratyakṣa*), inference (*anumāna*), testimony

17. *Vṛtti* corresponds to the Greek word *enérgeia*, which is employed by Dionysius in *De divinis nominibus*, (ed. Marietti), p. 24 for instance.

(*āgama*), error (*viparyaya*), *vikalpa*[18], sleep (*nidrā*) and attention or memory (*smṛti*)[19]. We refer them to the *sūtras* indicated and to their respective commentaries.

These processes of the mind may be described as being intellective-cognitive, considering the nature which Patañjali himself attributes to them in the *sūtras* mentioned.

As its translation indicates *vṛtti* is an activity, a function, an act of the mind. It is not a product in which this activity, so to speak, culminates. But this activity and its product are intimately and essentially bound. Even more they are indissolubly bound to each other. For instance, the *vṛtti anumāna* is the activity, the process, the act by means of which the mind constructs an inference or reasoning which implies a conclusion. This inferential or reasoning activity of the mind is expressed in the inference or the reasoning which results from it.

According to the *Sāṃkhya*, the *vṛttis* are actually the modifications of the mind, considering that the latter assumes the form of the object which it perceives. This remark explains the translation of *vṛtti* by "modifications". Nevertheless we prefer the expression "processes" because it corresponds more faithfully to our conception and also because *vṛtti*, although it can be conceived as a modification, is, in any way one considers it, a process, an activity, a function, an act of the mind.[20]

18. Regarding this term see *sūtra* I.9.
19. Regarding this term see *sūtra* I.11.
20. The *Sāṃkhya* conception of *vṛtti* was adopted by the Vedānta. Dharmarāja, a Vedāntist thinker of XVIIth century, defines *vṛtti* (*Vedāntaparibhāṣā*, p. 14) as follows: "yathā taḍāgodakaṃ chidrān nirgatya kulyātmanā kedārān praviśya tadvad eva catuṣkoṇādyākāraṃ bhavati, tathā taijasam antaḥkaraṇam api cakṣurādidvārā nirgatya ghaṭādiviṣayadeśaṃ gatvā ghaṭādiviṣayākāreṇa pariṇamate": "As the water of a tank, issuing through a hole, enters in the form of a channel a number of fields, and just like them assumes a rectangular or any other shape, so also the luminous mind, issuing through the eye etc., goes to the space occupied by objects such as a jar, and is modified into the form of a jar or any other object." (translation by Swāmi Mādhavānanda).

C. Restraint (Nirodha)

We have translated *nirodha* by "restraint". Other translations: "suppression" (H. Āranya); "inhibition" (Taimni); "restriction" (Woods); "hindering" (Ballantyne); "Unterdrückung" (Jacobi, *über das...*, p. 587); "Zur-Ruhe-bringen" or "Bewaltigung" (Hauer, *Der Yoga*, p. 239); "controlling" (Purohit).

"Restraint" then becomes the stopping, the cessation of the processes of the mind.

The restraint to which Patañjali refers in this *sūtra* can only be the *total* restraint of the mental processes, since, with the restraint, to which the *sūtra* refers, the "seer"[21] establishes himself in his own nature, as the following *sūtra* affirms. And the "seer" can only establish himself in his own nature when there does not exist any mental process with which he can identify himself according to the *Sāṃkhya* doctrine, the philosophical foundation of Yoga. Moreover, in accordance with the last *sūtra* of this book, the culminating point of the yogic process entails the total restraint of all the mental processes. It would be absurd for the "seer" to establish himself in his authentic nature in a moment prior to this culminating moment.

But, besides the *total* restraint there are also *partial* restraints, as those that occur in the course of the yogic process before this culminates in the total restraint, which is the aim of Yoga. The stopping, the cessation of the mental processes which constitute the restraint, are voluntary and transient. The yogin produces them in himself by means of his will and for a determined length of time. In this respect the restraint differs from the spontaneous and permanent cessation of the mental processes consequent upon death.[22]

The restraint of the mental processes constitutes the yogic trance, as will be shown in the course of the commentary on the First Book of Patañjali and particularly in the *sūtra* I.51.

D. Definition of Yoga

The *sūtra* gives us the definition of Yoga in a strict sense. But

21. Regarding this term see *sūtra* I.3.
22. See *sūtra* I.19.

the expression "*Yoga*" is also commonly used to indicate the practices necessary to bring about *nirodha* and the steps which lead up to it. The word *yoga* appears only once in the First Book (Sūtra 2). This Sūtra gives its strict definition, but the word *yoga* is also used to indicate the practices necessary to bring about *nirodha* and the steps which lead up to it. In Sūtras II.1 and II.28 *yoga* designates the method that produces *sāmadhi* and, by means of it, *nirodha*.

E. The Commentary of Vyāsa

Vyāsa thinkṣ that this sūtra refers to the initial stages of the restraint, or to the partial restraint (which he calls *samprajñāta yoga*), and also to the final stage, or to the total restraint (which he calls *asaṃprajñāta yoga*). We believe that this is a wrong interpretation, in view of the reasons we have given in paragraph C of this commentary.

3

तदा द्रष्टुः स्वरूपेऽवस्थानम् ॥

TADĀ DRAṢṬUḤ SVARŪPE 'VASTHĀNAM.

Then (is produced) the establishment of the seer (draṣṭṛ) in his own nature.

A. Then (tadā)

The expression *tadā*, "then", in the *sūtra* refers to the moment when the restraint mentioned in the earlier *sūtra* takes place, that is, the total restraint according to what has been affirmed in section C of the commentary of that *sūtra*.

B. The Seer (draṣṭṛ)

The expression *draṣṭṛ* literally means "he who sees", the seer. Before explaining what Patañjali means by this term, it is necessary to recall a few fundamental concepts, already mentioned in the Introduction of the *Śāṃkhya* philosophical system, which constitutes the very foundation of Yoga.

According to the *Sāṃkhya* there exists a primal matter (*prakṛti*) which is the origin of the totality of the sensible material reality. The mind is part of this material reality. In opposition to matter (*prakṛti*) stands the spirit (*puruṣa*) though we ought actually to say the *puruṣas* considering that the *Sāṃkhya* maintains the existence of an infinite number of *puruṣas*, spirits, individual souls. *Prakṛti* and *puruṣa* have an absolutely different nature. *Prakṛti* is devoid of consciousness, *puruṣa* is conscious. *Prakṛti* is the first cause, *puruṣa* is neither cause nor effect. *Prakṛti* is active, *puruṣa* is inactive. *Prakṛti* is constantly changing, *puruṣa* is immutable. *Prakṛti* is the object of knowledge, *puruṣa* is the subject of knowledge. *Puruṣa*, embodied in an individual, comes into contact with the external material world, by means of the mind, and of its functions or processes.

Embodied in the yogin—as in every man—is the *puruṣa,* the seer to whom this *sūtra* refers.

C. Identification of the Seer with his Mental Functions

In the normal state, that is, before the total and absolute restraint of the mental processes, there exists a connection between the Seer and the matter and, as a consequence of this, an identification of the embodied individual spirit with the mental processes: the embodied individual spirit appears as if it were the mental processes, it manifests itself in the form of the processes mentioned. See the commentary of *sūtra* I.4, section B.

So long as this false identification persists, the individual embodied spirit remains bound to error and to ignorance. And as a consequence of this identification and of this error there follow suffering and the realization of those actions which will result in the spirit remaining attached to matter. One manifestation of this bondage to matter is the successive reincarnations to which the spirit becomes subjected.

D. Freedom and Isolation of the Spirit. The Kaivalya

In order to free itself from suffering and from the reincarnations the Spirit must "dis-identify" itself from the mental processes; it must disentangle itself from them and return to its pristine and essential purity; it must isolate itself from matter and from all its manifestations, including, as we have said, the mind and its functions. Its goal must be *kaivalya* or isolation, a concept which Patañjali analyzes in Book IV.

E. Yoga as a Method to obtain the Freedom and Isolation of the Spirit

Isolation can only be brought about by means of the practice of Yoga, the essence of which—as the previous *sūtra* says—consists of the restraint of the mental processes and of their total and absolute suppression. One understand why Yoga lays so much emphasis on the restraint of the mental processes: the spirit becomes identified with them. By the elimination of these processes one after the other, the only entity that, by the method of reduction, ultimately remains, will be the Spirit, free and isolated in its total and absolute purity.

F. The Nature of the Puruṣa (Spirit, Seer)

According to the preceding explanations, it is understood that the true nature of the *puruṣa* to which the latter must return, by means of the practice of Yoga, is this state of freedom from matter, the state of total and absolute isolation in itself. When he gets this total and absolute isolation, the *puruṣa* has established himself in his own nature.

G. Vyāsa's Commentary

Vyāsa implicitly refers the expression *tadā* (now) to the stage of absolute and total restraint in which the isolation is produced. He does this in spite of his commentary on *sūtra* I.2 in which he affirms that the restraint, to which the *sūtra* I.2 refers, comprehends not only the total but also the partial restraint. See Section D of commentary on *sūtra* I.2.

4

वृत्तिसारूप्यमितरत्र ॥

VṚTTISĀRŪPYAM ITARATRA.

Short of this case (there is) the "identification" (sārūpya) (of the seer) with the processes (vṛtti).

A. Short of this Case (itaratra)

"Short of this case", that is, when there does not occur the total and absolute restraint (*nirodha*). When this restraint does not exist the seer identifies himself with the mental processes (*vṛtti*) to which we have briefly referred in the previous *sūtra* and which we shall now treat again in greater detail.

B. Identification (sārūpya) of the Seer with the Mental Processes (cittavṛtti)

The expression *sārūpya* has been translated in different ways: Taimni : "assimilation"; Bengali Baba : "conformity"; Rama Prasada : "identification"; Hauer : "Konform" (*Der Yoga*, p. 240); Vivekananda : "is identified"; Ballantyne : "is in the same form as"; Purohit : "conforms to"; H. Āranya : "appears to assume the form"; Woods : "takes the same form as".

Two states are possible for the *puruṣa* :

1. *Kaivalya* or isolation. In this state the *puruṣa* is isolated from matter; it is pure consciousness, which is realized on the level of unity; it does not suppose an object in front of it, it does not require any organ of knowledge and does not experience limitations of any sort. This state of isolation occurs, as we have said, at the moment of total *nirodha*.

2. When the total *nirodha* does not occur, the *puruṣa* is not isolated. It remains in contact with matter by the mediation of

the mind and of its functions. These functions or processes of the mind are the acts of consciousness which occur on the level of duality; they necessarily suppose an object in front of the subject; they are brought into being by means of organs and are subordinate to space, to time and to causality. They are acts of limited,[23] mediate and "impure" consciousness. In this second state the *puruṣa*, which is pure and unlimited consciousness, manifests itself in the form of the limited, mediate and "impure" consciousness constituted of the mental processes.[24] This *manifesting itself in the form* of the mental processes constitutes the *sārūpya* of the seer with these processes, that is, the "identification" of the *puruṣa* with them.

C. The notion of sārūpya according to Vyāsa and other commentators

For Vyāsa, "identification" consists in the *vṛttis* of the *puruṣa* not being distinct from the *vṛttis* of the mind (*vyutthāne yāś cittavṛttayas tadaviśiṣṭavṛttiḥ puruṣaḥ*). Following Vācaspati Miśra, Vijñānabhikṣu, *Vārtika ad loc.*, avers that the *vṛttis* of the *puruṣa* are the reflections of the *vṛttis* of the mind (*buddhi*) (*buddher viṣayākāravṛttīnāṃ puruṣe yāni pratibimbāni tānyeva puruṣasya vṛttayaḥ*). Vijñānabhikṣu further observes that these *vṛttis* do not produce a transformation (*pariṇāma*) in the *puruṣa* on account of his immutable nature. He gives a series of arguments to show that this reflection of the mental *vṛttis* does indeed exist in the *puruṣa*.

We do not concur with these interpretations, considering that Patañjali expressly refers to a *sārūpya* of the *puruṣa* with the *vṛttis* of the mind. Moreover, in relation to Vyāsa's interpretation, it is pertinent to add that Patañjali does not speak of

23. According to Dharmarāja, *Vedāntaparibhāṣā*, p. 8, all the *vṛttis* limit the pure consciousness (*vṛttiviśiṣṭam caitanyam*).

24. We find here a fundamental conception of Indian Culture: mind constitutes a limitation for consciousness and therefore it loses value. We must understand the word "impure", not in its moral meaning, but in an epistemological meaning, i.e.: submitted to the duality subject/object.

vṛttis of the *puruṣa*, and that it is not possible to affirm that there are *vṛttis* of the *puruṣa,* since the *vṛttis* constitute a modification and the *puruṣa* is changeless (*Yogasūtras* IV.18). It is probable that the interpretations of these commentators correspond to an elaboration of the *Sāṃkhya* doctrines posterior to Patañjali.

5

वृत्तयः पञ्चतय्यः क्लिष्टाक्लिष्टाः ॥

VṚTTAYAḤ PAÑCATAYYAḤ KLIṢṬĀKLIṢṬĀḤ

The processes (vṛtti) are five-fold, with kleśas (kliṣṭa) or without kleśas (akliṣṭa).

A. Different possible interpretations of the expressions kliṣṭa and akliṣṭa.

According to the Monier-Williams Sanskrit-English dictionary, the words *kliṣṭa* and *akliṣṭa* derive from the root *Kliś* which means "to torment, trouble, molest, cause pain, afflict". *Kliṣṭa*, the passive participle of this root means, according to the same dictionary, "molested, tormented, afflicted, distressed, wearied, hurt, injured, being in bad condition, worn, connected with pain or suffering". From the same root derives the word *kleśa*, which is noun of action and means in its general sense "pain, affliction, distress, pain from disease, anguish". In its technical sense, specific to the *Sāṃkhya-Yoga*, *kleśa* signifies five disturbances, which Patañjali treats in II. 3 and ff. The *kleśas* are : ignorance (*avidyā*);[25] consciousness of existence (*asmitā*); passion (*rāga*); aversion (*dveṣa*), attachment to existence (*abhiniveśa*). In Book I this expression (*kleśa*) occurs only once, in *sūtra* I. 24, but without any elucidation of its meaning.

On reconsidering the word *kliṣṭa* and relating it to the word *kleśa* we may say that *kliṣṭa* has two basic meanings : One of general acceptance "with pain, affliction, distress, etc." or rather "with *kleśas* in its general meaning", and another of a technical

25. Patañjali in *sūtra* II.5 defines *avidyā* as follows: anityāśuciduḥkhānātmasu nityaśucisukhātmakhyātir avidyā: *"to consider permanent, pure, agreeable and real what is impermanent, impure, painful and unreal is ignorance* (*avidyā*)".

acceptance: "with the five *kleśas*", giving to the word *kleśa* its technical meaning (ignorance, consciousness of existence, etc.). *Akliṣṭa* (*kliṣṭa* with the privative *a*-) means no-*kliṣṭa*.

After this brief statement about the words *kliṣṭa* and *kleśa* we shall examine their different interpretations.

I. *Kliṣṭa and akliṣṭa as "provoked by a kleśa" and "having for object khyāti or (discriminative) knowledge".*

This is the interpretation of Vyāsa the commentator "*kleśa-hetukāḥ...kliṭṣāḥ*" and "*khyātiviṣayā...akliṣṭāh*".

According to Vyāsa a *kliṣṭa* mental process would be a process the cause of which is one of the five *kleśas* mentioned earlier; and an *akliṣṭa* mental process would be a process the object of which is *khyāti* or (discriminative) knowledge. Discriminative knowledge is that knowledge which discriminates, for instance, between the real and the unreal, *puruṣa* (spirit) and *prakṛti* (matter), by differentiating one from the other, and not taking one for the other.

II. Kliṣṭa and akliṣṭa as "with kleśas (in the technical sense : ignorance, etc.)" and "without kleśas (in the technical sense)" or similar values as "affected by kleśas (in the technical sense)" and "non-affected by kleśas (in the technical sense)".

The above is the interpretation of Bhoja: "*kleśair...ākrāntāḥ kliṣṭāḥ*" and "*tadviparītā akliṣṭāḥ*". Hauer, *Der Yoga*, p. 243, agrees with Bhoja's interpretation. A mental process affected by a *kleśa* would be a process which continues while being accompanied by a *kleśa*. For instance, a perception accompanied by a feeling of desire or aversion.

III. Kliṣṭa and akliṣṭa as "with kleśas (in the general sense)" and "without kleśas (in the general sense)".

In relation to this interpretation it behoves us to consider the versions of Taimni, Vivekananda, Bengali Baba, Rama Prasada, Ballantyne, Max Müller, *The Six Systems*, p. 337, who translate the terms indicated by "painful" and "not painful". Purohit uses "painful" and "pleasurable". A mental process accompanied by a disagreeable or painful sensation would be a *kliṣṭa* or painful process; and an *akliṣṭa*, "non-painful" mental process, when it is accompanied by a pleasurable, agreeable or indifferent sensatation. For example, to see a loved person would be a non-painful, agreeable mental process (perception, *pratyakṣa*); to see an instrument of torture, would be a painful mental process (perception, *pratyakṣa*).

B. Criticism of Vyāsa's Interpretation (I)

As we have said, Vyāsa interprets *kliṣṭa* as "provoked by a *kleśa*" and *akliṣṭa* as "having for object (discriminative) knowledge". He certainly gives special importance to these terms. However, this interpretation must be subjected to the following criticisms :

(a) The meanings which Vyāsa attributes to the mentioned expressions are not the usual ones. The dictionaries do not give them. They appear only in Vyāsa and in those who follow his interpretation.

(b) On what does Vyāsa base himself to give to the terms mentioned the special meanings referred to? As Patañjali uses the said terms only in this *sūtra*, Vyāsa could not have found in the same Patañjali a foundation for his interpretation.

(c) Had Patañjali wanted to say that the mental processes are "provoked by the *kleśas*" and "having for object (discriminative) knowledge" would he not have used other words which express these concepts clearly and unequivocally, as *kleśahetuka* (provoked by the *kleśas*) or *khyātiviṣaya* (having *khyāti* as object), instead of using the term *kliṣṭa* and *akliṣṭa* with meanings which are not the proper and common ones, without any prior clarification, giving rise to ambiguity and equivocation ?

(d) The *sūtra* says that the mental processes are *kliṣṭa* or *akliṣṭa* that is, that all the mental processes can appear in the *kliṣṭa* or *akliṣṭa* form. Thus the *pramāṇa* (perception, inference, testimony) or means of arriving at correct knowledge, which constitute one type of mental process (see *sūtra* I.6) would be at times *kliṣṭa* and at other times *akliṣṭa*. The same holds with the other mental processes : error, *vikalpa*, *smṛti* and dream.[26] While taking note of this remark, the interpretation of Vyāsa leads us to a series of absurd conclusions. In fact there are *vṛttis* which can never be *kliṣṭa* as the dream *vṛtti* which can never have discriminative knowledge as object or like the error *vṛtti* (since the object of error is, as we shall see in I.8, the attribution to something of something which is not and since were error to have discriminative knowledge for objet, that is, were it to be constituted of the said knowledge, it would cease to be error). And Patañjali tells us that the *vṛttis* are at times *kliṣṭa* and at other times *akliṣṭa.* Moreover it is not easy to understand how some *vṛttis* can be generated by the *kleśas* as, for instance, the dream *vṛtti*. According to the prevalent theory in Indian thought (see Sinha, *Indian Psychology*, II pp. 364-365) dream is produced by causes of a physiological nature, as fatigue, the tension of the organism etc. How can it be affirmed that the *kleśas*—ignorance, consciousness of extistence, passion, aversion, attachment to existence— are the causes of dream?

(e) It is not possible to extract from the privative *a-*, from the root *kliś* (which means to torment, etc.) and from the suffix of the past participle *-ta*, which constitute the word *akliṣṭa,* the notion of *khyāti* (discriminative knowledge). Still less is it possible to give to the suffix *-ta* the meaning of "generated by". Moreover, if *kliṣṭa* really meant "generated by a *kleśa*", *akliṣṭa* would mean : "non-generated by a *kleśa*". Compare these with the English words *agitate, agitation, agitated. Agitated* means "with agitation", but not "generated by agitation" and *non-agitated* means "without agitation" and not "what has for its object, let us say, well-being, tranquillity".

(f) The present *sūtra* of Patañjali also appears in the *Sāṃkhya-sūtras* attributed to Kapila (II.33). In his commentary *Sāṃkhya-*

26. This is the only way to interpret the *kliṣṭākliṣṭāḥ* of the text. And in this way it is interpreted by the authors mentioned in points I, II, and III of section A of this commentary. They do not indicate neither suggest that this expression could be interpreted in another way, as for instance that some mental processes, as error, are always *kliṣṭa* and others, as the *pramāṇas*, are always *akliṣṭa*.

pravacanabhāṣya ad locum, Vijñānabhikṣu does not follow the interpretation of Vyāsa and interprets *kliṣṭa* and *akliṣṭa* as: "*duḥkhadāḥ sāṃsārikavṛttayaḥ*" and "*tadviparītā yogakālīna-vṛttayaḥ*".[27] Likewise Aniruddha, in his commentary on the same work, does not follow Vyāsa and gives the following meanings to the expressions *kliṣṭa* and *akliṣṭa* : "*kleśayuktāḥ rajastamomayyaḥ*" and "*sattvamayyaḥ dagdhakleśāḥ*".[28] Still less does Bhoja, in his commentary of the present *sūtra* of Patañjali, accept, as we have seen, the interpretation of Vyāsa. Thus, it is evident that Vyāsa's interpretation was not unanimously accepted and that important commentaries of the *Sāṃkhyasūtras* do not take into account this interpretation.

For the reasons indicated above, we believe that the interpretation of Vyāsa (I) is unacceptable.

C. Critique of Bhoja's Interpretation (II)

According to the observations made at the beginning of our commentary on the present *sūtra*, one may interpret the expression *kliṣṭa* as "with *kleśas*", "affected by *kleśas*", by giving to *kleśa* either a general, wide meaning, or a technical, restricted meaning.

With regard to Bhoja's interpretation, let us examine if it is possible to take, in the present *sūtra* of Patañjali, the word *kliṣṭa* in its meaning "with *kleśas*" or "affected by *kleśas*" (*kleśas* being understood in its restricted and technical sense) i.e. if it is possible to give to *kliṣṭa* the meaning of "with ignorance, consciousness of existence, passion, aversion and attachment to existence", or "affected by ignorance, etc.".

Undoubtedly since *kleśa* has in Patañjali, in those *sūtras* in which it appears, a technical meaning, it is quite probable that the word *kliṣṭa* related to *kleśa*, also has the restricted and technical meaning in this *sūtra*.

27. *"The vṛttis, which are proper of the saṃsāra and produce suffering"* and *"(the vṛttis) which take place in the moment of yoga and are contrary to the previous ones"*.

28. *"United to kleśas and made of rajas and tamas"* and *"made of sattva and with their kleśas destroyed"*. See point A of our commentary to *sūtra* I.16.

Besides that it is possible for the *vṛttis* to be either with *kleśas* in technical meaning or without *kleśas* in technical meaning. All the mental processes mentioned by Patañjali can be accompanied or be affected, always or sometimes, by one, several, or all the perturbations, technically called *kleśas*. So, for instance, the *vṛtti pratyakṣa* is normally accompanied by ignorance, consciousness of existence, passion, aversion and attachment to existence. For that reason it will be *kliṣṭa*. In the experience of *nirodha* (restraint) perception gradually dismisses these concomitants and becomes *akliṣṭa*. See Vijñānabhikṣu's opinion in the point B, (f) of our commentary. Similar observations are valid for the other processes.

D. Critique of Interpretation (III)

We believe that this interpretation cannot be accepted the more so as it does not impart a technical sense to the word *kliṣṭa* : this is so because the expression *kleśa,* to which it is related, has in Patañjali a technical meaning, as we have already indicated.

Nonetheless we must point out that the adjectives "painful" and "non-painful" as this interpretation understands *kliṣṭa* and *akliṣṭa* can be attributed to all the mental processes.

E. Our Interpretation

After considering the interpretations mentioned earlier as well as our criticism of the same, we are inclined to adopt the meanings "with *kleśas* (in the technical sense)" and "without *kleśas* (in the technical sense)" for the words *kliṣṭa* and *akliṣṭa.*

6

प्रमाणविपर्ययविकल्पनिद्रास्मृतयः ॥

PRAMĀṆAVIPARYAYAVIKALPANIDRĀSMṚTAYAḤ.

(The mental processes are :) the means to acquire right knowledge (pramāṇa), error (viparyaya), vikalpa, deep sleep (nidrā) and smṛti (attention-memory).

A. In this *sūtra* Patañjali enumerates the mental processes which must be the object of restraint to which *sūtra* I.2 refers. In I.7-11, Patañjali deals separately with them.

B. *Vikalpa* and *Smṛti*

Regarding these expressions, for which it is impossible to give an adequate translation which would comprehend their varied and multiple meanings, see *sūtras* I.9 and I.11, with their respective commentaries.

7

प्रत्यक्षानुमानागमाः प्रमाणानि ॥

PRATYAKṢĀNUMĀNĀGAMĀḤ PRAMĀṆĀNI.

The means of acquiring right knowledge (pramāṇa) are : perception (pratyakṣa), inference (anumāna), āgama (testimony).

In relation to the concepts used by Patañjali in this *sūtra,* it is necessary to make the following statements :

A. Perception (pratyakṣa)

In agreement with the commentators Vyāsa, Vācaspati Miśra, Bhoja and Vijñānabhikṣu and with the traditional interpretation which is associated with them, *pratyakṣa* indicates, in this *sūtra,* the perception through the senses of their corresponding objects.

However, we believe that we must give to the term *pratyakṣa* a wider meaning, considering that it comprehends not only the collection of material objects, but also that of the mental realities (*perceptiones animi*) and furthermore, the totality of the living experience which touches our consciousness, whatever be the nature of all of them.[29] This interpretation is all the more

29. Dharmarāja, *Vedāntaparibhāṣā,* p. 15, expressly declares that the experiences expressed as: "I am happy, I am unhappy, etc." are perceptions (ahaṃ sukhī duḥkhī ityādijñānasya pratyakṣatvam). The characteristic of this kind of experience-perception, in relation to other kinds of perception (sensorial, mental), is that, with regard to the experience-perception, it is not possible to speak of an object of that experience-perception. If I perceive in myself, if I experience a pain or a pleasure, it is not possible to separate my experience of pain or pleasure from that pain or pleasure themselves. They constitute only one phenomenon, one entity. Only for methodological reasons, in a figurative way, it is possible to separate and distinguish, in the experience-perception, the act of grasping (*grahaṇa*: my sensation of pain or pleasure) and its object (*grāhya, viṣaya:* the pain or pleasure felt in myself). And paraphrasing *sūtra* I.16 (see point E of our commentary of *sūtra* I.17), in which

adequate since it allows to consider, among the *vṛttis*, the perceptive mental processes, experiences, apprehensions, which are not sensorial and which Patañjali considers in his exposition of Book I, as referred to in *sūtras* I.10; I.17; I.18; I.19; I.36, 1.38, etc. See our commentaries of the said *sūtras*, especially I.10, E; I.17, D and E; I.18,D; I.19,I; I.36 and I.38,C.

In consequence *pratyakṣa* is the activity, the action, the process of the mind by means of which the latter knows something, either directly, or by the mediation of the senses.

B. Inference (anumāna)

Inference is the activity, the act, the process of the mind by means of which the latter fashions a reasoning which arrives at a conclusion. A traditional example in India is the following : *where there is smoke there is fire*; *there is smoke on the mountain*; *therefore, there is fire on the mountain.*

C. Āgama (testimony)

Āgama is the activity, the act, the process of the mind by means of which the latter knows something by means of the information conveyed to it by a trustworthy person or a sacred text. In his turn the trustworthy person, by means of a perception or an inference, had earlier acquired the knowledge of what is now the object of his communication.

The expression *āgama* has been translated in different ways : by "testimony" (Taimni, H. Āranya, Ballantyne, Max Müller, *The Six Systems*, p.337); by "verbal cognition" (Bengali Baba, Rama Prasada); by "verbal communication" (Woods); by "competent evidence" (Vivekananda); by "gesicherte Überlieferung" (Hauer, *Der Yoga*, p.240); "evidence" (Purohit).

Patañjali defines *asmitā*, we could say that the *śakti* of the experience-perception (that is to say: what the experience-perception embraces) and the *śakti* of the object of the experience-perception (that is to say: what the object embraces) are so to say identical, in the sense that the limits and the extension of an experience-perception are fixed by the limits and extension of the feelings of happiness, pleasure, fear, which constitute its object.

We have translated it by "testimony" although this translation does not satisfy us at all considering that *āgama* is not the communication transmitted by the authoritative person, but rather the cognitive process which this communication produces in him who receives it.

8

विपर्ययो मिथ्याज्ञानमतद्रूपप्रतिष्ठम् ॥

VIPARYAYO MITHYĀJÑĀNAM ATADRŪPAPRATIṢṬHAM

Error (viparyaya) is a false knowledge which does not correspond to the nature of that (= the object).

Error is a false knowledge which arises on the occasion of the perception of something, which does not correspond (*pratiṣṭha*) to the nature of the perceived object. The traditional example of error : a rope is seen and it is taken for a snake. The image of a snake, that comes forth on the occasion of the perception of the rope, does not correspond to the nature of the rope. On account of this lack of correspondence, this is a false knowledge.[30]

30. Śaṅkara, *Brahmasūtrabhāṣya*, Introduction, defines *adhyāsa*, which fundamentally corresponds to error, in the following words: atasmiṃs tadbuddhir iti: "*the buddhi (grasping) of 'that' in what is not 'that'* ". Padmapāda, *Pañcapādikā*, p. 23, defines *adhyāsa* as: atadrūpe tadrūpāvabhāsaḥ: "*The manifestation of the form of 'that' in the form of what is not 'that'* ".

9

शब्दज्ञानानुपाती वस्तुशून्यो विकल्पः ॥

ŚABDAJÑĀNĀNUPĀTĪ VASTUŚŪNYO VIKALPAḤ

Vikalpaḥ follows a knowledge of words (śabdajñānānupātin) and lacks a material correlate (vastuśūnya).

A. Contents of the expression vikalpa. The impossibility to translate it.

As we shall see later, when we shall analyze the examples of *vikalpa* given by the commentators, the expression *vikalpa* comprehends the activities of the mind, the results of which are : tautological expressions and judgements (examples 1 and 2); negative concepts (examples 3-5); fantasies (examples 6-9); abstract concepts (example 10).

There does not exist in the English language a word which connotes such a variety of manifestations of the mental life as are comprehended by '*vikalpa*'. For this reason we prefer not to translate the word '*vikalpa*'.

Vikalpa has been translated in different ways by different translators. Woods translates it by "predicate-relation"; Max Müller (*The Six Systems*, p.337), Taimini, Ballantyne, by "fancy"; H. Āranya (in his commentary) by "vague cognition", ("vague notion"); Purohit by "delusion"; Vivekananda by "verbal delusion"; Hauer (*Der Yoga*, p.240) by "begriffliches Denken"; Dasgupta (*A History of Indian Philosophy*, Vol. I, pp. 261 and 269) by "imagination", "abstraction", "construction", "different kinds of imagination"; Rama Prasada by "imagination". In a general sense these translations take into account only one of the varied and multiple aspects of *vikalpa*. These may be said to be correct but incomplete.

B. The Characteristics of Vikalpa Given by Patañjali.

In this *sūtra*, Patañjali indicates two characteristics of the mental process (*vṛtti*) called *vikalpa* : 1. it is *śabdajñānānupātin* : "it follows a knowledge of words"; 2. it is *vastuśūnya*: "it lacks a material correlate".

C. Analysis of the Characteristics of Vikalpa.

(a) *The vikalpa "follows (anupātin) a knowledge of words (śabdajñāna)"*

Every word produces a knowledge in the mind : on hearing the word,[31] its meaning is grasped. The concept and/or the image of the object, which it signifies, arise in the mind. This knowledge is a knowledge "created by words", a "verbal knowledge". Likewise the perception of an object produces in the mind the knowledge of this object; but this knowledge is an "objective knowledge", created, not by a word, but by an object.

The *vikalpa* follows a "verbal knowledge". In other words, the *vikalpic* activity is produced in the mind, emerging entirely out of verbal knowledges, subordinate to words, it is based on words, it depends on words. It is not necessary, for the production of the *vikalpic* activity, to have an object in front of oneself, as is the case in perception. Words are sufficient for this purpose. The place occupied by the object in perception, as the point of origin of the perceptive mental activity, is taken, in this case, by words.

Thus, by way of example of the perceptive process, if I see a cow, a knowledge is produced in my mind—the knowledge of the cow which I am seeing. The presence of this cow in front of me is necessary for the perception to take place and for the knowledge which accompanies it. An example of a *vikalpic* process : a knowledge is produced in my mind if someone utters

31. It has no importance whether the word is uttered by another person or by oneself, even only mentally. Of course, it is understood that the words must be words whose meaning is clear.

the word *centaur*. I grasp the meaning of this word and there arises in my mind the concept and/or the image of the fantastic animal, which this word signifies. It has not been necessary (nor would it be possible) for the animal designated by the word to be present in front of me, for the mental process to have taken place in me. The word only was sufficient.

It is thus evident that perception has to do with sense-objects. If the latter were to disappear, it would not be possible to have perceptive acts. On the other hand, *vikalpa* has to do with words. So long as words exist, the meaning of which is understood and which can be related among themselves according to the rules of language, the production of *vikalpic* acts remains possible.

(b) Vikalpa lacks a material correlate (vastuśūnya)

We have said that the *vikalpic* activity arises out of verbal knowledges. This is its first characteristic. Patañjali points out that, as the second characteristic of *vikalpa*, it "lacks a material correlate", that is, nothing actually existing corresponds to it in reality. *Vikalpa* is "empty of (a) thing" (the literal translation of *vastuśūnya*).

Thus, by reverting to the example of the *centanr*, on hearing the word *centaur*, a process is produced in the mind. I seize the meaning of this word (verbal knowledge) and there arises in my mind the concept and/or the image of the fantastic animal which this word signifies. To the (*vikalpic*) process, by virtue of which there arises in my mind the concept and/or the image of the fantastic animal *centaur* and which is actually manifested in the said concept and/or image, there does correspond nothing in reality: it does not really refer to anything, it does not have a material correlate; it is "empty of thing".

D. Examples of Vikalpa

Pursuing the argument we shall provide, with brief statements, examples of *vikalpa* given by different commentators and translators. We have said in the commentary on *sūtra* I.2 that every *vṛtti* is a mental activity which manifests itself, acquires reality, in a determined product. Further, this activity and its product are indissolubly linked. We may even emphasize that the activity and its product are distinct aspects of the same mental reality which, by methodological requirements, becomes separated and isolated.

The examples which we single out are examples of products of *vikalpic* activities, considering that the *vikalpa*, as we have said, is manifested in its product. It is only in relation to its products that one can establish a difference between the distinct types of *vikalpic* activity.

I. *The Head of Rāhu.* Rāhu is a monster that is only a head. Actually the only thing that exists is Rāhu, which is a head, or a head, which is Rāhu. There does not exist a head, as something distinct, which belongs to Rāhu. To say "the head of Rāhu" is tantamount to saying "the head of the head" or "Rāhu of Rāhu". On the other hand, it is a different matter to say "the sword of the soldier". The sword is something distinct from the soldier and, as such, can belong to him.

II. *Consciousness is the Nature of Puruṣa.* According to the Sāṃkhya doctrine, which is valid for Vyāsa. (from whom this example is taken) the *puruṣa* is consciousness. In reality what exists is a consciousness which is the *puruṣa,* or the *puruṣa,* which is consciousness. There does not exist a consciousness, as something separate and distinct, which would be the nature of *puruṣa.* To say : "Consciousness is the nature of *puruṣa*" is like saying : "Consciousness is the nature of consciousness" or "the *puruṣa* is the nature of *puruṣa*". But it is an entirely different matter to say : "salinity is the nature of sea water". Salinity is something distinct from sea water and is really its nature.

III. *The Puruṣa is inactive.*

IV. *The arrow remains fixed* (*= does not move*).

V. *The Puruṣa* is uncreated.

In these last three examples the words "inactive", "remains fixed", and "uncreated" express negative qualities. The only thing which they signify is the absence of determined qualities (activity, movement, birth). When they are applied, as predicates to a subject—as in the examples given—they do not indicate that something is inherent, as a quality in the subject, but that the said subject does not have the corresponding positive qualities (Vyāsa)[32].

VI. *Centaur*. We have already analyzed this example in early paragraphs.

VII. *The barren woman's son.*

VIII. *The castle in the air.*

IX. *The hare's horns.*

The argument used for the explanation of VI. *Centaur* holds good for the last three examples as well.

X. *The infinite*. This is a negative concept and the same reasoning may be used in relation to it as was used for "inactive", "remains fixed", and "uncreated".

Examples I-V are given by Vyāsa. Example II is given by Bhoja too. Example VI is given by Taimni, examples VII-IX are Bengali Baba's and X is H. Āranya's[33].

When we explained in the earlier paragraphs the characteristics of *vikalpa* offered by Patañjali, we analyzed the example *centaur* on considering that it holds these characteristics. The other examples to which we are now referring also evince these characteristics.

1. In fact the *vikalpic* activities which manifest themselves in the given examples do not have a material correlate. There does not exist a head which would belong to Rāhu; nor a consciousness which would be the nature of *puruṣa* (of examples I and II); nor anything which corresponds to the negative con-

32. It could be said that the three examples, which precede, correspond to aspects of "nothing" and that Vyāsa's explanation starts from the idea that "nothing" is the negation of being, that it is possible to speak meaningfully only about being, and that therefore it is not possible to affirm anything of "nothing".

33. For this example of *vikalpa* see our commentary of *sūtra* I.42, section D.

cepts : "inactive", "uncreated", "cease to move", "infinite" (of examples III, IV, V and X); nor do these exist : the centaur, the barren woman's son, the castle in the air, the hare's horns (of examples VI-IX).

2. On the other hand the *vikalpic* activities manifested in the examples previously mentioned are produced in the mind solely on the basis of a verbal knowledge—the knowledge of the words which constitute the examples.

E. Other vikalpas

Of course the *vikalpas* we have mentioned, taken from the examples given by commentators and translators, are not the only *vikalpas* that exist. There may be other mental phenomena which can be designated as '*vikalpa*', if they comply with the two characteristics of *vikalpa* indicated by Patañjali. See section D of our commentary on I.42. Other cases of *vikalpa* could be the general (or universal) concepts or notions (*genus*, *species*) which of course are included in the abstract concepts referred to in Section A: the mental monologue, the mental planning of a future activity.

10

अभावप्रत्ययालम्बना वृत्तिर्निद्रा ॥

ABHĀVAPRATYAYĀLAMBANĀ VṚTTIR NIDRĀ

Deep sleep (nidrā) is a process (vṛtti), the foundation (ālambana) of which is the experience (pratyaya) of non-existence (abhāva).

A. Nidrā (deep sleep)

The expression *nidrā* refers to deep sleep, that is, to sleep without dreams.

B. Ālambana (foundation)

The word *ālambana* literally means "foundation", "basis", "support", "that on which something depends". The experience of the inexistence of the other mental processes (*vṛtti*) is the support, the foundation of the mental process *sleep*. It may be said that this experience is the necessary condition, it is what is basically presupposed for deep sleep to be produced.

C. Pratyaya (experience)

In this *sūtra* Woods translates the expression *pratyaya* by "cause" (as in *sūtras* I.18 and 19) and by "presented-idea" in the other *sūtras* (II.20; III.2, 12, 17, 19, 35; IV.27) in which the word occurs. Hauer (*Der Yoga*, pp. 240 and 464) translates it by "impulse" ("Antrieb") in the present *sūtra* and by "re-presentation" ("Vorstellung" and expressions of similar import) in the others.

In our view it is an error to translate the term *pratyaya* in two or more distinct ways[34] in the Treatise of Patañjali. In the

34. Other translators incur in the same error, as Woods and Hauer. See our commentaries of *sūtras* I.11, I.19 and I.28.

first instance it is difficult to accept that in a single treatise the same expression be translated by two terms, so different in their meaning as "cause" and "representation", "idea". Moreover Patañjali generally uses the technical terms in a rigorous manner, by attributing to each of them always the same well determined meaning. Finally, because according to our opinion, the term *pratyaya* has a specific and fundamental, well defined meaning, which recurs in all the *sūtras* in which it appears. The meaning referred to is the following : etymologically *pratyaya* derives from *prati+I* which means "to go towards", "to go to meet"; it is a name of an agent formed by the suffix *-a*; the basic idea which it expresses is : "what goes towards someone", "what goes to meet someone". In the theory of knowledge in relation to which the expression *pratyaya* has been used, we must not lose sight of this original, basic meaning.

Ideas and images, as well as experiences, are *pratyaya* insofar as, so to say, they proceed up to the mind and present themselves before consciousness. *Sūtras* II.20; III.2, 12, 17, 19, 35 and IV.27 deal with ideas. For this reason it is right to translate in these *sūtras*, *pratyaya* by "representation", "idea", "presented-idea" (Woods), or by similar expressions. But *sūtras* I.10,18 and 19 refer to experiences. For this reason, in these *sūtras*, *pratyaya* must be translated by "experience", but without losing sight of the fact that in these *sūtras* as in the previous ones, the subject under consideration is one single process, by means of which *something reaches consciousness.*

D. Abhāva (non-existence)

We agree with Bhoja and the principal translators (Woods, Taimni, H. Āranya, Ballantyne, Jacobi, *Über das* ..., p. 592) that the non-existence to which this *sūtra* refers is the non-existence of the other *vṛttis* (processes) of the mind.

E. The Experience of Non-existence (abhāvapratyaya)

In harmony with the preceding explanations *abhāvapratyaya* is the experience of the non-existence of the other mental processes. The individual experiences that the other *vṛttis* do not exist. To clarify the thought of Patañjali one could say that the *abhāvapratyaya* is the experience of the emptiness left by the cessation of the other mental processes.

F. The Scope of this Sūtra

According to Patañjali deep sleep is a mental process. Consequently deep sleep is not a transcendental state. It is not possible to reach, in this state, the supreme goal of Yoga, the perfect isolation of the soul (*kaivalya*). More : the presence of the mental process of sleep is an impediment to this experience of isolation. Sleep as any other mental process must be restrained, that is, avoided, by the yogin who aspires to attain this end. The deep sleep has nothing in common with the state of trance which, as we shall see later, the yogin shall produce in himself with the help of the yogic practices and in which shall occur the isolation as the consequence precisely of the cessation of all the mental processes.

Perhaps the fact that Patañjali explicitly uses in this *sūtra* the term *vṛtti* in referring to sleep and gives to this mental process a definition (something which he does not do with perception, or with inference, or with testimony) would indicate that Patañjali wished to leave in the margin of any doubt that sleep is a simple mental process, something which cannot in any manner be considered as transcendent.

In his conception of sleep Patañjali contradicts the interpretation, frequently to be encountered, of some passages of the early Upaniṣads according to which deep sleep would be a transcendent state in which the spirit (*Ātman*) separates itself from matter (represented by the mind and the senses) and realizes, however transitorily, its reidentification with the Supreme Spirit (*Brahman*)[35].

G. Vyāsa's Commentary

In his commentary Vyāsa observes that on waking from deep sleep one can say : "I have slept profoundly, pleasurably".

35. In our article "Yoga y trance mistico en las antiguas Upanishads" we have proposed a new interpretation of these passages of the *Upaniṣads*.

This remembering, Vyāsa argues, implies that the mind has had during the deep sleep an experience which it remembers on waking. With this argument Vyāsa confirms the conception of sleep held by Patañjali[36].

36. Oddly Woods translates the word *pratyaya* in the *sūtra* by "cause" and, in the commentary of Vyāsa to the same *sūtra*, by "presented-idea". The interpretation of the word *pratyaya*, that we give in point C of our commentary, would have prevented Woods from incurring in the contradiction of translating the same word in two different ways in the *sūtra* and in Vyāsa's commentary, whom he follows in his translation of the *sūtras*.

11

अनुभूतविषयासम्प्रमोषः स्मृतिः ॥

ANUBHŪTAVIṢAYĀSAṂPRAMOṢAḤ SMṚTIḤ.

Smṛti is the non-complete disappearance (asaṃpramoṣa) of a perceived object (anubhūtaviṣaya).

A. *Translation of smṛti*

Smṛti is generally translated by "memory". See, in this regard, Vivekananda, Hauer (*Der Yoga*, p. 240),Bengali Baba, H. Āranya, Taimni, Woods, Purohit, Rama Prasada. We do not think that this translation is correct considering that it relates only to one aspect of the *smṛti* as we shall see subsequently in section D. We translate *smṛti* by "attention-memory", and thus we emphasize the two fundamental aspects of the *smṛti*. Unfortunately in English does not exist a word that covers the phenomenon indicated by the word *smṛti* in its totality, and embraces all its aspects. An adequate translation would perhaps be "retentive power" which Bengali Baba uses in the *sūtra* I. 20.

B. *Anubhūta-viṣaya* (*perceived object*)

The expression *anubhūta* literally means "experienced", "apprehended", "perceived". The expression *viṣaya* designates any object, when considered in relation to a human experience, specially in relation to perceptive knowledge, of a sensory or mental nature. So in I. 11 *viṣaya* is what has been "experienced", "apprehended", "perceived"; in I. 15 it designates what has been seen or heard; in I.33 *viṣaya* means the object of the benevolence and other feelings; in I. 37 *viṣaya* is that towards what mind is directed; in I. 44 *viṣaya* indicates the object of a *savicāra* or *nirvicāra samāpatti*, and in I. 49 *viṣaya* means the object of the intuitive knowledge (*prajñā*). See section B of our commentary on *sūtra* I,49 in which *viṣaya* is mentioned together with *artha*.

C. *Asaṃpramoṣa* (*non-complete disappearance*)

This expression has been translated as follows ; "das Nicht-gestohlenwerden" (Hauer, *Der Yoga*, p. 240); "absence of loss (i.e. retention)"(Bengali Baba); "not to slip away" (Vivekananda); "not letting go or allowing to escape" (Taimni); "the not letting go" (Ballantyne); "the not wiping out (Max Müller, *The Six Systems*, p. 338); "not adding surreptitiously" (Woods); "without stealing from anything else" (H. Āranya), and "not stealing away" (Rama Prasada).

We think that the literal sense of the word is : "the non-completed theft, the not-being completely stolen, taken away, while taking into account the meaning of the elements which compose it. That is, *a-* is a privative *a*; *-sam-* gives the idea of totality; *-pra-* the idea of "toward the exterior", "to great distance" and *-moṣa* means "stealing", "theft".

We have translated *asaṃpramoṣa* by "non-complete disappearance" for the sake of greater clarity and taking into consideration that this expression is close to the original.

With regard to the translations mentioned earlier we shall confine ourselves to observe that that of Hauer does hold on to the literal sense of the word, that those of Bengali Baba and of Vivekananda are acceptable but the others stray away from the said literal meaning, particularly those of Woods and of H. Āranya.

D. Interpretation of the Sūtra

In the present *sūtra* Patañjali rigorously defines the mental process *smṛti*. Consequently, we must consider as *smṛti* any mental process which falls under this definition. Traditionally, it is accepted that *smṛti* is the mental process memory in its aspects of retention and of remembering. In our view *smṛti* according to Patañjali encompasses both "attention" and "memory".

I. *Attention.* An act of attention is produced when an object is perceived and maintained in front of one's consciousness, that is, it is not allowed to be removed from the range of consciousness, it does not disappear from it and does not escape from it. The definition of *smṛti* given by Patañjali can be attributed to the phenomenon of attention thus described. Consequently we deem ourselves authorized to consider attention as falling under the expression *smṛti*. And it is this aspect of *smṛti* which is of the greatest interest for the aims of yoga.

The *sūtra* I.20 enumerates the following as the prerequisites for the production of the restraint (*nirodha*) of the mental processes: faith (*śraddhā*), energy (*vīrya*), *smṛti*, concentration (*samādhi*) and intuitive knowledge (*prajñā*). Each of these requisites is the necessary condition for the origination of the succeeding one. It is well understood that attention is indispensable for the concentration of the mind. On the other hand, if the expression *smṛti* signified solely "memory" and did not comprehend attention, the result would be that memory would come to be a requisite for concentration and one would not understand how memory—in either of its two aspects of retention and remembering—could contribute to bring about the concentration of the mind.

The traditional interpreters like Vācaspati Miśrā, Vijñānabhikṣu, Kṛṣṇavallabha, Woods, Bengali Baba, Purohit, who, in this *sūtra* take *smṛti* for "memory", find themselves constrained, when they again encounter the term *smṛti* in the *sūtra* I.20, to give to *smṛti* a meaning different from that of "memory", in spite of the fact that, according to their interpretation of the present *sūtra*, "memory" would be the sole meaning which Patañjali would have given to the expression *smṛti*.[37] These interpreters do thus make a double error : on one hand they do not maintain in all the *sūtras* in which this expression occurs the same meaning which, according to them, Patañjali himself has given to the term *smṛti*; on the other hand, they use a single technical word with two different meanings in two *sūtras* in close

37. Woods: "mindfulness", Benagali Baba: "retentive power", Purohit: "concentration", Vācaspati Miśra, Vijñānabhikṣu, and Kṛṣṇavallabha: "meditation" (*dhyāna*).

proximity one to the other.[38] These two errors are avoided when one considers that *smṛti* is a mental process which encompasses, according to the definition of the present *sūtras*, memory as well as attention. Other interpreters, like Taimni, find themselves compelled to have recourse to explanations which are totally unsatisfactory and in no way technical. See our commentary of *sūtra* I.20.

The difficulty which we encounter in the interpretation of *sūtra* I.20, when *smṛti* is taken to mean solely "memory" is one more argument in favour of our opinion that the translation "memory" does not cover the entire range of the expression *smṛti*.

Finally the fact that the Pāli term *sati*, the equivalent of the Sanskrit *smṛti*, is used in Buddhism, in the context of Yogic practices, with the meaning of "attention," is further an argument in favour of our interpretation.

II. *Memory*. We must first indicate what is the mechanism of memory according to Indian psychology. A perceived object does not only produce in the mind a *pratyaya*, that is, an idea or image, the form in which the object is perceived, but in addition to this, it leaves in the mind a *saṃskāra*, that is, a latent subliminal, unconscious impression. Indeed this is the form in which occurs the retention of the object in consciousness. When the *saṃskāra* is revived, it is reactivated and passes from the realm of unconsciousness to that of consciousness : memory, remembering is then produced.[39]

Thus, retention as well as remembering implies that the object has not completely disappeared from consciousness in which, in some way, it is maintained.

38. See our commentaries of *sūtras* I.10, section C and I.28 section B.
39. See our commentary of *sūtra* I.18, section F.

12

अभ्यासवैराग्याभ्यां तन्निरोधः ॥

ABHYĀSAVAIRĀGYĀBHYĀṂ TANNIRODHAḤ.

Restraint (*nirodha*) (*is realized*) *by means of abhyāsa and detachment* (*vairāgya*).

A. Definition of abhyāsa and vairāgya

In the *sūtras* I. 13 and I.15 Patañjali defines the terms *abhyāsa* and *vairāgya* respectively as "effort for stability" (*sthiti*) and "consciousness of the mastery possessed by one who is freed from desires of objects seen and heard".

B. General Observations

We must take into consideration that to realize the restraint (*nirodha*) of the mental processes (*vṛtti*) both means are necessary and that each one would separately be insufficient for such an effect. See our commentary of the *sūtra* I.15, Section C.

Both *abhyāsa* (effort for stability) and *vairāgya* (detachment) must be maintained during the course of the yogic process till *nirodha* at its highest degree is produced. But as soon as the highest *nirodha* is achieved then there can be neither the effort which constitutes *abhyāsa* nor the consciousness of mastery, which stands for *vairāgya*, since the highest *nirodha* is the absolute and total emptiness of consciousness.

C. Tan-(*their*).

Refers to the *vṛttis* dealt with in the preceding *sūtra*.

13

तत्र स्थितौ यत्नोऽभ्यासः ॥

TATRA STHITAU YATNO 'BHYĀSAḤ.

Of both, abhyāsa is the effort for stability (sthiti).

A. Abhyāsa

The present *sūtra* refers to one of the means indicated in the previous *sūtra* to obtain restraint (*nirodha*) of the mental processes: *abhyāsa* defined by Patañjali as "the effort for the stability (*sthiti*)"—obviously—of the mind.

We do not translate the term *abhyāsa*, because there is no English word that means: "effort for stability".

The word *abhyāsa* has been translated in the following way: "practice" (Rama Prasāda, Vivekanânda, H. Āranya, Woods, Purohit, Bengali Baba), "exercise" (Ballantyne), "Übung" (Hauer, *Der Yoga*, p.240).

Let us analyze the terms of Patañjali's definition.

B. Stability (sthiti) of the mind. Concept and means.

The mind is naturally unstable in this sense that in it flows a continuous flux, a constant series of mental processes and of emotional states.

The stability of the mind presents itself under two forms :

(a) The first form refers directly to the intellective-cognitive life. It consists in the fact that a sole mental process is maintained, preventing other processes to be produced; the mind stabilizes itself in a mental process, excluding the remaining ones. For instance, the yogin fixes his attention, with exclusion of anything else, on a sole luminous point or on some well determined sound, like the tic tac of a clock or the syllable AUM, which he repeats unceasingly. In this case, there is only a mental process, a visual or auditive perception; the mind has stabilized itself on it; the remaining mental processes are excluded. It is the stability obtained through the fixation, the concentration of the mind on a unique entity (thing, idea, image etc.); it constitutes the most effective means to obtain the stability and it can be called a *technical means.* In relation to this form of obtaining the stability see *sūtra* I.35-39.

(b) The second form of stability refers directly to the emotional life. It consists in a diminution of the intensity of the emotions, in the serenity of the mind. The yogin obtains the emotional stability, the mind's serenity, fomenting in himself some feelings of low tonality as indifference for what surrounds himself. His emotional life will have not the intensity of the life of a person who involves himself in the world. This emotional stability is a human attitude. On this point see *sūtras* I.33-34. Let us indicate that mind's serenity is one of the most exalted ideals of Indian culture.

This way to understand what *sthiti* is in its two forms, is founded on the study of *sūtras* I.35-39, which refer to the means to obtain intellective-cognitive stability, and of *sūtras* I.33-34, which deal with the form to obtain emotional stability. We remit to our commentary of the indicated *sūtras.*

These two forms of stability are intimately related between them. The first form necessarily will bring with itself the diminution or disappearance of the emotional states of the yogin and the second form at its turn will facilitate the fixation of the mind.

C. The stability (*sthiti*) *and the restraint* (*nirodha*)

The stability (*sthiti*) and the extreme restraint (*nirodha*), to which Patañjali is referring till this moment, are two different concepts. Taking into account Patañjali's terminological rigour, it is not possible to think that he is employing these two terms for the same concept. Less still is it possible to think that in *sūtra* I.12 he employs the word *nirodha* to express a determinate concept and in the following I.13 he uses another word (*sthiti*) to express the same thing. *Sthiti* is, according to what has been expressed in section A of the commentary to the present *sūtra:* 1. the immovilization of the mind produced by the mono-ideism provoked by the fixation of the mind on some object, and 2. the debilitation of the emotional life obtained through the fomentation of determinate sentiments. The *sthiti* carries with itself a mental process and/or a weakened emotional life/The total *nirodha* does not carry with itself either the one or the other.

D. The effort (yatna)

Patañjali defines *abhyāsa* as the "effort for stability". Explaining this definition it could be said that the *abhyāsa* is the eagerness, the desire, the will, to obtain the stability, the serious intention directed to that aim.

E. Vyāsa's commentary

According to Vyāsa the stability (*sthiti*) is the state or condition of a mind whose mental processes have ceased (*avṛttika*) and which flows with an imperturbable serenity. The majority of the commentators follows Vyāsa's interpretation.

Vyāsa's interpretation seems to us to be erroneous. In fact, if all mental processes (*vṛtti*) have ceased, it is the stage of total *nirodha*. It is not possible to speak at this moment of *sthiti*, since technically the stability presupposes, in Patañjali's concept, a *vṛtti*, a process that fixes the mind and/or a weakened emotional life, while during total *nirodha* consciousness is void of any content.

14

स तु दीर्घकालनैरन्तर्यसत्काराऽऽसेवितो दृढभूमिः ॥

SA TU DĪRGHAKĀLANAIRANTARYASATKĀRĀSEVITO DṚḌHABHŪMIḤ.

Now (the abhyāsa : effort for stability) becomes firm, when it is cultivated for a long time, uninterruptedly and with care.

In the first stages of the yogic practice the effort, the will of the yogin to obtain the stability will easily deviate from its goal under the influence of enternal stimuli (as for instance impressions originated around him) or internal stimuli (as for instance remembrances, emotions etc.). But that effort, that will of stability (*abhyāsa*), when it is trained in a prolonged, constant, and earnest way, will not be exposed any more to the external or internal stimuli, we have mentioned, will maintain itself firm and unshakeable, will keep itself fixed, and in this way will fully reach its goal : stability.[40] More still, the *abhyāsa*, and the stability that is obtained through it, with the course of time, and the practice, will transform themselves into habits of the yogin.

40. See Schultz, *El entrenamiento*, specially pp. 47-48, in relation to the general effects of training, one of which (fixation of mind) is referred to by Patañjali in this *sūtra*.

15

दृष्टानुश्रविकविषयवितृष्णस्य वशीकारसंज्ञा वैराग्यम् ॥

DṚṢṬĀNUŚRAVIKAVIṢAYAVITṚṢṆASYA VAŚĪKĀRASAṂJÑĀ VAIRĀGYAM.

Detachment (vairāgya) is the consciousness (saṃjñā) of mastery on the part of one who has liberated himself from the desire for objects either seen or heard of.

A. Concept of vairāgya (detachment)

Vairāgya is not simply the absence of desire, "detachment ". Patañjali says that *vairāgya* is the consciousness of being master, possessed by one who has liberated himself from desire. Three marks characterize *vairāgya* : 1. the absence of all desire,[41] 2. consciousness, 3. of mastery. To conform the *vairāgya* there must be control, subjugation of desire. This subjugation of desire is necessary in order to reach the absence of all desire, and it must last all the time. Moreover the yogin has the consciousness that he has subjugated his desires and that he goes on subjugating them.

The *vairāgya* supposes an act of the will aimed at the subjugation of desire and this act is of course conscious, as is also conscious the subjugation of desire which originates out of it. The absence of desire spontaneously produced by old age or illness is not *vairāgya*. *Vairāgya* is only that absence of desire produced by a subjugation which is voluntary and conscious.

Nevertheless, for the easiness of the exposition, we translate *vairāgya* by "detachment."[42]

41. Excepting of course the endeavour of the yogin in order to reach the ultimate aim of Yoga. See section C of our commentary of the *sūtra* I.51.

42. This ideal of detachment constitutes one of the most powerful ideals of India, one of those ideals that is most characteristic of its culture. From

B. Seen or heard of objects

By "objects seen" we must understand everything that forms part of the empirical reality in which we live, and by "objects heard of", those objects whose existence is not grasped by our senses and depends only on the authority, on the traditions of each culture, as for instance anything of supernatural kind which is offered by different religions as a reward for their followers. As examples of the first ones, Vyāsa mentions the following ones : women, food, drinks, power; as examples of the second ones : heaven, the discarnate state (as that of the gods), the resolution into primary matter.

C. The abhyāsa and the vairāgya. The vairāgya as a means to obtain nirodha (restraint)

The *vairāgya* is, together with *abhyāsa*, one of the two means to obtain *nirodha*, i.e. the restraint of mental processes (I.12).

The *abhyāsa* looks for the stability of the mind in its two forms : the intellective-cognitive one and the emotional one. The *vairāgya* attacks principally the desire, makes the yogin immune to the external and internal stimuli which in normal conditions enchain man; the *vairāgya* renders the yogin indifferent to anything.

It is obvious that the absence of desire, the detachment from everything, facilitates the obtention of the emotional stability, of the mind's serenity, and allows the mind to concentrate itself more easily. At its turn the *abhyāsa*, the effort for stability, which manifests itself in the mind's concentration on a determinate entity and in the fomentation of feelings of low tonality, necessarily hinders the activity of desire or attenuates its action. It is easy to see the close relationship between these two means.

As we have indicated in the commentary of *sūtra* I. 12, on judging by the way in which that *sūtra* is composed, it seems that in Patañjali's opinion both means are necessary to produce *nirodha*. In fact, it seems difficult, or even impossible, that det-

---

the *Upaniṣads* onwards it is an object of traditional teaching and in a general way it is promoted by all the classic doctrines of India.

achment (*vairāgya*), by itself, alone without the *sthiti* (stability)—specially without the *sthiti* produced by the mind's concentration—could be able to provoke the stopping of all the mental processes (*nirodha*). It seems also difficult, or even impossible, that a yogin, dominated by desires and therefore liable to external and internal stimuli, could perform, in an adequate way, an effort aiming at that stability (*abhyāsa*) from which originates the restraint of all the mental processes.

16

तत्परं पुरुषख्यातेर्गुणवैतृष्ण्यम् ॥

TATPARAṂ PURUṢAKHYĀTER GUṆAVAITṚṢṆYAM.

Superior to that (*vairāgya*) *is the indifference* (*vaitṛṣṇya*) *for the guṇas as a consequence of the knowledge* (*khyāti*) *of the spirit* (*puruṣa*).

Before giving our interpretation of the present *sūtra*, we shall refer to some concepts of the Sāṃkhya philosophy that are necessary for its comprehension.

A. *The guṇa theory*

The concept of *guṇa* derives from the philosophical system Sāṃkhya. As we have already indicated in our commentary of the *sūtra* I.3, according to that system, there exists a primordial matter, the *prakṛti*, from which originates empirical reality. This matter is constituted by the three *guṇas* : *sattva*, *rajas* and *tamas*. Although the word *guṇa* usually means "quality", in the Sāṃkhya's context this word does not indicate the qualities of the matter, but its factors, elements or substances that constitute it. Each of these *guṇas* has its own characteristics and functions : *sattva's* function is the manifestation, thanks to this *guṇa* objects appear before consciousness. It is *sattva* which produces pleasure, happiness, bliss. *Rajas* is the origin of all activity and movement; to it are due the disorderly effort and pain. *Tamas* is the source of inertia and from it derive apathy, indifference, error. "*All things are composed of these three guṇas and their differences are due to the different combinations of these guṇas. The nature of a thing is determined by the preponderance of a particular guṇa. Things are called good, bad or indifferent; intel-*

ligent, active or slothful; pure, impure or neutral, on account of the predominance of sattva, rajas or tamas respecrtively."[43]

B. The knowledge (khyāti) of the spirit (puruṣa)

The "knowledge of the spirit" is the knowledge that *puruṣa* is different from *prakṛti.*

This knowledge is a *sui generis* knowledge, for which in truth the word "knowledge" should not be employed. It has nothing to do with rational discursive knowledge neither with any of the rational processes, as inference, argumentation etc. It has nothing to do either with intuition or any kind of knowledge by experience, and of course it has no relation at all with erudition and accumulation of information. The "knowledge", to which this text refers, is the state in which the "seer", i.e. the *puruṣa,*[44] frees himself from everything that is extraneous to him, recovers his original and own nature, isolates himself in himself. *Cognoscere = esse.*

C. Consequences of isolation (kaivalya)

When knowledge is produced for *puruṣa,* that is to say: when the *puruṣa* has established himself in his own nature (I.3), and has reached the isolation (*kaivalya*) from matter, then *puruṣa* and *prakṛti* enter into a state of mutual indifference : matter ceases to appear before *puruṣa* and *puruṣa* has no attraction for matter or, what is the same, for the *guṇas* that constitute it—it is as one does not exist for the other, and *vice versa.* (*Sāṃkhya-kārikā* 69 and 71 ; *Sāṃkhyasūtra* III.65 and 70).

D. Traditional construction and translation of the sūtra

All the interpreters and translators consider that in this *sūtra* the word *vairāgya* (detachment) must be understood as implied

43. Sharma, *A critical Survey,* p. 155.

44. As we have indicated in I.3, the "seer" is the *puruṣa.* Rigorously the word "seer" can be employed in regard to the *puruṣa* only before isolation while there is the duality subject-object. When isolation is produced and unity is reached, only the word *puruṣa* can be employed to designate him.

and they apply to that word the adjective *tatparam* : "superior to that". In their opinion this *sūtra* defines another kind of *vairāgya*, the so called "superior *vairāgya*" in opposition to the *vairāgya*, dealt with in the previous *sūtra* : the *vairāgya* superior to the previous one is the indifference (or any similar concept) in front of the *guṇas*, indifference produced by the knowledge of the *puruṣa*.

E. Our construction and translation of the sūtra

We do not accept to consider that the word *vairāgya* is implied in this *sūtra* and we consider that the word *tatparam* : "superior to that" is a predicate of *guṇavaitṛṣṇasya*: "indifference for the *guṇas*". This *sūtra* does not deal therefore with a superior *vairāgya*, but with a new concept, the *vaitṛṣṇya*, and indicates that this *vaitṛṣṇya*, produced by the knowledge of the *puruṣa*, is superior (*param*) to the *vairāgya* (*tat*) which has been defined in the previous *sūtra*. The reasons which induce us to choose this construction and not to accept the traditional interpretation will be exposed in sections H and I of this commentary.

F. Traditional interpretation

All traditional interpreters understand that the superior *vairāgya*, referred to according to them in this *sūtra*, is a kind of *vairāgya* more intense than that the yogin gets in the course of his practices and which consists in the absence of desire or attraction for the *guṇas*, the last elements of the original matter, whose characteristics and functtons have been described before. As the *guṇas* combined in different proportions constitute all the manifestations of reality, detachment for the *guṇas* means detachment for matter in its totality. Besides that, as the *guṇas* have different characteristics and functions, the detachment for the *guṇas* is also detachment for those characteristics and functions.

The detachment for the *guṇas* would be superior to the detachment for either seen or heard of objects (empirical or supra-empirical reality), to which previous *sūtra* refers, because it is of a more general character and because its object is the essence of reality, its ultimate fundament.

G. Our interpretation of the sūtra. The indifference (vaitṛṣṇya)

The *vaitṛṣṇya* to which this *sūtra* refers, corresponds to the state of indifference into which the *puruṣa* enters *ipso facto* just in the moment in which the knowledge of his own nature, i.e. isolation *(kaivalya)*, is produced in him. See section C of this commentary.

The *vairāgya*, to which previous *sūtra* refers, is a process which is produced in the yogin who aims to his own liberation, an attitude that he adopts and which is a means to get the restraint of mental processes *(nirodha)*. The *vaitṛṣṇya* is a process that takes place in the seer as a consequence of the isolation which he has obtained through the absolute and total restraint of the mental processes. It may be said that the *vairāgya* of the previous *sūtra* takes place on a psychological level and that *vaitṛṣṇya* occurs on a metaphysical level.

This *vaitṛṣṇya* is higher *(param)* than *vairāgya* referred to by the previous *sūtra* *(tat)*, considering that it is produced not during the course of the yogic practice which is necessary for realizing the total restraint of the mental processes and to the subsequent isolation, but when the supreme goal of yoga, constituted by the said restraint and the isolation, has already been reached.

H. The Grounds of our Translation and Interpretation

From a grammatical point of view and in conformity with the *sūtra* style, the two constructions of the *sūtra*, indicated in the preceding paragraphs D and E, are possible. But considerations of a logical nature urge us to give preference to our construction of the *sūtra* and, as a result, to our interpretation.

The preceding *sūtra* refers to "*the consciousness of mastery of one who has freed himself from the desire for objects seen or heard*". The present *sūtra* deals with "*the indifference to the guṇas (which originates) from the knowledge of the spirit*". Between these two definitions there exists a *substantial* and not merely *qualit-*

ative, accessory difference. It is evident that both definitions cannot refer to a single concept. Actually it is a matter of two essentially different concepts and not of two forms of one single concept, forms which would be different only in degrees of quality, as a higher and a lower *vairāgya* would be.

Now indeed, "indifference (*vaitṛṣṇya*) to the *guṇas*" can only correspond to that state which *puruṣa* reaches in the face of matter at the moment of isolation (*kaivalya*). Once the discriminative knowledge has been produced, this state of indifference to matter, the state whereby matter is abstracted, is the only state possible for *puruṣa*. It is not possible to give another meaning to the expression *vaitṛṣṇya*.

I. Critique of the Traditional Interpretation

In contrast to the traditional interpretation, in addition to the reasons given as a fundament of our interpretation, we may bring forth the following considerations. If the present *sūtra* refers to a type of *vairāgya*, then we could replace in it the expression *vairāgya* by its corresponding definition (given by Patañjali himself in the I.15). We would then have, with the translation given by the traditional interpreters : " 'consciousness of mastery of him who has freed himself from the desire for objects seen or heard' higher than the previous one (or higher than that of *sūtra* I.15) is the indifference to the *guṇas* (which originates) from the knowledge of spirit". It is absurd to establish an equivalence between "consciousness of mastery" and "indifference", especially if we bear in mind the terminological rigour of Patañjali. Moreover the traditional interpreters consider this higher *vairāgya* as being produced when the yogin has reached the supreme knowledge and has arrived at the final goal of yoga, *kaivalya*. It is contradictory to maintain that, in this stage of the yogic process, when the mind has become empty of all content, there be a consciousness of mastery; that when *puruṣa* has isolated itself, there be in it this consciousness.

17

वितर्कविचारानन्दास्मितानुगमात्सम्प्रज्ञातः ॥

VITARKAVICĀRĀNANDĀSMITĀNUGAMĀT SAṂPRAJÑĀTAḤ.

Due to the accompaniment of vitarka (analysis of gross objects), vicāra (analysis of subtle objects), ānanda (bliss) and asmitā (consciousness of existence), (the citta-vṛtti-nirodha : restraint of the mental processes) is saṃprajñāta (with knowledge).

A. Concept of that to which the present sūtra refers

Most commentators and translators consider that this *sūtra* refers to *samādhi* (concentration of the mind), an expression which appears for the first time in the *sūtra* I.20. We agree with Kṛṣṇavallabha and Hauer (*Der Yoga*, p. 241) and take this *sūtra* as referring to *nirodha*. First, because up to now Patañjali has been dealing with *nirodha* and there is no justification for substituting in this *sūtra* the said concept by another which has neither appeared nor been mentioned—in which case that would go against the usage of the *sūtra* style. Second, the commentators and translators who refer this *sūtra* to *samādhi* see themselves constrained to refer *sūtra* I. 20 also to *samādhi*, thus condemning Patañjali to posit an incongruency in this *sūtra*, that is *samādhi* is preceded by *samādhi*.

B. Vitarka (Analysis of Gross Objects)

Vitarka is translated by : "deliberation" (Woods), "reasoning" (Vivekananda and Taimni), "supposition" (Bengali Baba), "rationale Überlegung" (Hauer, *Der Yoga*, p. 241), "philosophical curiosity" (!) (Rama Prasada), "consciousness of sentiment" (Purohit).

We have translated it by "analysis (of gross objects)" by reason of the following considerations.

Without doubt *vitarka* is a mental activity. Indeed that is how it is interpreted by Vyāsa (*vitarkaḥ cittasyālambane sthūla ābhogaḥ*), Vācaspati Miśra (*svarūpasākṣātkāravatī prajñā ābhogaḥ*) and Vijñānabhikṣu (*viśeṣeṇa tarkaṇam avadhāraṇaṃ vitarkas...*) in their commentaries on the present *sūtra*; and this is what emerges from the translations of the expression *vitarka* indicated earlier.

Moreover with regard to what can be inferred by what Patañjali says in *sutra* 1.44 compared to I.42, *vitarka* is a mental activity *related to gross objects*. Besides the commentators mentioned earlier, as well as Bhoja in his commentaries on the present *sūtra*, also relate *vitarka* to gross objects.

In agreement with Vācaspati Miśra and Vijñānabhikṣu (*Yogasāra-saṃgraha*, p. 17) we must understand by *vitarka* the mental operation by means of which the subject posits before his consciousness all the "gross" particularities and constitutive parts of a "gross" object : it is the "making-evident" (*sākṣāt-kāra*) of the "gross" (*sthūla*). The concept of "gross" object comes from the Sāṃkhya doctrine and we have to understand the *mahābhūta* in its context.

Again to explain this term we must refer briefly to the Sāṃkhya doctrine. According to the Sāṃkhya, *prakṛti* or primeval matter, on account of the proximinity of the *puruṣa* or spirit, evolves as follows : *prakṛti* is transformed into *mahat*, also called *buddhi* (cosmic intellect); *mahat* or *buddhi* is transformed into *ahaṃkāra* (cosmic consciousness); *ahaṃkāra* is transformed into the ten *indriya* (organs of sense and of activity: ears, skin, eyes, tongue, nose, voice, hands, feet, organs of excretion, organ of generation—these denominations do not designate the physical parts of the body, but the faculties which correspond to them), into the *manas* (mind) and in the five *tanmātra* (essences of sound, touch, colour, taste, smell); in their turn the five *tanmātra* transform themselves into the five *mahābhūta* (gross elements) which are : space, air, fire or light, water, earth.

Out of the context of the Sāṃkhya doctrine and terminology we may, in a general way, say that the "gross" object is anything that falls under our senses. H. Āranya gives the following examples of the "gross" object : cow, jar, yellow, blue. Rām Sharmā gives the following : sun, moon, star, Rāma, Kṛṣṇa, Śiva, Durgā and other divinities.[45]

The preceding explanations do justify our affirming that *vitarka* is an analytical and particularising activity of the mind directed to a "gross" object. The mind gradually proceeds to apprehend anything "gross" which constitutes and individualises the "gross" object which it has in front of it[46].

Vitarka implies, on the part of the mind, an act of attention on the "gross" object; it *spontaneously* accompanies every act of attention on a "gross" object in its first stages (See *sūtras* I. 41-44). It is understood that if the mind is fixed on a "gross" object all the "gross" particularities and constitutive parts of the object will gradually render themselves present to consciousness.

As *nirodha* is produced by the fixing of the mind and the fixing of the mind connotes an intense and prolonged act of attention, *nirodha* will, in its first stages, be accompanied by *vitarka*.[47]

45. We must understand, in the case of divinities, that the "gross" objects are the images of the divinities or the same divinities incarnated under some form.

46. See Saint François de Sales, *Traité de l' amour de Dieu*, Book VI, Chapter V: "*Meditation considers in detail and piece by piece the objects that are capable to move us; contemplation gives rise to a completely simple and concentrated glance on the object it loves*".

47. The word *vitarka* appears again in *sūtra* I.42 (*savitarka*) with the same meaning as it has in this *sūtra*. See in our commentary of I.42 our critique of the interpretation, given by tradition, of that word in *sūtra* I.42; that interpretation differs from the interpretation, given also by tradition, of the same word in the present *sūtra*. The rejection of this traditional interpretation fortifies the interpretation we are giving of *vitarka*. Outside the First Book of the *Yogasūtras* the word *vitarka* is employed in *sūtras* II.33 and 34 with a different meaning, which cannot be accepted in the present *sūtra*. See note 16 of the Introduction.

C. Vicāra (Analysis of Subtle Objects)

The term *vicāra* has been translated by : "reflection" (Woods and Taimni); "discrimination" (Vivekananda); "clear vision" (Bengali Baba); "sinnende Betrachtung" (Hauer, *Der Yoga*, p. 241); "consciousness of discrimination" (Purohit); "meditation" (Rama Prasada).

We translate it by "analysis (of subtle objects)". We agree with Vyāsa, Vācaspati Miśra and Vijñānabhikṣu in their commentaries of *sūtra* I.17 and with the translators mentioned earlier that *vicāra* is a *mental activity* and, according to the express statement of Patañjali in I.44, it is an activity *related to subtle objects*.

Following Vācaspati Miśra, *ad loc.*, and Vijñānabhikṣu (*Yogasārasaṃgraha*, p. 18) mentioned earlier, we must understand *vicāra* as the mental activity by means of which the subject brings before consciousness all the "subtle" particularities and constitutive parts of a "subtle" object. It is the "making evident" of the "subtle" (*sūkṣma*).

Similarly, in agreement with the Sāṃkhya the subtle object is *prakṛti*, *mahat* or *buddhi*, *ahaṃkāra*, *manas*, the *indriya* and the five *tanmātra*, that is, primal matter and all its derivatives with the exception of the gross elements.[48]

Out of the context of the Sāṃkhya doctrine, examples of "subtle" objects are : images, ideas, sensations, emotions. *Ānanda* and *asmitā* which we mention below are likewise "subtle" objects.

Like *vitarka*, *vicāra* is an analytical and particularising activity except that it is related to a "subtle" object. It implies an act of attention on a "subtle" object, it *spontaneously* accompanies every act of attention on a "subtle" object in its earliest stages and equally accompanies *nirodha* in its beginnings.[49]

48. The *puruṣa* is excluded from this classification of objects into "gross" and "subtle", since it cannot be an object. Let us remember that for the Sāṃkhya mind is a part of the material reality.

49. Cf. Schultz, *El entrenamiento*, p. 95: "*We can do that a subject completely concentrate himself on a sensorial experience and thereby, in a certain way, that he consider it as under a magnifying glass. In the daily life of the*

D. Ānanda (Bliss)

By *ānanda* is meant the sentiment of joy, of bliss, of well being, of placidness. This sentiment accompanies *nirodha* in its first stages and is the result precisely of calmness, of relaxation which the restraint of the mental processes bears in its wake. We have here a fact which is easily experienced, and which is commonly observed by those who practise yoga. In n. 2, p. 15 of *The Conception of Buddhist Nirvāṇa*, Stcherbatsky says : "The late prof. O. Rosenberg has himself practised some yoga-meditation in a Zen Monastery in Japan. He used to compare the agreeable feeling of ease which he then experienced to the effect produced by music specially when executed personally. Attention is then fixed and a light feeling of ecstasy makes you forget all troubles of life." Swami Sivananda, *Practical Lessons in Yoga*, p. 160, says : "Regular meditation...makes the mind calm and steady, awakens an ecstatic feeling".[50]

E. Asmitā (Consciousness of Existence)

The term *asmitā* has been translated in the following way : "sense of personality" (Woods); "I-sense or feeling of individual personality" (H. Āranya, in his commentary); "sense of pure being" (Taimni); "egotism" (Ballantyne); "egoism" (Bengali Baba and Rama Prasada); "unqualified egoism" (Vivekananda); "consciousness of personality" (Purohit); "Ichbewusstsein" (Hauer, *Der Yoga*, p. 241); "sense of being" (Dvivedī).

---

common subject such a process comes into account whenever one desires that the sensorial experiences acquire vivacity and strength, either in the case of details of the apparatus of movement and support in one's own body (phonation, etc.) or in order to intensify external sensorial impressions. So for instance we can transform into an object of concentration's exercises any sonorous, cromatic experience or tactual sensations. Thereby two aims can be obtained: on one side, through the concentration's exercises it is possible to complete, increasingly and in its totality, the experience in question, polishing, deepening, making it clearer; and on the other side, the subject can reach in himself, in the corresponding situations, a state of depth and deeper and accentuated experiences".

50. Schultz, *El entrenamiento*, pp. 80:90, refers to *"the beneficent influence"* and *"extraordinary sensation of well-being"* which is poroduced by his own method of autogenous training.

Literally *asmitā* means "I-am-ness". It is a word formed by *asmi* = "I am" and *-tā*, a suffix which forms abstract nouns and corresponds to the *-ness*, or *-hood*, or *-ty* in English.

We must understand by the word *asmitā*: "the consciousness of (I) am", "the consciousness of the (I) exist". Though the term *asmitā* refers fundamentally to the notion of "to be", "to exist", it involves the notion of 'I' expressed by the verbal declension of the first person singular *-mi*. The word *asmitā* does not refer merely to being, or to existence, but actually to the consciousness of being, of existence, since the term *asmi*, which forms part of the word, is specific to a subject which proclaims his existence. With this word the subject expresses his consciousness, his sensation, his sentiment of the fact that he exists.

For these reasons we have adopted the translation "consciousness of existence".

In the *sutra* II.6, Patañjali defines the *asmitā* in the following way : "*the identity* (*ekātmatā*) *as it were of the power* (*śakti*) *of him who sees* (*dṛś*) *and of the power of the act of seeing* (*darśana*)". It may be pointed out that "he who sees" is the *puruṣa* as subject of knowledge. In other words *dṛś* designates "consciousness". The "act of seeing" designates "the cognitive processes".[51] The word *śakti* which literally means "power", designates in this case "the faculty, the ability, the possibility, the extent". Thus "the *śakti* of him who sees" and "the *śakti* of the act of seeing" refer respectively to the extent, to the limits, of consciousness and of the act of knowledge.

The identity of the power of him who sees (*dṛś*) with the power of the act of seeing (*darśana*) consists of the following:

Every individual is conscious of the fact that he exists. This consciousness of existence necessarily presupposes the sensations, emotions, volitions, ideas; it does not occur without them.[52]

51. Compare the use of the word *draṣṭṛ* in *sūtra* I.3 section B of our commentary. *Draṣṭṛ* as well as *DṚŚ* and *darśana*, which properly refer to the action of seeing, are applied by extension, not only in Patañjali but in the Indian thinking in general, to any cognitive process.

52. A constituent part of consciousness is the vague and diffuse sensa-

This consciousness of existence, so to speak, emerges from the sensations, emotions, volitions, ideas; it has them as supports and expresses itself through them; it is limited by them which determine its extent, it encompasses all that they encompass (See note 29). This subordination and dependence with regard to the sensible, emotional, volitive and intellective activities to which pure consciousness is subjected when it manifests itself in the consciousness of existence is, in Patañjali's view, an identification, "as it were", of consciousness with these activities.

The concept of *asmitā* has a close relationship with that of *sārūpya*. *Sārūpya* would represent the objective aspect (the simple fact of pure consciousness appearing under the form of the mental processes) and *asmitā*, the subjective aspect (the

---

tion of one's own body, of the organic interiority, of physical limits, in short, of the somatic individuality. We think that this aspect of consciousness of existence is very important in relation to Yoga. We reach this conclusion taking into account the great capacity of somatic introspection reached by many yogins, which is nothing else than an intense development of the awareness of one's own body. It is said about one yogin that he was able to perceive the operations of his brain, his heart and other organs, the circulation of his blood and the "subtle rythms" of his body and that he could hear also the palpitations of his heart and pulse (Evans-Wentz, *Tibetan Yoga*, p. XLI). It is said about the great yogin Milarepa that he had the power to observe the physiological processes of his own body (*ibidem*, p. 24). Another reason for that opinion is the fact that the capacity of somatic introspection seems to be a previous and necessary requisite fot the mastery that many yogins have on their own nervous and circulatory systems, which generally are outside any conscious control . Rele refers, in the beginning of his book *The Mysterious Kundalini*, the experiments performed by the yogin Deshbandhu in The Bombay Medical Union. Deshbandhu could stop the circulation of blood in his hands and paralyze, almost completely, the movements of his heart. See similar cases in Th.Brosse, *Études instrumentales* and the articles mentioned in note 7. Schultz, *El entrenamiento*, p. 291, says referring to some practises employed in hypnosis: "*Thereby one stimulates that process which should be designated, in general terms, as "somatization" and which is characterized by an internal, perceptive-affective, intense concentration on one's own corporality. This concentration is of a more general and diffuse kind, in the case of hypnotism, and it takes place then on the entire body; in the case of autogenous training it is more systematic and it is not necessarily stimulated or accompanied by any operation coming from outside and practised in the member which is exercised*".

consciousness of existence conditioned by the limitation constituted by the mental processes) of a single phenomenon: the limitation of pure consciousness due to the human condition. See the commentary of the *sūtra* I.4, section B. *Asmitā*, consciousness of existence, still persists during the first stages of *nirodha* in the yogin who has concentrated his mind on an object.

F. Saṃprajñāta (with knowledge)

In this *sūtra* Patañjali limits himself to saying that when *nirodha* has as its concomitants *vitarka* or *vicāra* or *ānanda* or *asmitā*, it is *saṃprajñāta*, that is "with knowledge"—in other terms, it is sufficient that a single one of the elements indicated be present for *nirodha* to be "with knowledge". In fact *vitarka* and *vicāra* imply the knowledge of a "gross" and of a "subtle" object, respectively, *ānanda* and *asmitā* imply an experiential knowledge which is "subtle" in itself and which also refers to "subtle" objects like bliss and existence.

In our view *nirodha* with *vitarka*, *vicāra*, *ānanda* and *asmitā* does not constitute the only case of *saṃprajñāta nirodha* or restraint with knowledge, as will be seen in the commentary of the following *sūtra*.

18

विरामप्रत्ययाभ्यासपूर्वः संस्कारशेषोऽन्यः ॥

VIRĀMAPRATYAYĀBHYĀSAPŪRVAḤ SAṂSKĀRAŚEṢO 'NYAḤ.

Another (nirodha : restraint) is preceded by abhyāsa (effort for stability) in the experience (pratyaya) of the cessation (virāma) (of vitarka, vicāra, ānanda and asmitā) and during it there remains a saṃskāra (subliminal impression).

Before commenting on the different terms of this *sūtra* it is proper, for the sake of clarity, that we refer briefly to the theory of the *samāpattis*.

A. Theory of the Samāpattis

Patañjali develops the theory of the *samāpattis* in the *sūtras* I.41-51. We shall elucidate the precise meaning of this expression in the commentary of the said *sūtras*. For the time being, concerning the effects of the commentary of this *sūtra*, it is sufficient for us to show that the term *samāpatti* can be taken to mean "concentration of the mind". The different *samāpattis* express different stages of concentration. The *samāpattis* are the following :

Sūtra 42 : *Samāpatti* with *vitarka* (concentration with analysis of a gross object)

Sūtra 43 : *Samāpatti* without *vitarka*

Sūtra 44 : *Samāpatti* with *vicāra* (concentration with analysis of a subtle object)

Sūtra 45 : *Samāpatti* without *vicāra*

Sūtra 46 : In the *samāpatti* without *vicāra* is produced *prajñā* or intuitive knowledge

Sutra 50 : *Prajñā* produces a *saṃskāra* which hinders the formation of other *saṃskāras*

Sūtra 51: With the restraint of the *saṃskāra* mentioned, the total restraint is produced; it is the concentration of the mind at its highest stage.

B. Cessation (*Virāma*)

In the opinion of the commentators and translators who follow Vyāsa, this *sūtra*, at the mention of "cessation", would indicate the "cessation of all the functions (*vṛtti*) of the mind". In our opinion the *sūtra* refers to the cessation of the mental activities *vitarka* (analysis of gross objects), and *vicāra* (analysis of subtle objects), and of the sensations *ānanda* (bliss) and *asmitā* (consciousness of existence).

Our interpretation is primarily justified on grounds of proximity: the term *vṛtti* has been mentioned many times earlier and Patañjali ends his references to the *vṛttis* in the *Sūtra* I. 11; after which he turns to other themes: the means to obtain *nirodha* (I.12-16) and different types of *nirodha* (I.17-20). Had reference, in this *sūtra*, been made to the cessation of the *vṛttis*, then *vṛtti-virāma* should have been said, for the sake of clarity. On the contrary, the indicated mental activities and sensations have been just mentioned in the previous *sūtra*. Besides, in conformity with the *sūtra* style for the comprehension of a *sūtra* are to be understood concepts drawn from the *sūtras* immediately preceding it.

Moreover, if *virāma* signified the cessation of all the mental processes, as the traditional interpretation has it, this cessation would then constitute the total *nirodha*, the final aim of yoga (see *sūtra* I.2). How could Patañjali say, in this *sūtra*, that there exists another *nirodha* preceded by that total *nirodha*, which is the ultimate limit of the yogic effort?

Lastly, our interpretation makes it possible to have a better assessment of the classification of the *nirodhas*, given by Patañjali in the present *sūtras* I.17-18, with the theory of *samāpattis*, which is fundamental to yoga and dealt with in the *sūtra* I.41 and ff. About this argument in favour of our interpretation, see section H of our commentary on this very *sūtra*.

C. Experience (pratyaya)

As we have shown in our commentary of the *sūtra* I.10 C, we interpret *pratyaya* as meaning "experience".

D. The Experience of Cessation (virāmapratyaya)

Conforming to the explanations which precede, *virāmapratyaya* is simply the experience which the yogī has of the cessation of the mental activities and of the sensations, mentioned in the earlier *sūtra*. When these activities and sensations have ceased, there arises, so to say, a "void" in the consciousness of the yogī and the latter seizes, experiences, lives the "void" mentioned.[53]

E. Abhyāsa (Effort for Stability)

Abhyāsa constitutes one of the means to produce *nirodha* of the mental processes, as explained in *sūtra* I.13.

In the present *sūtra*, the *abhyāsa* in the experience, in the living of cessation is the effort to maintain the mind stable in the said experience; the will that the sole contents of consciousness be this experience. The mind is fixed, so to say, in the void left by cessation.

F. Preceded by (pūrva)

For the "other" *niodha* to be produced, it is necessary that there should have already occurred *abhyāsa* in the experience of the cessation of the elements indicated in the previous *sūtra.*

The path covered up to this moment has then been: (1) restraint with knowledge (*sūtra* I.17), (2) cessation of the elements concomitant with the restraint with knowledge which have been earlier mentioned (the first part of the present *sūtra*) and (3) effort for stabilizing the mind in the experience of this cessation (the second part of the present *sūtra*).

G. Saṃskāra (Subliminal Impression)

Extending the explanation given in the *sūtra* I.11, we say that any expression of the mental life (the mental processes enumerated

53. Oddly Taimni, without respecting the norms of Sanskrit language, translates *virāmapratyaya* by "cessation of *pratyaya*".

in *sūtra* I.6, the emotions, the passions, the habits, the desires, the volitive acts, etc.) deposits in the mind a *saṃskāra*, or a latent subliminal impression. These latent subliminal impressions constitute the predisposition, the "seed" of other new manifestations of mental life; they rest in what may be called the unconsciousness in a potential form and will necessarily actualize themselves, "yield their fruits", either in this life, or in another life. While these *saṃskāras* exist, there exists the bondage to existence, to the cycle of reincarnations. For this reason Yoga claims, on one hand, to impede the formation of new *saṃskāras* and, on the other, to uproot, "to burn" the already existing "seeds".

Now we have to determine to what *saṃskāra* or *saṃskāras* does Patañjali refer in the expression *saṃskāraśeṣa*.

According to traditional interpretation the term *saṃskāraśeṣa* would mean: "in which only subliminal impressions (*saṃskāras*, in the plural) are left" (Woods, Vivekananda; Bengali Baba, H. Āranya) and the *saṃskāras* which are left would be the *saṃskāras* produced by *nirodha* (restraint) itself (Vyāsa, *ad* I.51, H. Āranya).

For us the word *saṃskāraśeṣa* means: "in which is left a *saṃskāra* and this *saṃskāra* which remains is for us the *saṃskāra* produced by *prajñā* mentioned in *sūtra* I.50. The reasons on which we base our opinion are the following:

We cannot accept the traditional interpretation expressed earlier, as it is contrary to a principle of the doctrine of yoga accepted by this traditional interpretation, and thus falls into a contradiction with itself. Actually in the total and absolute *nirodha*, which occurs in the stage indicated in the *sūtra* I.51, there are no *saṃskāras*: they are all destroyed, whatever be their origin (Vyāsa *ad* I.18; I.51 and IV.29; Bhoja *ad* I.18; Vijñānabhikṣu, pp. 34 and 35; Taimni, pp. 124 and 432).[54] But the traditional interpretation considers, in commenting on the present *sūtra* (I.18), that *nirodha*, to which the *sūtra* refers, corresponds to the total and

54. To avoid this contradiction some traditional interpreters, as Vijñānabhikṣu and Taimni, are obliged to divide the final stage in two sub-stages, one with *saṃskāras* and another without *saṃskāras*. In this way they manifest the weakness of their position and corroborate our interpretation.

absolute *nirodha* and does, nevertheless, on determining the meaning of the word *saṃskāraśeṣa* admit the existence of *saṃskāras* in the final stage of the yogic process, in violation of the principle mentioned earlier and in contradiction with itself.[55]

Further, the interpretation which we propose lends to the present *sūtra* (I.18) greater congruence with the theory of the *samāpattis* exposed earlier. We explain it in the following paragraph.

H. The Position of the nirodha of the previous sūtra and of the nirodha of the present sūtra in the theory of samāpattis

According to traditional opinion the *nirodha* of the previous *sūtra* (I.17) is that which occurs in the *samāpatti* with *vitarka* and with *vicāra* (I.42 and 44). The *nirodha* of the present *sūtra* (I.18) would constitute, as already indicated, the stage mentioned in *sūtra* I.51: It would be the total *nirodha* which accompanies the concentration of the mind at its highest stage.

Insofar as the previous *sūtra* (I.17) is concerned, we agree with the traditional interpretation. But we believe that the *nirodha* of the present *sūtra* (I.18) is that which occurs during the *samāpatti* without *vicāra* (I.44)[56], which is followed by the total *nirodha* referred to in the *sūtra* I.51. Thus this *sūtra* does not describe the final stage of the yogic process, but actually a previous albeit more advanced stage which is described in *sūtra* I.17.

We justify our view in the following manner:

1. As we have seen in Section B of our commentary on this same *sūtra*, the *cessation* to which this *sūtra* refers is not the cessation of all the *vṛttis*, but the cessation of the *vitarka* and *vicāra* activities mentioned in the previous *sūtra*. Now, the cessation of all the *vṛttis* constitutes the essential condition for the production of the total *nirodha* (I.2 and I.51). As the cessation of the *vṛttis* does not exist, we have not yet entered the final stage of the yogic process, total *nirodha*.

55. See also Sinha, *A History* II, p. 165n, and *Indian Psychology* I, p. 351.

56. And also during the *samāpatti* without *vitarka* on account of the identification of both done by Patañjali. See section A of our commentary of *sūtra* I.44.

The cessation of the activities indicated (*samāpatti* without *vicāra*) is the necessary condition for the occurrence of the total *nirodha* of the *sūtra* I.51. But it is not a sufficient condition, since it bears with it the emergence of a new mental activity constituted by intuitive knowledge (I.48). For the total *nirodha* to emerge it is necessary that this intuitive knowledge disappears in its turn together with the *saṃskāra* to which it gives rise (I.50 and I.51).

2. Again as we have seen in Section G. of our commentary on this same *sūtra*, the reference to one *saṃskāra* or to *saṃskāras* (*saṃskāraśeṣa*) does not allow a reference of this *sūtra* to total *nirodha*, in which the *saṃskāras* do not exist. On the other hand this *sūtra* can be properly referred to for the stage before total *nirodha*, or when the *vicāra* has ceased (*samāpatti* without *vicāra*) and *prajñā* has emerged, which produces a *saṃskāra* (I.48 and I.50).

I. The Other (*anya*)

Patañjali limits himself to saying that the *nirodha* dealt with in the present *sūtra* is the "other"[57]

The traditional interpretation takes the term *anya* in its meaning of "opposed" (to the previous) and consequently thinks that this *sūtra* deals with *samādhi* (concentration of the mind) without knowledge (*asaṃprajñāta*)—the final stage of the entire yogic process.

Our view is different from the traditional. We believe that *anya* must be taken in the sense of "other" without the connotation of "opposition to the previous", and that it signifies "other *nirodha saṃprajñāta*", that is, "other type of restraint with knowledge".[58] Our opinion derives from our exposition in the previous section of this commentary.

57. Let us remember that for the traditional interpretation this *sūtra* as well as the previous one (I.17) refer to *samādhi* and not to *nirodha* (restraint). See our commentary of *sūtra* I.17, section A. This divergence does not affect the explanation given in this section H.

58. It is not contrary to the norms of *sūtra* style to understand as implicit in this *sūtra* the ideas of *nirodha* and *saṃprajñāta* (restraint with knowledge), which we take from the previous *sūtra*.

Virāmapratyayābhyāsapūrvaḥ saṃskāraśeṣo 'nyaḥ I.18

The knowledge which accompanies *nirodha* relates, in the *sūtra*, to intuitive knowledge. Thus the previous *sūtra* has dealt with one type of restraint with knowledge; this *sūtra* deals with another type of restraint with knowledge.

19

भवप्रत्ययो विदेहप्रकृतिलयानाम् ॥

BHAVAPRATYAYO VIDEHAPRAKṚTILAYĀNĀM.

The experience (pratyaya) of their condition (bhava) (is the nirodha—restraint of the mental processes) of the disembodied ones (videha) and of those who dissolve in the primordial matter (prakṛtilaya).

To understand this *sūtra* it is necessary to bear in mind the following philosophical principles of the Sāṃkhya-Yoga.

A. "Gross" Body, "Subtle" Body and Spiritual Entity

Man is made of a material structure which comprehends, on one hand, the "gross" body (flesh, bones, hair, etc.) and, on the other, the "subtle" body, composed mainly of the mind (*citta*) and the senses, and of a spiritual entity (*puruṣa*). This subtle body functions thanks to the spiritual entity and it is through the subtle body that the spiritual entity comes into contact with the external world. In the mind (subtle body) are accumulated the subliminal impressions left behind by all the mental processes (see our commentary on *sūtra* I.11), and the karmic residues, or the consequences not yet consummated of the actions which have been accomplished. The mind carries with it, from one existence to another, these subliminal impressions and these karmic residues.

B. The Reincarnations

Man[59] is normally chained to the cycle of reincarnations. The primordial cause of this bondage is ignorance: man ignores his

59. As we shall see what really transmigrate is the spiritual entity together with the subtle body.

authentic nature and identifies himself with what is not (with the mental processes, *vṛtti*). See the *sūtras* I.4 and I.17 and our commentary on these *sūtras*, sections B, C and E respectively.

C. Liberation

Man can free himself from the cycle of reincarnations by eliminating its cause, ignorance, by means of the methods which Yoga and the other doctrines of India place at his disposal. The individual who has succeeded in destroying ignorance dies, at his death, for the last time and shall not be reborn.

D. The Destiny of the Gross Body after Death

When a man dies, his gross body dissolves into his original material elements: earth, water, light (or fire), air and space.

E. The Destiny of the Subtle Body and of the Spiritual Entity after Death

Regarding the subtle body and the spiritual entity, after death, two possible situations are posited, from the point of view of individual destiny.

1. In the case of the non-liberated man who dies, his spiritual entity remains bound to the cycle of reincarnations, taking birth and dying time after time. During this transmigratory process persists the spiritual entity accompanied by the subtle body. What determines the fate of the individual in his new reincarnation is the fact of the subtle body carrying with itself the subliminal impressions and the Karmic residues.

2. In the case of the man freed in life (*jīvan-mukta*) his spiritual entity, at the moment of death, withdraws within itself, "establishes itself in its own nature" and the subtle body, for its part, without the support of the spiritual entity, regresses, on account of its being a material entity, to its primal source, the primordial matter (*prakṛti*), and definitively dissolves in it.[60]

60. A third situation is produced in the cosmic level. World is submitted to a cyclic process of evolution (*sarga*) and dissolution (*pralaya*). When a cosmic dissolution takes place, automatically takes place also the dissolution into the primordial matter of the subtle body of all individuals. We must

F. Automatic nirodha (Restriant)

When the dissolution of the gross body in its elements is realized, as well as the dissolution of the subtle body in the primal matter (the latter dissolution presupposes the previous or simultaneous dissolution of the gross body), the mind does automatically stop functioning and the mental processes are suspended. Then there arises an automatic *nirodha* or restraint of the mental processes, *ipso facto*, without the intervention of the will and of the effort of the individual as is the case of the *nirodha* dealt with in the following *sūtra*.

We may now explain the present *sūtra* in the light of the preceding remarks.

G. The videha (Disembodied Ones) and the automatic nirodha

In our view, Patañjali refers, by means of the term *videha* (disembodied), to the human beings who die without having reached freedom. They lose their gross body. Their subtle body and their spirit pass on to a new reincarnation. When they die and their mind stops functioning the automatic *nirodha* is produced.

H. The prakṛtilayas (which dissolve in the primal matter) and automatic nirodha

By means of the expression *prakṛtilaya* Patañjali refers to the beings whose subtle body dissolves in the primal matter, as is the case of those who die[61] as *jīvan-mukta*[62] (liberated in life). As we have already shown, the dissolution of the gross body precedes the dissolution of the subtle body and, with the dissolution of the subtle body, is produced the automatic *nirodha*.

---

understand that in the evolution that follows the cosmic dissolution, the spiritual entities, which have not been already liberated, return to the cycle of reincarnations and that during the cosmic dissolution the spiritual entities experience a quasi-*kaivalya* (isolation).

61. As it is also the case for all the liberated or not liberated beings affected by a cosmic dissolution.

62. If the man, who has reached liberation during his life (*jīvan-mukta*), is not already, in the moment he dies, in a state of *nirodha*, since in that case there would not be place for an automatic *nirodha*.

I. Bhava-pratyaya (Experience of One's Condition)

We have already indicated in the *sūtra* I.10 that *pratyaya* means: "what comes to consciousness", "experience".

Bhava means "state", "condition", "form of existence".

Bhava-pratyaya literally means: "the experience of the condition".

The meaning of the present *sūtra* is, according to the explanation given in the preceding paragraphs, the following: automatic *nirodha* is produced when the individual enters into the condition, state of *videha* or *prakṛtilaya.* The state of *videha* or *prakṛtilaya* constitutes the *nirodha* of those who enter into it. But for the automatic *nirodha* to be produced it is necessary that this state reaches the consciousness of the individual, comes within the compass of consciousness, becomes subjectively interiorized within the consciousness and passes through it. So long as this does not happen the automatic *nirodha* cannot arise. Likewise deep sleep, as the *sūtra* I.10 says, is not the mere absence of the other mental processes (*citta vṛtti*), but it is the experience (*pratyaya*) by the individual of this absence.

J. The Interpretation of Vyāsa and of Bhoja

Vyāsa explains the expression *videha* as *deva*, god. We do think it right to consider the Hindu gods as "*videhas*", as "incorporeal", since the Hindu view affirms that the gods do have bodies, although these be of a divine nature. Still, if it is admitted that the gods are *videhas*, there is no reason to restrict this term to the gods, as it can be used also for any human being who dies and persists in the cycle of reincarnations. Moreover, it is difficult to think that the gods, because of their being gods, would experience a *nirodha*, since the gods, according to the Hindu view, live their divine life fully on the intellectual and emotional level.

Bhoja restricts the term *videha* to a certain type of yogīs: to those who have not gone beyond the concentration on *ānanda* (see the commentary of Bhoja on I.17). This interpretation is unacceptable to us as it represents an arbitrary restriction of the expression.

Vyāsa is scarcely explicit in his commentary on the term *prakṛtilaya*. It seems to refer to a certain type of yogīs whose subtle body would dissolve in the primal matter for a certain length of time at the end of which these yogīs would return to the cycle of reincarnations[63]. During this time these yogīs would experience a sort of *kaivalya* (*kaivalyam iva*).

In this commentary on I.17 Bhoja restricts the term *prakṛtilaya* to those yogīs who have not succeeded to go beyond the concentration on *asmitā*.

Our opinion is that these interpretations are not acceptable, because there is no basis for the limitations read into the concepts of *videha* and *prakṛtilaya*.

63. Gauḍapāda, in his commentary of the *Sāṃkhyakārikās* 45 refers to the dissolution of primordial matter as a consequence of detachment (*vairāgya*), indicating that this dissolution is only transitory and does not mean liberation, *mokṣa*.

20

श्रद्धावीर्यस्मृतिसमाधिप्रज्ञापूर्वक इतरेषाम् ॥

ŚRADDHĀVĪRYASMṚTISAMĀDHIPRAJÑĀPŪRVAKA ITAREṢĀM.

(The nirodha) of the others is preceded by faith (śraddhā), energy (vīrya), attention (smṛti), concentration of the mind (samādhi), intuitive knowledge (prajñā).

A. The nirodha (restraint) of the others

In the preceding sūtra Patañjali has referred to a *sui generis* form of the production of the *nirodha*: in the *videhas* (disembodied) and in the *prakṛtilayas* (those who dissolve in the primal matter) *nirodha* is automatically prodnced by the simple fact of reaching these respective conditions, indeed at the very moment when the latter conditions are attained. The only requisite for this *nirodha* is this condition, this form of existence.

In the present *sūtra* Patañjali speaks of another form of attaining the *nirodha*: the form which corresponds to the "others". The "others" are those who are neither *videhas* nor *prakṛtilayas*, consequently, all yogīs.

The *nirodha* of the *videhas* and of the *prakṛtilayas* implies death and it may be therefore averred that the preceding *sūtra* refers to *nirodha post mortem.* The *nirodha* to which this *sūtra* refers, that of the yogīs in general, is a *nirodha ante mortem.*

If the *nirodha* of the *videhas* and of the *prakṛtilayas* is produced, as we say, in an automatic, spontaneous form, the *nirodha* of the "others", of the yogīs in general, is produced in a different form. It presupposes a series of requisites on the yogin's part : faith, energy, attention, concentration of the mind, intuitive knowledge.

B. Faith (śraddhā)

We understand "faith" as the acceptation of Yoga, that is, the trust in the reality and the excellence of the goal which it pursues (i.e. *kaivalya*=isolation) and in the effectiveness of its methods to reach this goal : conviction, trust, devoid of all doubt and accompanied by a sentiment of mental calmness. Faith is necessary in the yogin for him to enter the path of yoga and to maintain himself in it.

C. Energy (vīrya)

We have translated the term *vīrya* by "energy". It could also be translated by "vigour", "strength". It is necessary for the yogin to have a certain energy, a certain strength, a certain basic vigour. The yogin cannot be an indolent man, without physical resistance, weak, without will, considering that the yogic practice (for instance, the concentration of the mind on a single object or maintaining oneself for a long moment in a particular posture) requires effort, persistence, dedication, and implies physical and psychical loss.

Of course, with the yogin having spent a long time in yoga, the yogic practices will become each time more automatic, more habitual, more unconscious. As a result these practices will require of the yogin less energy, less effort of his conscious will.

D. Smṛti (Attention)

In *sūtra* I.11 the meaning of the expression *smṛti* has been established. The definition which Patañjali gives of *smṛti* at times signifies 'attention', at other times 'memory', since it refers to an element common to both—the fact that a perceived object does not leave consciousness and maintains itself in front of it. The *smṛti*-attention, according to the preceding, is the foundation of mental concentration which could certainly not take place without a concomitant act of attention.

The traditional commentators who take *smṛti* in *sūtra* I.11 only as 'memory', when they comment this *sūtra*, see themselves compelled to have recourse to interpretations which are unacceptable.

Thus Vācaspati Miśra takes *smṛti* in the sense of *dhyāna* ("meditation"). Other commentators like Vijñānabhikṣu, Kṛṣṇavallabha, follow his interpretation. But there exists no basis for understanding *smṛti*-memory (the only aspect of *smṛti* which these authors accept) as *dhyāna*, 'meditation', since the definition of the word *dhyāna* given by Patañjali in III.2 has nothing to do with 'memory'. Moreover Vācaspati Miśra gives to the technical term *smṛti* two different meanings : 'memory' in *sūtra* I.11 and 'meditation' in the present *sutra*. In our opinion, as we have said it in the commentary of *sutra* I.10, it is not correct to translate the same technical term in the *Yogasūtras* in different ways, especially when Patañjali himself gives a precise definition of it. Probably Vācaspati Miśra has chosen *dhyāna*, 'meditation', to replace by it *smṛti*-memory, since in the exposition of the yogic method which Patañjali develops in the Second Book and at the beginning of the Third Book, *dhyāna* precedes *samādhi*, concentration of the mind.

Woods, who translates *smṛti* in the *sūtra* I.11 by "memory", interprets *smṛti* in the present *sūtra* with another meaning, that of "mindfulness", which is akin to "attention". Thus Woods too makes the same mistake as does Vācaspati Miśra by translating the same technical expression in two different, distinct forms. It would appear that Woods has had recourse to this interpretation by considering the meaning which the term Pāli *sati*, equivalent to the Sanskrit *smṛti*, has in the Buddhist texts, in conformity to the traditional interpretations.[64]

Taimni's position is different from that of the other authors already mentioned. Taimni translates, in the present *sutra*, the term *smṛti* by "memory", in the same way as in *sūtra* I.11, but he stresses that he interprets *smṛti* not in its ordinary psychological meaning, but in a special sense. *Smṛti* is for Taimni the remembrance of the past experiences, the memory of which is useful for the yogin's progress. Taimni's interpretation is unacceptable as it arbitrarily restricts the definition which Patañjali gives for "*smṛti*", since it understands by the expression *anu-*

64. See note 3, p. 45 of Woods' translation.

bhūtaviṣaya ("object perceived or experienced") of the *sūtra* I.11, only the determined experiences of the past, thus limiting the scope of the term *anubhūtaviṣaya.* For Patañjali *smṛti* is the not being removed from consciousness of a perceived object, whatever be the latter. For Taimni *smṛti* would be to maintain alive the memory only of determined experiences. Further it is not clear how the remembrance of the past experiences could be a direct determining condition of *samādhi*, the concentration of the mind, as attention is. On the contrary, it appears that a remembering activity, whatever be its contents, on account of its discursive nature, does in no way favour the concentration of the mind.

E. Concentration of the Mind (*samādhi*)

Patañjali deals with *samādhi* in later *sūtras*, especially in I.41-51. The more important details will be tackled in the commentaries of these *sūtras.* Meanwhile we limit ourselves to providing only a rough idea of what is *samādhi.*

Samādhi is an intense and prolonged concentration of the mind. The mind is fixed on a specific object (thing, sound, image, idea, etc.). As a consequence of this act of intensified attention the object occupies the entire field of consciousness, presents itself, alone and isolated, with an unaccustomed intensity, to consciousness. On account of the monoideism that the concentration produces, the functions of the mind cease : there are no ideas, no reasonings, no sentiments, no volitions, no memories. The senses stop functioning and odours, tastes, forms disappear. The external world ceases to affect the yogin; it does not reach him; it has been eliminated. The yogin himself stops perceiving himself, feeling himself, experiencing himself. He is totally calm, serene, indifferent, unchanging, alone before the object which shines in front of him with an extraordinary presence. One instant more and the same object disappears and the individual sinks in a state of vacuity and of total and absolute isolation. It is the yogic trance.

There are different stages of *samādhi* (concentration of the mind) to which correspond different stages of restraint (*nirodha*) of the mental processes. The more intense is the concentration, the more profound and general will the restraint be. To the highest stage of concentration corresponds the total and absolute restraint (last *sūtra* of Book I).

F. Intuitive Knowledge (prajñā)

Prajñā arises as a consequence of an intense concentration (*samādhi*) of the mind on a determined object, at the moment when the latter shines before consciousness with an extraordinary presence. *Prajñā* emerges before the highest stage of concentration (*samādhi*), before the total and absolute restraint (*nirodha*). *Prajñā* is an intuitive knowledge of the object on which the mind has been concentrating. *Prajñā* is the true knowledge of the object, according to Patañjali in I.48.[65] See the commentary on the *sūtra* mentioned.

G. Pūrvaka (Preceded By)

We may agree with Vyāsa and the other commentators that each of the requisites, mentioned in this *sūtra*, is a condition which determines the one following it. Faith (*śraddhā*) is necessary to put energy (*vīrya*) in the practice of Yoga; in its turn energy is necessary to the effort required by attention (*smṛti*). We have already shown that attention is necessary for the concentration of the mind (*samādhi*). In fine, *prajñā* (intuitive knowledge) can only emerge in an advanced stage of concentration.

The present *sūtra* shows that the requisites mentioned are in their turn the determining condition of the *nirodha* (restraint). As these requisites reckon among them *prajñā* which occurs before total *nirodha* (see section F of the same commentary) it is necessary that it be understood that the *sūtra* is actually alluding

65. This intuitive knowledge, although it has some points of contact with any intuitive knowledge, has some special characteristics, owing to the circumstances in which it is produced.

to *nirodha* at its highest stage (I.51). However, we must observe that *śraddhā*, *vīrya*, *smṛti* and *samādhi* also are a determining condition of the diverse stages of *nirodha* which precede the total *nirodha*.

21

तीव्रसंवेगानामासन्नः ॥

TĪVRASAṂVEGĀNĀMĀSANNAḤ.

For those of intense fervour (saṃvega) (nirodha) is near.

A. The Concept of saṃvega (Fervour)

Patañjali has in the *sūtra* I.20 pointed out the conditions necessary in the case of the yogins in general for the attainment of *nirodha*. If the yogin has faith and energy, if he develops attention (*smṛti*) and if, by means of adequate practice, he reaches *samādhi* and *prajñā* is produced, the yogin will *neccssarily* obtain *nirodha* in its several stages (as has been elucidated in the commentary on *sūtra* I.20).

In *sūtras* I.21-31, Patañjali discusses the means to accelerate or facilitate the attainment of *nirodha* : (1) fervour and (2) surrender to the Lord.

The present *sūtra* and the followling one refer to the first of those accelerating means : fervour (*saṃvega*), enthusiasm, vehemence, exaltation, introduced by the yogin in the actualisation of his practices. The yogin who spends only a short time in concentration and unenthusiastically completes it, will progress more slowly than he who spends all his time in it and pours all his fervour into it.

Fervour does not eliminate the necessity of the pre-conditions indicated in *sūtra* I.20 for the realisation of restraint (*nirodha*), that is, by itself fervour does not produce the restraint of the mental processes (*cittavṛttinirodha*). To attain restraint the yogin must possess faith, energy and attention; he shall have to realize concentration of the mind and intuitive knowledge must arise in him. This is absolutely necessary.

B. Saṃvega (fervour) and vīrya (energy)

Vīrya (mentioned in *sūtra* I.20) is the physical and psychic energy which the yogin must *necessarily* have to realize the yogic practices which lead him to *nirodha*. *Vīrya* is a *sine qua non* condition.

Saṃvega is, so to say, a stimulus of a psychical nature, like fanaticism. It may or may not happen. But when it happens it does enhance the realisation of the yogic process. Above all it bears upon *vīrya*, upon the energy which the yogin pours into his practices, thereby increasing and multiplying it.

22

मृदुमध्याधिमात्रत्वात्ततोऽपि विशेषः ॥

MṚDUMADHYĀDHIMĀTRATVĀT TATO 'PI VIŚEṢAḤ.

Due to the fact that (fervour = saṃvega) can be mild, moderate or intense, (there arises) also a difference from it (tatas).

The idea expressed in this *sūtra* is the following : due to the fact that fervour can have several grades there exist differences, in function of these diverse grades, in the rapidity with which *nirodha* is attained; a greater fervour, a higher speed in the attainment of *nirodha*, and so on successively.

23

ईश्वरप्रणिधानाद्वा ॥

ĪŚVARAPRAṆIDHĀNĀD VĀ

or from the surrender to the Lord.

A. Meaning of the sūtra

The meaning of the present *sūtra* is : *Due to the fact that the surrender to the Lord can have different grades (mild, moderate or intense) there also exist differences, in function of these different grades, in the rapidity with which the restraint (nirodha) of the mental processes is attained.*

B. Basis of the Previous Interpretation

These are the reasons which justify our interpretation of the present *sūtra* : (1) We think that the *vā* ("or") of this *sūtra* correlates the ablative *-praṇidhānāt* with *tatas* (lit. : "from it") of the previous *sūtra,* which, in its turn, stands for *saṃvegāt* ("from fervour"). (2) It is necessary to complete the present *sūtra* with concepts expressed in the previous one and implied in the latter : *mṛdumadhyādhimātratvāt* and *viśeṣa*—and all this in accordance with the *sūtra* style.

Consequently the complete form of the *sūtra* would be : (*mṛdumadhyādhimātratvāt*) *īśvarapraṇidhānād vā* (*viśeṣaḥ*) and its literal translation would be : "or (there arises also a difference) from the surrender to the Lord (due to the fact that it can be mild, moderate or intense)".[66]

66. We do not think that *vā* unites this *sūtra* with I.12, as Hauer, *Der Yoga*, p. 225, maintains, firstly owing to the distance that separates both *sūtras* and secondly because *abhyāsavairāgyābhyām* ("through *abhyāsa* and

C. Scope of this sūtra

In the *sūtras* I.21 and I.22 Patañjali tells us that the more intense be the fervour (*saṃvega*)—the enthusiasm, the determination—which the yogin evinces in the practice of Yoga, the sooner will the restraint of the mental processes occur. There is a correlation between the level of fervour and the closeness of *nirodha.*

The present *sūtra* expresses, in an extremely condensed and elliptical form, the same idea, with regard to the surrender to the Lord : the more the surrender to the Lord be intense, the nearer will the restraint of the mental processes be. Thus there exists the same correlation between the level of intensity of the surrender to the Lord and the closeness of the *nirodha*[67].

D. The Lord

The Lord (*Īśvara*) is a spirit the main characteristics of which are given in the following *sūtras.* The concept of "Lord" is further enhanced by the well known commentators, who contribute to it a greater number of characteristics than those mentioned by Patañjali. The presence of the concept of a God in Patañjali's system, which transforms it into a theistic system, marks it as being different from the non-theist Sāṃkhya. Further the surrender to the Lord is a concept which is singularly religious and links Yoga with religion.

E. Nature of the Surrender to the Lord

When the individual surrenders himself entirely to the Lord,

---

vairāgya", I.12) must be considered as an instrumental (see commentary of Vyāsa) and consequently cannot be coordinated with *īśvarapraṇidhānāt* which is in ablative.

67. Hauer, *Der Yoga,* p. 225, and following ones, relying in his interpretation of particle *vā* indicated in the previous *sūtra,* considers that the surrender to the Lord is a third means (together with *abhyāsa* and *vairāgya* of I.12) to obtain the *nirodha,* restraint.

We consider that Hauer is wrong, since we consider that his interpretation of particle *vā* is erroneous, as we have indicated in note 66 and also because Patañjali in I.12 indicates in a very precise way that the only means to get *nirodha* are *abhyāsa* (effort for stability) and *vairāgya* (detachment).

he concentrates on this transcendent entity that is the Lord. All his thoughts, emotions and activities are projected on to this supra-mundane entity, which totally absorbs him.[68]

F. The Surrender to the Lord and Vairāgya (Detachment)

As a consequence of this surrender to the Lord, the individual becomes detached from the world; the world does not interest him; he can act, but without any consideration for the fruit of his actions. His *vairāgya* varies in intensity according to that of his self-surrender to the Lord. According to the *sūtra* I.12 *vairāgya* is one of the two necessary and indispensable means to obtain the restraint of the mental processes. The self-surrender to the Lord furnishes thus one of the fundamental means required to arrive at *nirodha.*

Although Patañjali does not expressly say that the surrender to the Lord produces *vairāgya*, the effect described may nevertheless be attributed to him, if we consider the following : (1) Of its own nature, the surrender to the Lord does indeed necessarily bring about, as effect, detachment from the world; (2) Moreover it is common knowledge that, in a context similar to that of Yoga, in Christian mysticism, devotion to God produces this effect in the soul of his devotees.[69]

G. Surrender to the Lord, abhyāsa and samādhi

In the preceding paragraphs we have referred to the surrender to the Lord in its relation to *vairāgya,* one of the two means to obtain *nirodha,* in conformity to the *sūtra* I.12. But the surrender to the Lord is also related to another aspect of the yogic activity : the concentration of the mind (*samādhi*) which constitutes the essential element of Yoga (see our commentary on *sūtra* I.20) and which is produced by means of concentrating the mind and maintaining it stable (*abhyāsa*) on a single object or entity. This concentration of the mind will in its turn

68. We must remember such religious personalities as Rāmakriṣṇa, Santa Teresa de Jessú, San Juan de la Cruz, San Francesco d'Assisi.

69. See Unterhill, *Mysticism*, pp. 185 and 189.

produce the restraint of the mental processes, which is the ultimate goal of Yoga.

In fact the Lord can be the object on which the particular yogin fixes, stabilizes his mind. Furthermore for him who has completely surrendered himself, the Lord shall be the object on which he will feel bound to fix and stabilize his mind. The fascination which the Lord exerts on the person who has devoted, surrendered himself to Him, would make it impossible for him to choose another object upon which he could fix and stabilize his mind.

In *sūtra* I.28 Patañjali will mention two ways in which the yogin, in the context of his surrender to the Lord, can fix and stabilize his mind : the repetition of the syllable AUM (the symbol of the Lord) and "meditation" on its meaning.

This fixation and stabilization of the mind becoming each time more intense will lead, by means of the yogic process described by Patañjali in the following *sūtras*, to the concentration of the mind (*samādhi*) which will bring about the restraint of the mental processes, the ultimate goal of yoga.

However, in opposition to the case of *vairāgya*, Patañjali explicitly states that from the surrender to the Lord emerges the concentration of the mind (*samādhi*) (see *sūtras* II.1-2 and II.45). Though Patañjali does not say so, we must understand that this concentration, which arises out of the surrender to the Lord, will be produced according to the yogic process described in earlier paragraphs, which constitutes the essential method of Yoga.

H. Fervour and Self-Surrender to the Lord

As we have shown in an earlier section there exists a parallelism between the fervour (*saṃvega*) and the surrender to the Lord (*īśvarapraṇidhāna*) in the sense that, corresponding to a more or less intense fervour, or to a more or less complete surrender, obtaining restraint (*nirodha*) will take place sooner or later. Nevertheless it behoves us to establish the fundamental difference between both. Fervour or enthusiasm or resolution evinced by the yogin is simply a tonality which accompanies the yogic activity making it more or less intense. On the other hand, the surrender to the Lord is not a tonality which *accompanies* the yogic activity, it *produces* the *vairāgya*, one of the fundamental and necessary factors which lead to the restraint of the mental processes.

I. The Importance of the Lord

With regard to the theme of the importance of the Lord in Patañjali's system what we must first of all take note is that it is possible to practise Yoga and realize its goal (restraint of the mental processes, *cittavṛttinirodha*, and *kaivalya*, or the total isolation of the Spirit produced in it) without having recourse to the Lord, or without surrendering one's self to the Lord. Actually the yogin can fix his mind on an object which need not be the Lord and succeed in achieving concentration of the mind and the restraint of the mental processes. In the *sūtras* I.35-38 Patañjali indicates a series of objects which can serve as the basis for fixing the mind and in the *sūtra* I.39 further points out that this can be effected on any object desired by the yogin. In Buddhism, which does not affirm an *īśvara*, the concentration of the mind is realized on other types of objects. For its part, *vairāgya* or detachment from the sensible world can be produced as the result of a philosophical meditation, of a disgust for the world, of an exercise of the will, without necessity for the individual of concentrating on one transcendent entity. By its emphasis put on impermanence, unsubstantiality, and suffering of the world, of contingent reality, Buddhism generates detachment in its followers.

In the light of the preceding argument the Lord, in Yoga, is but a secondary element which could be left out.

But it acquires a great importance for the yogin who, as a result of religious inspiration, surrenders himself to the Lord. The surrender to the Lord shall produce in him—as already explained—a detachment. Moreover, fixing and stabilizing his mind on the Lord, he shall succeed in achieving the concentration which will be followed by restraint. Besides, the surrender to the Lord will fill the yogin with fervour in the actualization of his yogic practices.

In any way the Lord does not, in Patañjali's yoga, play as important a role as that which God does in Western Christian mysticism. In the Yoga of Patañjali, the Lord has, for the religious yogin, only the functional value of making possible and facilitating the obtaining *nirodha*. But the ultimate aim of the efforts of the yogin is to attain, by means of this restraint, the complete isolation of the spirit immanent in him, and not the mystical union of the yogin with the Lord.

J. *Vyāsa's Interpretation*

According to Vyāsa in I.23, when the yogin surrenders himself to the Lord, the latter inclines to him and favours him. It is difficult to concur with this interpretation, considering that it is not possible to specify what is the nature of this "inclination" and this "favour" on the part of the Lord. Moreover, being a *puruṣa, Īśvara* is on this account essentially an entity isolated in itself, indifferent, changeless, without thought, without emotions, without activity—an entity to which it is impossible to ascribe an attitude of grace towards the person who surrenders himself to it.[70]

70. We are not satisfied by M. Eliade's interpretation (*Yoga* pp. 73-76) on the basis of the concept of "metaphysical sympathy"(?) between the Īśvara (the Lord) and the *puruṣa* who is looking for liberation through Yoga. This "sympathy" according to Eliade would be due to the structural correspondence that exists between them.

24

क्लेशकर्मविपाकाशयैरपरामृष्टः पुरुषविशेष ईश्वरः ॥

KLEŚAKARMAVIPĀKĀŚAYAIR APARĀMṚṢṬAḤ
PURUṢAVIŚEṢA ĪŚVARAḤ.

The Lord (Īśvara) is a particular spirit (puruṣa) which is affected neither by the kleśas, nor by the consequences (vipāka) nor by the accumulations (āśaya) of actions.

In this *sūtra* and in the two following ones Patañjali undertakes to sketch the characteristics of the Lord, whose functions in Yoga have been described by us in the commentary of the preceding *sūtra*.

A. The Lord (Īśvara)

We have to conceive the Lord as a personal deity, similar to the supreme divinities of the great Hindu religions, like Viṣṇu, for example. Man is in a relation of dependence on him. All that precedes is implicit in the expression *Īśvara*, used to designate the supreme gods of Hinduism and in the self-surrender (*praṇidhāna*) which the yogin must realize (I.23).

B. Particular (viśeṣa)

In the Sāṃkhya all the *puruṣas* (spirits) are alike. By means of the term *viśeṣa* (particular, special, peculiar, *sui generis*), Patañjali makes a distinction between the *puruṣas*. The special *puruṣa*, *Īśvara*, is postulated in contrast to the other *puruṣas*. In Section E of the commentary on this same *sūtra* we shall see why *Īśvara* is a special *puruṣa* and in what sense this is so.

C. Non-Theistic Sāṃkhya and Theistic Yoga

The Sāṃkhya, philosophical foundation of Yoga, is a dualistic and non-theistic system. While being equal among themselves the *puruṣas* (spirits) stand against matter (*prakṛti*). None of these *puruṣas* has the status and the function of a personal god. What distinguishes the Yoga from the Sāṃkhya is that Patañjali postulates the existence of a special *puruṣa*, conceived as the Lord, as a personal god.

Why does Patañjali part from the basic Sāṃkhya system and posit the existence of an *Īśvara* ?

Either Patañjali acknowledges a new stage in the evolution of the Sāṃkhya doctrine—a stage marked by the appearance of a theistic element. The transformation of an atheistic Sāṃkhya into a theistic Sāṃkhya by means of the elevation of one of the *puruṣas*—*Īśvara*—to a position of supremacy, would correspond to the transformation—which one encounters in the Upaniṣads of an impersonal Absolute devoid of qualities (*Brahman*) into a personal Absolute with qualities (*Īśvara*). We may see in these two parallel processes the influence of the religious sentiment of the masses in India. The non-dualistic Vedānta, in its explication of the Upaniṣadic doctrines, will maintain the coexistence of *Brahman* and of *Īśvara* by interpreting the latter as a conditioned manifestation of the former. As the commentary on the following *sūtras* will show, the configuration of *Īśvara* in Patañjali's Yoga seems to have been made according to the conceptions of Vedānta. Or the *sūtras* referring to *Īśvara* did not exist in the original text or compilation of the *Yogasūtras* attributed to Patañjali, but constituted instead an interpolation done by some theistic author who would have found little satisfaction in a purely Sāṃkhyan and, consequently, atheistic Yoga.

D. *Characteristics of Īśvara*

The characteristics of the particular *puruṣa* who is *Īśvara*—as indicated in this *sūtra*—are as follows :

1. Unaffected by the *kleśas*. As already mentioned in the commentary of the *sūtra* I.5 the *kleśas* are : ignorance (*avidyā*), consciousness of existence (*asmitā*), passion (*rāga*), aversion (*dveṣa*) and attachment to existence (*abhiniveśa*) (II.3).

2. Unaffected by the consequences (*vipāka*) and

3. Unaffected by the accumulations (*āśaya*) of actions. According to the fundamental assumptions of the majority of the philosophical doctrines of India, every action (*karma*) does not exhaust itself or end in itself, but it leaves a residue, an impression (in the mind, for the majority of the doctrines). These residues or impressions accumulate, form a store (*āśaya*), a stock of potentialities. These residues or impressions in a particular moment, in this life or in another, do actualize themselves, fructify, ripen (*vipāka*), produce a good or bad result according to the moral nature of the realized action. For the Lord, there exist neither "accumulations" nor "ripenings" of the actions which He can bring to conclusion.

E. The Particularity and Pre-eminence of Īśvara

The characteristics mentioned by Patañjali in this *sūtra* pertain to every *liberated puruṣa*. What is specific to *Īśvara* is that *at no time*—neither in the past, nor in the present, nor in the future—has He been, is, or will be affected by the *kleśas*, the consequences and the accumulations of actions (Vyāsa). This is in stark contrast to what happens to the other *puruṣas* who, at some time in their existence, before attaining liberation (*kaivalya*), are affected by the *kleśas*, the consequences and the accumulations of the actions.

Indeed, because it does not succumb to the power of the *kleśas*, the consequences and the accumulations of the actions, this particular *puruṣa* is superior to the other *puruṣas* and on account of this deserves to be qualified as "Lord", an expression which indicates his hierarchical superiority.

The following *sūtra* will provide new justifications for the specificity and primacy of *Īśvara*, by maintaining that *Īśvara* bears the highest possibility of having total knowledge, which is not the case with the other *puruṣas*.

F. The Present Sūtra and Vedānta

A parallel may be established between the position of the *Īśvara* of Yoga with regard to the other *puruṣas* and the position of *Brahman-Īśvara* with regard to the other *Ātmans* (individual spiritual principles) in the doctrine of non-dualistic Vedānta : *Brahman* and the *Ātmans* are identical, of the same nature. But *Brahman-Īśvara* is never bound by ignorance (*avidyā*), while the *Ātmans* are bound so long as they do not attain liberation.

25

तत्र निरतिशयं सर्वज्ञबीजम् ॥

TATRA NIRATIŚAYAṂ SARVAJÑABĪJAM.

In Him the seed(bīja) of omniscient (sarvajña) is unsurpassed.

A. Sarvajña (omniscient)

The term *sarvajña* which appears in the compound *sarvajña-bijam* is a masculine adjective and means "who knows all", "omniscient".

B. Bīja (seed)

Bīja literally means "seed". The ideas which symbolically express this word are those of : (a) origin, cause, source; (b) possibility, potentiality. In this *sūtra* it must be taken in the latter sense.

C. Paraphrase of the Sūtra

Therefore, by taking into account the meanings of the words *sarvajña* and *bīja* the translation of the *sūtra* is : "In Him the seed of omniscient is unsurpassed". Paraphrased the *sūtra* means : in *Īśvara* there lies, in its plenitude, the seed, the potentiality, the possibility of being omniscient.

D. Interpretation

The meaning of the *sūtra* is as follows : there are two possible situations for the *puruṣa* (spirit). First, when the *puruṣa* is associated with *prakṛti* (matter). In this condition it is the *puruṣa* that knows and the *prakṛti* is the object of its knowledge. Second, when the *puruṣa* has been liberated, has been isolated from *prakṛti* and is in a state of complete isolation, *kaivalya*—the supreme goal of the yogin. In this condition there is no knowledge for the *puruṣa*, the *puruṣa* does not know, it is beyond all knowledge, being disconnected from the *prakṛti* which constituted the unique object of its knowledge. But there always exists in the *puruṣa* the possibility to know, which constitutes the essential quality of its nature, in opposition to the nature of *prakṛti*, and which would become actualized, if *puruṣa* enters into a new contact with the *prakṛti*. The knowledge, actualized while the *puruṣa* was in contact with the *prakṛti*, has been converted into a potential knowledge, into a possibility to know, into a seed of knowledge.

E. The Omniscience of Īśvara

As we have just said, the *puruṣas*—when they come into contact with *prakṛti*—have the possibility to know, to be subject to knowledge. But their knowledge is limited to one part or aspect of *prakṛti*, and this by the limitations which its own incarnation engenders in them. If He enters into contact with matter, *Īśvara* will have the possibility of omniscience, of being subject of a knowledge of all. In other words His knowledge will be the knowledge of *prakṛti* in its totality, without any sort of limitation.

F. Niratiśaya (unsurpassed)

The potentiality or possiblity (*bīja*) of omniscience is greatest in *Īśvara*. It could never be subject to any increase.

G. The Present Sūtra and Vedānta

According to Jacobi ("Über das...,p.618) the Sāṃkhya does not refer to the concept of omniscience and words like *sarvajña* ("omniscient") and *sarvajñatva* (omniscience) do not appear in the more important Sāṃkhyan literature. One may understand why this is so : when the *puruṣa* is liberated, isolated, it has nothing to do with *prakṛti*, there exists for it, on that account, neither object of knowledge nor knowledge. When the *puruṣa* is incarnated, the limitations of its own incarnation allow it only a partial knowledge.

In the non-dualistic Vedānta, omniscience is one of the qualities of *Īśvara* (qualified and personal form of *Brahman*, the Absolute).

Patañjali does not say that *Īśvara* of Yoga is omniscient, as this omniscience would suppose a *constant* contact with *prakṛti* which, by its very nature, is the object of all knowledge. It would further suppose that, in consequence, *Īśvara* does never experience the state of isolation. It is for this reason that Patañjali affirms in *Īśvara* the existence of only a seed or possibility of omniscience.

The doctrine which the present *sūtra* upholds would seem to accommodate the conception of the Vedāntic *Īśvara* with the fundamental principles of the Sāṃkhya.

26

पूर्वेषामपि गुरुः कालेनानवच्छेदात् ॥

[SA] PŪRVEṢĀM API GURUḤ KĀLENĀNAVACCHEDĀT.

He is the preceptor of the Primal ones also, because He is not limited by time.

This *sūtra* mentions two new characteristics of *Īśvara*, to which we shall refer now.

A. Is Not Limited by Time (kālenānavacchedāt)

The first characteristic of *Īśvara* consists in that for Him time does not exist: *Īśvara* has no beginning or end. This characteristic is not specific of *Īśvara*, because the other *puruṣas*, when they have become isolated from *prakṛti*, also are beyond time, which is a manifestation of *prakṛti*.

B. Preceptor (Guru) of the Primal Ones (purveṣām)

Precisely for not being limited by time *Īśvara* has been able to be the *Guru* of the Primal Sages. The word "Primal ones" indicates the creating gods, like *Brahmā*, who have appeared at the beginning of the present cosmic period and in the previous cosmic periods (Vyāsa and Bhoja, *ad loc.*). *Īśvara* has been their *guru* for having transmitted to them the teachings contained in the Vedas.

C. Īśvara and Prakṛti

In order to have been able to be the preceptor of the Primal ones *Īśvara* has had to give up *kaivalya* (isolation) and come into contact with *prakṛti* (matter) to the realm of which belonged the Primal ones, as well as the activity of the *guru*.

As a result of His relationship with *prakṛti*, *Īśvara* enters into contact with time; He becomes temporal. It is then that the seed of omniscience (see *sūtra* I.25), which has been lying dormant in Him, becomes actualized and *Īśvara* is the omniscient *guru*. But in conformity with *sūtra* I.24, *Īśvara*, in spite of being in contact with *prakṛti*, is not affected by the *kleśas*, the consequences and accumulations of actions.

D. The Present Sūtra and Vedānta

The conception of a *puruṣa* who abandons his position of *kaivalya* to become, in the beginning of each cosmic cycle, the *guru* of the first created gods, is not in accordance with the principles of Sāṃkhya, for which a liberated *puruṣa*, as is *Īśvara*, is a *puruṣa* who has, for all times, set himself beyond *prakṛti* and, as such, is devoid of all activity.

27

तस्य वाचकः प्रणवः ॥

TASYA VĀCAKAḤ PRAṆAVAḤ.

The mystic syllable AUM designates Him.

A. The Syllable AUM

AUM is the symbol of the Lord. It must be borne in mind that, according to Indian thought, the link which binds the symbol to the symbolised is not an accidental or conventional relation. Indeed there exists an absolute identity of essence between both.[71] Consequently AUM and *Īśvara* are essentially identical. The *Taittirīya Upaniṣad* says: "AUM *is all*".

B. The Present Sūtra and Vedānta

In the Upaniṣads AUM designates *Brahman*. Undoubtedly Patañjali is labouring under the influence of Vedānta when he uses this syllable in this *sūtra* to designate that yogic *Īśvara*. The process of conforming the yogic *Īśvara* according to the mould of the Vedāntic *Īśvara* culminates in the use of the symbol AUM as the name of the yogic *Īśvara*.

This conception, alien to the Sāṃkhya, would seem to be one more proof of Patañjali's intention to accommodate the conception of the Vedāntic *Īśvara* with the principles of the Sāṃkhya on which he bases himself. The *Īśvara* of Vedānta, as the conditioned aspect of *Brahman*, is the creator, preserver and destroyer of the universe. He preserves the moral order and reveals the sacred teachings which expound this moral order and favours all those who, full of devotion, come near to him. *Brahman* is not in

71. See Fernando Tola, *Doctrinas Secretas de la India, Upanishads*, note 28 of the *Chāndogya*.

contact with the world and with men. But *Īśvara* is. Patañjali could not accept an *Īśvara* as the creator, preserver and destroyer of the world, for these functions are fulfilled, in the Sāṃkhya, by *prakṛti*, out of its own dynamism. But he attributes to his *Īśvara* the functions of the preceptor who reveals the sacred teachings. In this form the yogic *Īśvara* is in contact with matter and preserves something of the function of maintaining the universe.

28

तज्जपस्तदर्थभावनम् ॥

TAJJAPAS TADARTHABHĀVANAM.

Repetition (japa) of it and the evocation (bhāvana) of its meaning (artha) (must be made).

This *sūtra* indicates the two practices that should be made in the context of the Lord.

A. The repetition (japa) of the syllable AUM

The first of these practices shall consist in the rhythmic and uninterrupted repetition many times of the syllable AUM. This repetition can be either oral or mental. The *Mantra Yoga*—a branch of yoga—has developed the practice of *japa* by using different *mantras*, that is, formulas of one or more syllables, usually devoid of meaning, among which AUM is the most celebrated. In India the belief in the religious, mystical and magic value of the *mantras* has always been, and still is, a commonplace. To have the desired effect the *mantra* must be repeated countless times. The appendix of *Swami Brahmananda El eterno compañero* recommends how the *japa* or the repetition of the *mantra* must be practised: "*The aspirant may begin on the first day of the new moon by repeating the mantra a thousand times. The following day he repeats it two thousand times. The next day three thousand times, and in this way he continues increasing the number of repetitions till the day of the full moon, when he reaches fifteen thousand. After this, on the day following the full moon the japa is reduced to fourteen thousand and thus successively till he reaches a thousand on the following new moon. This practice can be continued during one, two or three years as the aspirant wishes or according to the directions of the guru.*" The belief in the supernatural power of the *mantras* has had, and still has, exaggerated expressions. By being repeated a large number of times, a *mantra* can yield material benefits or supernatural powers. Pandit (*Kuṇḍalinī Yoga*, p. 26) relates the case of a yogin who repeating a *mantra* associated with fire, was able to cause the latter to destroy a group of people who had treated him disrespectfully.

B. The Evocation (bhāvana) of the Meaning (artha) of the Syllable AUM

The expression *bhāvana* of the present *sūtra* has been translated in many ways : Woods and Ballantyne, "reflection"; Rama Prasada, "understanding"; Taimni, "meditation"; Vivekananda, "meditating"; Purohit, "meditate"; Bengali Baba, "development"; Hauer (*Der Yoga*, p. 241) "innere Vergegenwärtigung"; H. Āranya, "contemplate". These same translators give to the expression *bhāvana* a different meaning in the *sūtras* II. 33 and 34: Woods, "cultivation"; Ballantyne, "calling up"; Rama Prasada, "habituation" and "the habit to thinking to"; Taimni, "(constant) pondering"; Vivekananda, "thinking"; Purohit, "cultivate"; Hauer (*Der Yoga*, p. 247) "Erwägung"; H. Āranya, "thought". Only B. Baba maintains in II. 33 and 34 the same meaning for the term *bhāvana*.

As we have written earlier with regard to the words *pratyaya* and *smṛti* in the commentaries of the *sūtras* I. 10 and I. 11, it is not correct to translate a single term used by Patañjali in a different way each time it appears in a different *sūtra*. In our view *bhāvana* means, in the three *sūtras* in which it is used, one single thing: "the fact of producing, of manifesting, of rousing"; "production", "evocation".[72]

C. Meaning (artha)

Artha is simply *that which is designated by the word*, the "object" that is designated, that is signified, that is meant by the word, hence: the "meaning" of that word. What is designated by a word, its "object", its "meaning", can be a material, concrete thing, a notion or a supernatural being as "the Lord", etc.

72. The basic meaning of *bhāvana* is "the act of producing".

In the present *sūtra artha* is thus the "object" (=the Lord) designated by the word AUM, its "meaning", as we have translated it. In *sūtras* I.42 and 43, as we shall see, *artha* is the object on which the yogin has concentrated his mind.

In section B of our commentary on *sūtra* I.11, we have explained that *viṣaya* means also *object*, but "object" considered in relation to a human experience. *Artha* indicates also *object*, but without relation to anything—the "object" considered in itself. Thus in the present *sūtra* (I.28) *artha* signifies the object referred to by the word; *sūtra* I.42 enumerates the elements (*śabda, jñāna, artha, vikalpa*) that are present in the *samāpatti with vitarka*, without establishing any relation among these elements; *sūtra* I.43 indicates which element *remains*—the *artha*—in the *samāpatti* without *vitarka* from the elements independently enumerated in I.42. In all these cases the *artha* is considered in itself; no relation is established to any human experience. For *sūtra* I.49, in which *artha* is also mentioned (together with *viṣaya*), we remit to our commentary thereon. As for *sūtra* I.32 *artha* is used in a prepositional use that has no reference to the technical meaning of the word. Of course any *artha*, any *thing in itself*, when coming in relation to a cognitive act, becomes a *viṣaya*.

The syllable AUM is bound to the notion of "Lord". For a person who is a stranger to India or who is ignorant of Indian culture, this syllable contains nothing or very little. But it is pregnant with meaning, it is full of content for the devotee, the Hindu philosopher or initiate. For the latter it is, as it were, the epitome and essence of all that successive generations of devotees have felt, of all that the successive generations of the thinkers and mystics of India have thought, experienced and expressed. In them the syllable AUM evokes the notion of a being, pure and immaculate, all-powerful, creator and ruler of the world, protector of the good, scourge of the evil ones, receptacle of all knowledge, the great teacher of the sages of the past, etc., etc. And when the devotee, the philosopher, the initiate give themselves over to greater religious experience, the more they surrender themselves to devotion and the syllable AUM becomes the most proper symbol for the Lord, most closely associated with Him-

This rich and profound notion of the Lord would, with like power and intensity, present itself to their minds, when they pronounce the sacred word AUM or when they hear it being pronounced.

D. The Practice Recommended by Patañjali: Evocation of the Meaning

The practice which Patañjali recommends consists of repeating the syllable AUM (*japa*) with evocation (*bhāvana*) of its meaning (*artha*).[73] This does not mean the merely mechanical repetition of AUM devoid of meaning. When the syllable AUM is repeated, the notion of the Lord becomes present in the mind.

Thus, *bhāvana* is not a discursive, analytical meditation in which the mind determines successively the several spiritual and metaphysical qualities and moral attributes which conform the concept, that is, the essence of divinity. Beneficent from a religious point of view, a process of this nature would, however, be counter-productive for the effects of yoga, because it bears within itself a mental dispersion.

Bhāvana is the evocation in one single act, *totum simul*, of the entire mental world, enriched by the contributions of successive generations, which the syllable AUM, so to say, brings with itself.

73. *Sūtras* II.33 and 34 advise, in order to check bad thoughts, the production (*bhāvana*) of thoughts that are contrary to them.

29

ततः प्रत्यक्चेतनाधिगमोऽप्यन्तरायाभावश्च ॥

TATAḤ PRATYAKCETANĀDHIGAMO 'PY ANTARĀYĀBHĀVAŚ CA.

Hence (tataḥ) (are produced) the acquisition (adhigama) of an introverted consciousness (pratyakcetanā) and the non-existence of the obstacles (antarāyābhāva).

B. Effect of the Exercises Alluded to in the Previous Sūtra

In the present *sūtra* Patañjali indicates the effects brought about by the repetition of the syllable AUM (*japa*) and the evocation of the meaning of the syllable AUM (*bhāvana*).

B. The Acquisition (adhigama) of an Introverted Consciousness (Pratyakcetanā)

The repetition of the syllable AUM and the evocation of its meaning—as explained in the commentary on the preceding *sūtra*—bring in their wake an introversion, an absorption into oneself, an interiorisation of consciousness (*pratyakcetanā*).

On one hand, by dint of repeating the syllable AUM and evoking its meaning, the mind stops giving any attention to the objects of the external world, it stops dispersing itself. Further, the mental repetition of this syllable and the evocation of its meaning constitute a return of consciousness to a product of the mind, to something which lies within its internal compass.

To the word *pratyakcetanā* we have given a literal meaning. Translations similar to ours are those of: Taimni, "turning inward of consciousness"; Vivekananda, "introspection"; Hauer (*Der Yoga*, p. 242) "Geisteshaltung der Einkehr". Hauer notes, *ibidem*, p. 466, that *pratyakcetanā* corresponds more or less to C.G. Jung's "introversion".

C. Another Interpretation and Criticism of the Expression pratyakcetanā

Vyāsa thinks that with the practice of *japa* and of *bhāvana* (mentioned earlier) the yogin acquires the knowledge of his own nature (*svarūpa-darśana*). By basing themselves on this rather freely interpreted text of Vyāsa, a few authors and translators have given a different meaning to the compound *pratyakcetanādhigama*. Thus Rama Prasada translates: "understanding of the individual self"; Bengali Baba: "attainment of the inner soul"; Ballantyne: "knowledge of the rightly intelligent (spirit)"; H. Āranya: "realisation of the individual self".

We think that this interpretation is not acceptable, for the following reasons: 1. *Pratyak* means "moving in an opposite direction" and *cetanā*, "consciousness". The meaning of the compound *pratyakcetanā* then is "consciousness which moves in an opposite direction", that is, a consciousness which does not follow its natural movement, towards the exterior or towards the objects, a consciousness turned towards the interior. There is no reason to lend to this compound a meaning which does not arise from its constituents. 2. The introversion of the consciousness is the normal and necessary effect of the practices of *japa* and of *bhāvana*. These practices do effectively bring about the stabilization of the mind, its fixation on the syllable AUM and on its meaning, that is, on an idea, an object of the inner world, whereupon the consciousness, absorbed in itself, separates itself from the outer world and becomes introverted. 3. In agreement with Vyāsa himself *ad* I.28, through *japa* and *bhāvana*, the mind becomes fixed (*cittam ekāgraṃ saṃpadyate*). In I.28 Bhoja endorses Vyāsa by saying that *japa* and *bhāvana* are a means for the fixation of the mind (*ekāgratāyā upāyaḥ*). But *ekāgratā* of the mind is a stage in the yogic process, which pre-supposes the subject-object duality and finally leads to the total *nirodha* or trance which marks the attainment of the isolation (*kaivalya*) of the Spirit. Translations such as: "attainment of the inner soul', "realisation of the individual self", etc. would allow one to understand that it is in this *intermediate stage* that the *final goal* is reached. And this final goal would not be the goal of Patañjali's

Sāṃkhya-Yoga, but rather that of the doctrines belonging to the Vedāntic tradition. 4. Finally we may point out that the disappearance of the obstacles, the second effect of *japa* and of *bhāvana* indicated by the present *sūtra*, constitutes likewise a secondary consequence within the yogic process. According to the interpretation of the translators who base themselves on Vyāsa, the present *sūtra* would be considering the attainment of the final goal and a secondary result on the same level, as if they were two realities of like nature and equal importance.

D. The Non-existence of the Obstacles (*antarāyābhāva*)

Patañjali enumerates the obstacles and their concomitants in the following two *sūtras*. The obstacles are the dispersions (*vikṣepa*) of the mind. Naturally dispersion is contrary to the restraint (*nirodha*) of the mental processes, the final goal of Yoga. Mental fixation—which *japa* and *bhāvana* comprise—eliminates the obstacles and, as a result, the dispersion constituted by the latter.

For more elaborate details on each of these obstacles we refer to the following two *sūtras*.

30

व्याधिस्त्यानसंशयप्रमादालस्याविरतिभ्रान्तिदर्शनालब्धभूमि-
कत्वानवस्थितत्वानि चित्तविक्षेपास्तेऽन्तरायाः ॥

VYĀDHISTYĀNASAṂŚAYAPRAMĀDĀLASYĀVIRATI-
BHRĀNTIDARŚANĀLABDHABHŪMIKATVĀNAVAS-
THITATVĀNI CITTAVIKṢEPĀS TE 'NTARĀYĀḤ

Sickness, apathy, indecision, negligence, idleness, non-cessation, erratic perception, the absence of initiative, inconstancy—these dispersions (*vikṣepa*) *of the mind are the obstacles* (*antarāya*).

A. As we have shown in the commentary of the preceding *sūtra*, the "obstacles" are circumstances which produce the dispersion (*vikṣepa*) of the mind. In Section G of this commentary, we shall describe in what way the obstacles are factors of dispersion. It is this dispersing effect which does lend a unity to the apparently heterogeneous enumeration of the obstacles which Patañjali makes in this *sūtra*. One must always bear in mind this distinctive characteristic of the obstacles in the interpretation of each one of them. From among the possible interpretations of each of the expressions used by Patañjali to designate these obstacles we must select the one which best conforms to the said characteristic.

The obstacles enumerated by Patañjali are states, modes of being, of behaviour, attitudes specific to man, which may be encountered in a person devoted to yoga or not. The obstacles must not be defined exclusively in terms of yoga, but in general terms, in agreement with the specific reality which corresponds to each of the expressions which designate them. Thus, for instance, the term *pramāda* designates "negligence" in general and not as Kṛṣṇavallabha defines it : "*the lack of effort with regard to the means which lead to samādhi*". Patañjali does not give to these terms a special, restricted meaning. We must then take them in their general broad sense, because, as says Vijñānabhikṣu, *Vārtika ad* I.32, it is not correct to give to a word having a general meaning, without a previous restriction, a particular meaning (*bādhakaṃ vinā sāmānyaśabdasya viśeṣaparatvānaucityāt*). Furthermore just as the first expression of the enumeration *vyādhi* is taken in its general sense of "sickness" without any limitation, likewise it is necessary to take the other expressions of the enumeration in the sense which they normally have.

Of course, if these obstacles are to be found in a yogin, they would actually affect his yogic practices.

B. The First Five Obstacles

1. *Vyādhi* (sickness). Vyāsa explains: "*disorder of the humours*,[74] *the secretions*[75] *and of the organs* (*of the body*).

2. *Styāna* (apathy). Vyāsa and Bhoja explain: "*the inability of the mind for action*". Other versions: "languor" (Woods, Taimni, Ballantyne, Rama Prasada), "incompetence" (H. Āranya), "mental laziness" (Vivekananda). "lack of enthusiasm" (Purohit), "debility" (Bengali Baba), "dullness" (Dvivedī), "Verstarrung" (Hauer, *Der Yoga*, p.242).

4. *Pramāda*[76] (negligence). Bhoja explains: "*the disposition to non-performance* (*ananuṣṭhāna*), *indifference to the means which lead to samādhi*". Kṛṣṇavallabha: "*the absence of effort with regard to the means which lead to samādhi*". These explanations give an idea of what we must understand by *pramāda*, although they suffer from the defect—which we have already mentioned— of restricting its meaning, by defining the expression exclusively in function of yoga. Other versions: "heedlessness" (Woods), "carelessness" (Taimni, Rama Prasada, Dvivedī, Ballantyne), "delusion" (H. Āranya), "irregularity" (Purohit), "inadvertence"

74. Air, phlegm and bile according to Indian medical conception.

75. As for instance that which allows digestion of food.

76. We speak of *saṃśaya*, to which number 3 corresponds in Patañjali's enumeration, after number 5.

(Bengali Baba), "lack of enthnsiasm" (Vivekananda), "Unbesonnenheit" (Hauer, *ibidem*).

5. *Ālasya* (indolence). Vyāsa explains : "*the inertia produced by the heaviness of the body and of the mind*" and Vijñānabhikṣu, *Vārtika ad loc* : "*heaviness of the body on account of kapha* (phlegm, one of the humours of the body), etc., *heaviness of the mind on account of tamas* (see *sūtra* I.16 A); *these two causes producei nactivity* (*apravṛtti*) *and then on-performance of the means which lead to samādhi.* Other versions : "listlessness" (Woods), "laziness" (Taimni, Ballantyne), "lethargy" (Vivekananda, Purohit), "sloth" (Bengali Baba, H. Āranya, Dvivedī, Rama Prasada), "Gleichgültigkeit" (Hauer, *ibidem*).

The last three terms (2, 4 and 5) refer to entities which are close to one another and this renders it difficult to establish the nuances which distinguish them. Hence we can understand the indecision which characterises the translations.

6. *Saṃśaya* (indecision). Vyāsa explains : "*thought which oscillates between the two extremes* : '*this could be like this*', '*this could not be like this*'". Other versions: "doubt" (Woods, Taimni, Ballantyne, Vivekananda, Bengali Baba, Purohit, H. Āranya, Dvivedī), "indecision" (Rama Prasada), "Zweifelsucht" (Hauer, *ibidem*).

C. Non-cessation (*avirati*)

Vyāsa as well as Bhoja explain the term *avirati* as *cittasya viṣayasaṃprayogātmā gardhaḥ*: "*the greed of the mind, the essence of which is the contact with sense-objects*". Kṛṣṇavallabha says : *cittasya viṣayaprāptyabhilāṣā*: "*the mind's desire for the acquisition of objects*". Vijñanabhikṣu (*Yogavārtika*) : "*saṃprayogātmā sannikarṣajanyo gardho 'bhilāṣa* : "*greed, desire the essence of which is contact, and which arises out of proximity*". With the modern translators this term is given the following versions : Woods : "worldliness"; Taimni and Dvivedī : "worldly-mindedness"; Hauer (*Der Yoga*, p.242): "Genuss-sucht"; H. Āranya : "non-abstention", adding, in his commentary, "*remaining aloof from worldly affairs and giving up interest therein, remove non-abstention*"; Rama Prasada and Bengali Baba :

"sensuality"; Purohit : "yearning for sensual pleasures"; Vivekananda : "clinging to sense-enjoyments"; and Ballantyne : "addiction to objects" which he explains in his commentary as "*a greediness consisting in attachment of the mind to objects of sense*".

We translate *avirati* by "non-cessation". Mental and physical activity is the characteristic state of man. There normally runs in the mind a constant and continuous flux of ideas, of sensations which reach it through the senses, of emotions. These ideas, sensations and emotions constitute the activity of the mind. Action, movement, constitute the activity of the body. *Avirati* would be the non-cessation, the non-detention of this mental and physical activity, the state of always thinking or feeling, of always acting, of being in movement, of physical and psychological agitation. We do not think that the term *avirati* bears a moral connotation. Yoga would consider as an obstacle the fact of not being able to put an end to the activity of the mind and of the body, whatever be the nature of this activity.

We prefer this interpretation as it better connotes the original, etymological meaning of *avirati*. The expression *avirati* is formed by the privative *a-* and the word *virati*. The primal meaning of *virati* is "cessation", "pause", "detention". It is derived from the root RAM (with the prefix *vi-*) which essentially means "to cease". Thus according to its etymology *avirati* is "non-cessation".

The traditional commentators and the translations mentioned above—most of which are inspired by the former—give to the term *avirati* three basic meanings : 1. desire (Vyāsa, Bhoja, Kṛṣṇavallabha and Vijñānabhikṣu), 2. desire for, attachment to sensual things (Hauer, R. Prasada, Bengali Baba, Purohit, Vivekananda and Ballantyne), and 3. worldliness, worldly mindedness (Woods, Taimni and Dvivedī). It is clear that these interpretations and translations are far removed from the original, basic meaning of the root RAM.

Moreover *virati* and *virāma* are derived from the same root RAM (in different degrees of vocalic alternance) with the same prefix *vi-* and the suffixes *-ti* and *-a* which denote names of action.

The meaning of *virāma* then is—needless to argue—"cessation". It is not clear why its synonivem *virati*, by the simple fact of the addition of a privative *a*-, instead of signifying "non-cessation" should acquire the meaning of "desire", "desire for sensual things", "worldliness".

Furthermore the dictionaries of Böhtlingk and Monier-Williams give for *virati* only the meaning of "cessation" or similar ones; therefore *avirati* can only mean: "non-cessation". For synonyms of *virati* Amarasiṃha gives the words *ārati* and *avarati* and mentions, for these three words, the basic meaning of "to stop", "to cease" (*uparāma*). Only Apte mentions, with regard to *virati*, a third and final meaning—in addition to "cessation" and its kindred versions—"indifference to worldly attachments" and, as the authority for this meaning, refers to Bhartṛhari, *Vairāgya* 95 (*mahī ramyā śayyā*..). But in this stanza of Bhartṛhari *virati* does not necessarily need to be translated by "indifference to worldly attachments" for it could as well be translated by "cessation (of activities)" or by some such word as "quietude".

Moreover, our translation may be buttressed by the following consideration : *sūtras* I.29 and I.32 mention the fixation of the mind on one entity as the means of eliminating obstacles. See our commentaries on *sūtras* I.29 (particularly section D) and I.32. If the term *avirati* means "desire" or "attachment"and if Patañjali had intended to mention the means to eliminate it, he would have indicated the practices pertaining to *vairāgya* (*Yogasūtras* II.29 and ff),[77] which constitute the *specific* means to suppress the desire in all its forms; he would not have mentioned— as he does—the fixation of the mind on a single entity, the essential finality of which is to produce the concentration of the mind and which, only *as a secondary consequence*, eliminates the obstacles. (*Vide* our commentary of the *sūtra* I.32.) But, if we take *avirati* as meaning "non-cessation" (of the psycho-physical activity), on there being no specific means to eliminate the non-cessation, the sole means which deserves mention is the concentration of the

77. See C. Dragonetti, "El método yóguico".

mind, one of whose secondary effects constitutes the said elimination.

Furthermore, if in this *sūtra*, *avirati* means "desire" or "attachment", Patañjali would not have included it among the obstacles, since it would have been unnecessary, as on dealing with *vairāgya* (in the *sūtras* I.12 and I.15) and with the practices which lead to it (in the *sūtras* II. 29 and ff.), he refers in a sufficient and specific way to desire, giving to it the corresponding importance within the general framework of yoga. And this importance is greater than that of a simple obstacle.

Finally, in the sense of "desire", *avirati* has, neither in virtue of its nature nor that of its importance, no place in the enumeration of the obstacles. The other obstacles are negative and static attitudes; they are deficiencies, wants; while the desire is something positive, dynamic. Besides desire holds—in yoga[78]—an importance of the first order. So long as desire persists it is impossible to attain the restraint of the mental processes (*nirodha*), the ultimate goal of yoga. Patañjali mentions two means to obtain *nirodha* : *vairāgya* and *abhyāsa*. One of these two means—*vairāgya*—specifically brings about the suppression of desire. In the sense of "non-cessation" *avirati* does, both in importance and in its nature, stand on a par with the other obstacles.

But, whether, as we propose, the term *avirati* be taken in the sense of "non-cessation" or that it be taken in the sense of "desire", as the traditional interpretation has it, we think that this term (*avirati*) does not bear any moral connotation. It is not a matter only of the non-cessation of the activities which are opposite to the moral, nor the desire for objects which are opposite to the moral or which are alluring to the senses. Yoga condemns without any qualification the non-cessation of any activity whatsoever or the desire for any object whatsoever.

We base the latter point of view on the opinion of the commentators Vyāsa, Bhoja, Vijñānabhikṣu and Kṛṣṇavallabha, whose definitions of *avirati* rest on the margin of the moral,

78. As in Indian philosophy in general.

because they use the word *viṣaya*, object of the senses, without any qualification, and *viṣaya* by itself indicates an object in general.[79] Moreover we must bear in mind the technical and amoral characteristic of Yoga, for which everything remains subordinate, as a simple means, to the supreme end of the total restraint of the functions of the mind and which rejects as being harmful to the practices, which it teaches, the morally reprehensible or otherwise, only insofar as it hinders the realization of these practices. It is in this sense that sickness, totally removed from the moral, is considered to be an obstacle. If we give to *avirati* a moral connotation, the present *sūtra* would appear to condemn only the non-cessation of the activities which are contrary to the moral, while not condemning the non-cessation of any other sort of activity. But then the latter non-cessation is as harmful to the effects of yoga as is the former, because the mental and physical activity—constituted of a ceaseless flux of ideas, sensations and emotions, and of the exertions of man in the external world—becomes a factor of dispersion which hinders stability and renders difficult "the acquisition of an introverted consciousness" referred to in *sūtra* I.29. On the contrary, if we give to *avirati* its broad sense, this *sūtra* then condemns the non-cessation of any type of activity whatsoever, on account of the dispersing characteristic which it has, to the margin of its nature, be the latter moral or not, sensual or not.

D. *Erratic Perception* (*bhrāntidarśana*)

We translate the term *bhrāntidarśana* by "erratic perception" and by "erratic perception" we mean that perception which is unable to maintain itself on a determined point, which moves from one object to another.

Vyāsa defines *bhrāntidarśana* as follows : "*erroneous knowledge*"; Bhoja : "*erroneous knowledge like silver in mother-of-pearl*";[80] Vijñānabhikṣu : "*erroneous knowledge, the conviction*

79. Let us remember that for Indian psychology mind is the sixth sense, whose objects are the ideas.

80. Classical example in India: a pearl-oyster is seen and it is taken for silver.

opposed to the meaning determined by the guru, etc."; Kṛṣṇavallabha : "*erroneous knowledge like 'being method of the samādhi is not specific to yoga'*". For these authors, *bhrāntidarśana* is substantially a *viparītaṃ jñānam*, an "erroneous knowledge" and it can be either a mistaken perception or a false conception.

In a general sense the modern translators and commentators adopt the interpretation mentioned earlier. Thus, Woods and Ballantyne : "erroneous perception"; Dvivedī : "false notion"; Bengali Baba : "wrong understanding"; Taimni : "delusion"; H. Āranya : "false knowledge"; Purohit : "hallucination"; Rama Prasada : "mistaken notion"; Vivekananda : "false perception"; and Hauer (*Der Yoga*, p.242) "philosophisch-Irrlichtelieren".

Our translation, we submit, is preferable because the expression *bhrānti* originally means : "the wandering about, roaming about". It is only by extension that it means "error", "confusion", "perplexity", and *darśana* originally designates : "seeing", "ocular perception", "vision". Again, only by extension, does it mean : "understanding", "doctrine", "philosophical system". Further we believe that an erratic perception has more of the nature of a dispersing obstacle to the mind than does an erroneous philosophical conception, as for instance : not believing in the existence of the spirit (*puruṣa*); or than does a mistaken perception like the *locus classicus* of "seeing a rope and believing that it is a snake". Besides, if Patañjali were referring to an erroneous knowledge, he would have simply used the term *viparyaya*, the technical term he actually uses in *sūtra* I.8, to designate such a form of knowledge or its equivalent *viparītajñāna*.

E. The Lack of Initiative (*alabdhabhūmikatva*)

The compound *alabdhabhūmikatva* literally means "the fact of being a person for whom a *bhūmi* has not been attained", or, more simply, "not attaining a *bhūmi*". Of the objects denoted by the word *bhūmi* we must bear in mind the following : "earth", "situation", "position", "step", "degree", "stage".

Vyāsa explains this expression as follows : "*not attaining a stage* (*bhūmi*) *of the concentration of the mind* (*samādhi*)". Bhoja and Kṛṣṇavallabha understand it in the same sense. Most translators explain it by borrowing from Vyāsa. Thus : "failure to attain any stage (of concentration)" (Woods); "not attaining concentration" (Vivekananda); "Unfähigkeit, die Versenkungsstufen zu erreichen" (Hauer, *Der Yoga*, p.242); "not attainment of any yogic stage" ("yogic stage" meaning the different stages of concentration) (H. Āranya); "failure to attain any stage (of concentration)" (Ballantyne); "failure to attain a step" (Purohit); "not attainment of the plane" (Bengali Baba); "non-achievement of a stage" (Taimni).

It seems to us that this interpretation suffers from the defect of taking *bhūmi* in a restricted sense, that is, the "stage of concentration". In the *sūtras* I.14; II.27; III.6, in which the expression *bhūmi* occurs, it does not, according to Patañjali, signify the stages of concentration; accordingly there is no reason to attribute this meaning to it in the present *sūtra*. Actually the word *bhūmi* appears in a compound in the *sūtras* I.14 and II.27 : *dṛḍhabhūmi* and *prāntabhūmi*, respectively. The first literally means "(a person or thing) whose *bhūmi* (fundament, base) is solid", i.e. "a firm (person or thing)"; and *prāntabhūmi* signifies "(a person or thing) whose position or situation (*bhūmi*) is set at the extreme limit". In *sūtra* III.6, the word *bhūmi* can be translated by "stage", and *solely by the fact of being determined by the pronoun 'tasya'* (which replaces the expression *saṃyama* of the two *sūtras* III.4 and 5 which precede it) signifies the stages of *saṃyama*, between which stretch the different levels of concentration. In itself *bhūmi* only means "stage". Further, the compound *alabdhabhūmikatva* appears in this *sūtra* in a series of expressions each with a general meaning. For example, the words *vyādhi* and *ālasya* simply mean "sickness" and "sloth", in their broad sense, and could be used in any context. See Section A of this commentary. Therefore it is necessary to give to *alabdhabhūmikatva* a general sense conforming to that of the remaining expressions of this *sūtra*.

As it is not possible to give a restricted interpretation to the compound *alabdhabhūmikatva*, it is only proper to give to it a general, broad meaning. The expression *alabdhabhūmikatva* simply means "the fact of being a person who cannot take earth (*bhūmi*)"—that is, it means the impossibility of establishing a base in anything, of resting one's feet in something, of holdings on to anything, starting something, "the lack of initiative" understood in this sense. It can be compared to the Sanskrit expression *padaṃ LABH* : "to gain a footing" (Monier-Williams, Apte).

F. Inconstancy (anavasthitatva)

The compound *anavasthitatva* means literally "the fact of being a person who does not maintain himself established." If the previous obstacle hinders someone from taking position in something, from starting something, the present obstacle hinders him from maintaining himself in it. Like all the other obstacles mentioned in this *sūtra* the expression *anavasthitatva* has a general meaning. All the expressions signify the general weaknesses of human nature, which in the perspective of yoga hinder the realisation of the yogic practices. These expressions do not exclusively refer to yoga, they are not technical terms of yoga.

Vyāsa explains the term *anavasthitatva* by *"the fact that the mind does not maintain itself in the stage (bhūmi) attained."* Bhoja, Vijñānabhikṣu (*Vārtika*) and Kṛṣṇavallabha explain it in the same manner. Other translations are : "instability in the state (when attained)" (Ballantyne); "instability" (Taimni, Rama Prasada, Dvivedī, Bengali Baba); "instability to stay in a yogic state" (H. Āranya); "failure to maintain that step" (Purohit); "falling away from the state when obtained" (Vivekananda) ; "Unfähigkeit, darin zu beharren" (Hauer, *Der Yoga,* p.242).

G. The "Obstacles" As Factors of Dispersion

As we have shown earlier the obstacles disperse the mind; we shall now briefly outline how each of these obstacles acts as a factor of dispersion.

Sickness. Ill-health or suffering produced by sickness distract the yogin by drawing his attention to these sensations of ill-health and pain. Vijñānabhikṣu (*Vārtika*) further observes that the preoccupation to obtain the means to stop the sickness constitutes in itself an element contrary to yoga (*vyādhyādigocarā vā tannivṛttyupāyagocarā vā cittasya vṛttayo bhavanti yogabhraṃśikā ityarthaḥ*). This explains why the post-pātañjala yoga gives such great importance to the health of the yogin that the treatises on yoga often give the impression of being books on preventive medicine.

Apathy, negligence, sloth. In the states of apathy, negligence, sloth the vital impulse, the nervous tension, are reduced. The mental control is relaxed and the mind seems abandoned to itself, subjected to the disordered and spontaneous flux of ideas, sensations and emotions. What takes place is, so to say, akin to drowsiness, fatigue, intoxication. One ceases being master of one's thought; the mind becomes, at the whim of its own dynamism, full of unrelated contents.

Indecision. In a state of indecision the mind vacillates between several possibilites. Such an unsteadiness constitutes in itself a factor of dispersion. Besides every alternative that offers itself gives rise to clusters of mentally conflicting ideas and emotions which, on forcing the mind to shift from one to the other, do necessarily disperse it.

Non-cessation. It is obvious that the non-stopping of the mental and physical activity, the persistence of this activity, unceasingly crams the mind with different contents, which action maintains it in a state of permanent dispersion.

Erratic perception. The senses applied to different objects necessarily imply a constant mobility of the mind and, as a result, its dispersion. Moreover there arises the possibility that the representation of each one of the diverse objects be accompanied by different emotional states which in turn intensify the distraction of the mind.

Lack of initiative, and inconstancy. The inability to establish oneself in something, to start something, and the impossibility to maintain oneself in what one has succeeded to attain, to continue doing what one has started, denote efforts which prove to be fruitless and which must be repeated; changes of situations, vacillations, which give rise to various, manifold contents of the consciousness, all of which bring in their wake a dispersion of the mind.

H. The Concept of "Obstacle"

The "obstacles" cause the dispersion of the mind, whereby they render the mental concentration difficult and even create such a state in which such concentration becomes extremely difficult. See Vyāsa's commentary on *sūtra* I.1. When they render difficult the concentration of the mind, the obstacles actually hinder the realisation of the restraint of the mental processes, which must of necessity be preceded by concentration. See *sūtra* I.20.

Strictly speaking the "obstacles" may be called "obstacles" of *samādhi* and *nirodha* and of yoga in general. But we prefer to view them as the "obstacles" of *nirodha,* since Patañjali has up until now been dealing with *nirodha.*

I. Elimination of the Obstacles

The obstacles mentioned by Patañjali, which render restraint difficult, can be eliminated by *abhyāsa* in one single entity (see *sūtra* I.32), the forms of which are *japa* and *bhāvana* (see *sūtras* I.28 and I.29). We also refer to our commentary of *sūtra* I. 32.

31

दुःखदौर्मनस्याङ्गमेजयत्वश्वासप्रश्वासा विक्षेपसहभुवः ॥

DUḤKHADAURMANASYĀṄGAMEJAYATVAŚVĀSA-PRAŚVĀSĀ VIKṢEPASAHABHUVAḤ.

Pain, mental unease, agitation of the body, inspiration and expiration, are the concomitants of the dispersions (*vikṣepa*).

A. Daurmanasya (*mental unease*)

The expression *daurmanasya* has been translated in several ways, most of which indicate a state of depressive feeling : "despondency" (Woods); "dejection" (H. Āranya and B. Baba); "sulkiness" (Purohit); "distress" (Ballantyne); "Trübsinn" (Hauer, *Der Yoga*, p. 242); "mental distress" (Vivekananda); "despair" (Taimni, Rama Prasada and Dvivedī).

By *daurmanasya* Vyāsa understands : "*the agitation of the mind because of the non-realisation of a desire*" (*icchāvighātāc-cetasaḥ kṣobhaḥ*). This interpretation is followed by the commentary attributed to Śaṅkara, by Kṛṣṇavallabha and by Ram Sharma.

We prefer the translation "mental unease" for *daurmanasya*, according to the etymology of the word. Our interpretation agrees with that of Bhoja who defines *daurmanasya* as "*the unease of the mind due to external or internal causes*" (*bāhyā-bhyantaraiḥ kāraṇair manaso dauṣthyam*).

B. Aṅgamejayatva (*Corporal Agitation*)

Different translations of this term are available : "unsteadiness" (Woods); "unsteadiness of limbs" (B. Baba); "tremor of the body" (Vivekananda); "trembling" (Ballantyne); "shakiness" (Rama Prasada); "restlessness" (H. Āranya);

"nervousness" (Purohit, Taimni, Dvivedī); "Gliederzittern" (Hauer, *Der Yoga*, p. 242).

The commentators Vyāsa and Bhoja interpret *aṅgamejayatva* as "*the agitation, the trembling of the body*".

C. Śvāsa and Praśvāsa (inspiration and expiration)

It may be said that there exist three types of breathing: (1) the more or less regular, normal breathing, which occurs in the ordinary living condition of every individual; (2) the agitated, irregular breathing which generally accompanies the emotional states of excitement or depression and of disease. This sort of breathing, as well as the preceding one, may be qualified as "spontaneous"; and (3) the *prāṇāyāmic* breathing i.e. the breathing ruled by *prāṇāyāma* or the conscious control of breathing, designed to introduce in it a determined rhythm and to regulate the volume of the air inspired. *Prāṇāyāma* or breath control plays a very important role in the practice of yoga, as will be seen in the commentary on *sūtra* I.34.

With the expressions "inspiration" and "expiration" (*śvāsa-praśvāsa*), the present *sūtra* refers to the spontaneous, uncontrolled breathing (consequently, to normal breathing and to agitated, irregular breathing).

The commentators Vācaspati Miśra (*anicchataḥ*), Vijñānabhikṣu (*Vārtika* : *puruṣaprayatnaṃ vinā svayameva*) and Kṛṣṇavallabha consider that Patañjali does, in this *sūtra*, refer to the spontaneous, non-volitive breathing. Vācaspati Miśra and Kṛṣṇavallabha further expressly stress that the breathing, mentioned in the present *sūtra*, is the breathing which is contrary to *prāṇāyāma*. Of the translators H. Āraṇya, Rām Śarmā and Harikṛṣṇadās Goyandakā do, in their remarks, point out that the breathing referred to in this *sūtra* is uncontrolled breathing.

Less appropriately so, the translators Purohit, Dvivedī, Ballantyne and Vivekananda think that, in this *sūtra*, Patañjali is speaking of irregular breathing, that it is only an aspect of an uncontrolled breathing.

D. Vikṣepa-sahabhū (*Concomitant of the Dispersions*)

By the expression *sahabhū* Patañjali means—according to his commentators—that suffering, etc., are produced as a result of the emergence of the mental distractions (Bhoja) : *kutaścinnimittād utpanneṣu vikṣepeṣu ete duḥkhādayaḥ pravartante,* that they arise from the distractions (Vijñānabhikṣu, *Vārtika* : *vyādhyādivikṣepodbhavāḥ*); that they are their accompaniments (Kṛṣṇavallabha : *vikṣepānucarā ityarthaḥ*).

It is understood that each one of the dispersions is *necessarily* accompanied by one or more concomitants; but only some of them can be accompanied by all the concomitants. Moreover, in the case of uncontrolled breathing, all the dispersions are involved.

Thus sickness can give rise to all the concomitants. It is not evident that apathy, negligence, sloth produce pain or agitation of the body, but they do generate mental unease.

The commentators do not provide explanations on this matter which actually should be the object of experimental research which would establish the clinical data specific to the relationship between the dispersions and their concomitants.

32

तत्प्रतिषेधार्थमेकतत्त्वाभ्यासः ॥

TATPRATIṢEDHĀRTHAM EKATATTVĀBHYĀSAḤ.

To ward them off, abhyāsa (effort for stability) on a single entity (must be practised).

A. The Position of this sūtra in the Exposition of Patañjali

In I.2, Patañjali defines yoga as "the restraint (*nirodha*) of the mental processes". In I. 12, he mentions the two means (*abhyāsa* or the effort for stability and *vairāgya* or detachment) to obtain this restraint. In I. 20 he enumerates the requisites previous to restraint. In I. 21 and I. 23 he points out two factors which accelerate the attainment of *nirodha*: fervour (*saṃvega*) and surrender to the Lord (*īśvarapraṇidhāna*). I.30-31 refer to the obstacles which stand in the way to *nirodha*. I. 32 mentions the means to eliminate the said obstacles : the stabilizing of the mind in one single entity; and in I. 33-39, Patañjali will indicate the means whereby the stability referred to is attained. We thus hold the thread of Patañjali's explanation.

But Patañjali interrupts this general exposition by introducing a digression which begins with I. 24 and ends with I. 29. This digression is related to the concept of *Īśvara* (Lord) which appears in I. 23. In this digression, Patañjali points out the characteristics and the name of the Lord, the practices which must be realized in the context of surrender to the Lord (*japa* : repetition of the syllable *AUM* and *bhāvana* : evocation of the meaning of the syllable *AUM*, I. 28) and the effects of these two practices (I. 29), one of which is precisely the disappearance of the obstacles—obstacles which constitute the subject of the general exposition, coming immediately after the digression about the Lord (I. 30).

It may be observed, therefore, that the digression about the Lord is skillfully connected with the general exposition by means of the theme of the obstacles. Actually, the digression ends in I. 29 by saying that with *japa* and *bhāvana* the disappearance of the obstacles is brought about. And *sūtra* I. 30 which takes up again the main thread of the general exposition, enumerates these obstacles.

B. To Ward Them Off (*tat-pratiṣedha-artham*)

In the present *sūtra* Patañjali affirms that, by means of *abhyāsa* over a single entity, the warding off (*pratiṣedha*) of the obstacles is obtained. It is surprising that *sūtra* I. 29 states that *japa* and *bhāvana* which are forms of *abhyāsa* on a single entity, produce the non-existence (*abhāva*) of the obstacles. The presence of the two expressions of such divergent meanings, as are *pratiṣedha* (warding off) and *abhāva* (non-existence), in two *sūtras*, placed one so near to the other, to indicate the effect which the practice *abhyāsa* has on the obstacles, can serve as an argument to consider the digression about the Lord in *sūtras* I. 24 to I. 29, as an interpolation in the original text.

C. Abhyāsa

We refer to *sūtra* I. 13 in which Patañjali defines the term *abhyāsa* and to our commentary *ad locum*. We recall only that *abhyāsa* is the effort, the determination, the will to reach the stability of the mind, the intention directed to such a goal.

D. A Single Entity (*eka-tattva*)

The mind must be rendered stable, fixed on a single entity. This entity can be any object—"gross or subtle"—whatsoever. The Lord can be this object, though it need not necessarily be so.

Vācaspati Miśra thinks that the Lord is the "sole entity" mentioned in the *sūtra* (*ekaṃ tattvam īśvaraḥ prakṛtatvād iti*). Kṛṣṇavallabha and Rāma Śarmā follow Vācaspati's interpretation.

But Vijñānabhikṣu rejects with reason this interpretation. He states (*Vārtika ad* I. 31) that had Patañjali wished to indicate that fixing the mind on the Lord constitutes the means to ward off the obstacles, he would have said, instead of *ekatattvābhyāsa, īśvarābhyāsa "abhyāsa* on the Lord", so that his statement would not lend itself to any doubt (*yadi hīśvarapraṇidhānam eva kevalam antarāyābhāvahetur iti vakṣyamāṇasūtrārthaḥ syāt, tadā ekatattvābhyāsa iti sāmānyopasaṃharo na yujyeta, nissaṃdehārtham īśvarābhyāsa ityeva vaktuṃ yuktatvād iti bhāvaḥ*). In the commentary on *sūtra* I. 32 he adds that it is improper to give to a word having a generic meaning—without any previous restriction—a specific meaning. (See Section A of our commentary on I. 30.) Further he says that if *ekatattvābhyāsa* exclusively referred to the Lord, then this *sūtra* would be redundant, since it would have expressed the same idea as does the earlier *sūtra* I. 29. Bhoja, H. Āranya, Harikṛṣṇadās Goyandakā follow the interpretation of Vijñānabhikṣu.

In the present *sūtra* Patañjali says *in general terms* that the *abhyāsa* on a single entity is the means to eliminate the obstacles. *Sūtra* I. 29 establishes that a particular case of *abhyāsa* on a single entity—as *japa* or *bhāvana* is—leads to the same goal. The enunciation of the general principle contained in I. 32 renders I. 29 unnecessary, which refers to a particular case. This superfluity of I. 29 can serve as another argument to support the view that the digression about the Lord is nothing but an interpolation.

E. How Does Ekatattvabhyāsa Act in Favour of the Elimination of the Obstacles

As has been explained in Section G of our commentary of *sūtra* I. 30, the obstacles are dispersions of the mind, insofar as, from each one of them, there arises a constant flux of manifold and diverse representations (*pratyaya*) to the consciousness. It may be said that the obstacles generate a polyideism.

When the mind strives to establish itself in only one entity, and becomes fixed on it, the representation of this sole entity takes up the entire field of consciousness, and prevents other representations from intruding into it. Indeed this is what happens in every act of attention : only one representation monopolises the consciousness in a more or less intense way, to the exclusion and inhibition of the other representations which could reach it.

Thus, for example, in the case of sickness, by means of the monoideism which the *abhyāsa* fosters, the sensations of disease and pain do not reach the consciousness. We recall the "ecstatic anesthesia" of the mystics. See Underhill, *Mysticism*, pp. 329 and 360.[81]

81. Cf. Schultz, *El entrenamiento*, p. 95: *"Anyhow there is no doubt about the possibility to suppress pain through autogenous concentration, as we have described it here and as we have had the occasion to observe in a very large material of subjects of common type".*

33

मैत्रीकरुणामुदितोपेक्षाणां सुखदुःखपुण्यापुण्यविषयाणां भावनातश्चित्तप्रसादनम् ॥

MAITRĪKARUṆĀMUDITOPEKṢĀṆĀṂ SUKHADUḤKHA-PUṆYĀPUṆYAVIṢAYĀṆĀṂ BHĀVANĀTAŚ CITTAPRASĀDANAM.

Serenity of mind (*cittaprasādanam*) (*arises*) *from the production* (*in the yogin*) *of benevolence, compassion, satisfaction, indifference towards happiness and sorrow, merit and demerit* (*respectively*).

A. Position of this sūtra

From this *sūtra* to I. 39, Patañjali is concerned with the means of attaining the stability (*sthiti*) of the mind, in its double—intellective-cognitive and emotional—aspect. In I.33 and I. 34 he will deal with the emotional stability; and with the intellective-cognitive stability in the following *sūtras*. See our commentary on *sūtra* I. 13, Section B.

B. Benevolence (*maitrī*), *Etc.*

Maitrī (benevolence). Other translations : "friendliness" (Woods, Taimni, Rama Prasada); "friendship" (Bengali Baba, Vivekananda); "sympathy" (Dvivedī); "amity" (H. Āranya); "Freundschaft" (Hauer, *Der Yoga*, p. 242).

Karuṇā (compassion). Other translations : "tenderness" (Ballantyne); "mercy" (Vivekananda); "Mitleid" (Hauer, *ibid.*).

Muditā (satisfaction). Other translations : "joy" (Woods, Bengali Baba); "gladness" (Taimni, Vivekananda); "complacency" (Ballantyne, Rama Prasada, Dvivedi); "good-will" (H. Āranya); "Frohsinn' (Hauer, *ibidem*).

Upekṣā (indifference). Other translations : "disregard" (Ballantyne); "neutrality" (Bengali Baba); "Gleichmut" (Hauer, *ibidem*).

Sukha (happiness). Other translations : "pleasure" (Bengali Baba); "Lust" (Hauer, *ibidem*).

Duḥkha (sorrow). Other translations : "Pain" (Woods, Bengali Baba); "misery" (Taimni, Rama Prasada, Dvivedī); "grief" (Ballantyne); "Leid" (Hauer, *ibidem*).

Puṇya (merit). Other translations : "virtue" (Taimni, Ballantyne, Bengali Baba, Rama Prasada, Dvivedī); "frommes Werk" (Hauer, *ibidem*).

Apuṇya (demerit). Other translations : "vice" (Taimni, Ballantyne, Bengali Baba, Rama Prasada, Dvivedī); "unfrommes Werk" (Hauer, *ibidem*).

C. Meaning of this sūtra

This *sūtra* suggests that the yogin, who develops in himself the sentiments mentioned in the *sūtra*, shall obtain serenity of mind, one of the forms of stability. The yogin who has developed in himself these sentiments, shall see himself free from the violent disturbances of the mind, he shall not react vehemently to improper conduct; he shall exist at the level of sentiments expressed on a low key. He shall adopt an attitude which is affable, mildly compassionate, smiling, or, in many cases, indifferent to the people around him.

It must be understood that the sentiments recommended by this *sūtra* have to be maintained on a low key so that they do not unbalance the yogin and, at the same time, bind him, or compromise or identify him emotionally with the situations in which he finds himself. The yogin must always be emotionally distant. It is understood that an exalted sentiment of compassion would be contrary to the serenity of the mind which the yogin endeavours to attain.

D. The Moral Value of the Sentiments Mentioned

We must observe that benevolence in the face of bliss, compassion in the face of sorrow, satisfaction in the face of meritorious conduct, indifference in the face of demerit, of other persons, are not sentiments which are recommended for their intrinsic moral value, but as means whereby the yogin attains the spiritual peace which is required for his task, all this in agreement with the a-moral characteristic of Yoga. It is also for this reason that the tendency will be towards indifference—the sentiment recommended in certain cases—becoming generalized so that it extends to all cases.

E. Effects of the serenity of the mind (cittaprasādana)

A serene mind is a stable mind from the emotional point of view. The serenity of the mind will facilitate the attainment of the intellective-cognitive stability produced by means of fixation, of the concentration of the mind on a single entity.

34

प्रच्छर्दनविधारणाभ्यां वा प्राणस्य ॥

PRACCHARDANAVIDHĀRAṆĀBHYĀṂ VĀ PRĀṆASYA.

Or (it arises) from the expulsion of the air breathed in and the retention of the air absorbed.

A. The Prāṇāyāmic Breathing

This *sūtra* actually refers to the *prāṇāyāmic* breathing, that is, the regulated breathing, opposed to the normal, ordinary, spontaneous breathing. See *sūtra* I.31. In II.49-53, Patañjali refers to *prāṇāyāma* in greater detail. The texts of the Haṭha Yoga—especially the *Haṭhayogapradīpikā*, the *Gheraṇḍasaṃhitā* and the *Śivasaṃhitā* among others—do, in accordance with the general tendency of Haṭha Yoga, deal extensively with *prāṇāyāma* or the controlled breathing. The modern expositions on Yoga bear, in a general sense, detailed chapters on these practices. We may, in this context, mention, as a special case, Swami Kuvalayānanda's *Prāṇāyāma*.

The *prāṇāyāmic* breathing depends on the will of the yogin in what refers to the volume of air absorbed, the number of inspirations (*pūraka*) and expirations (*recaka*) per unit of time, the duration of the inspirations and expirations and the duration of the retentions (*kumbhaka*). Of course, once the desired control is attained, the regulated breathing becomes automatic, as happens with all the yogic practices.

Prāṇāyāmic breathing is rhythmic, that is, the volume of air absorbed and the duration of each stage of breathing (*pūraka, kumbhaka, recaka*) shall be the same for as long as the yogin wishes it.

The yogin can each time make the rhythm of his breathing

slower and progressively reduce the volume of air absorbed till extreme limits are reached.

Further, in the first stage of the *prāṇāyāma* or controlled breathing, the mind must of necessity concentrate on the same respiratory process (that is, attention follows the process of intake, retention and expulsion of air absorbed) to establish specifically the desired rhythm and volume of air absorbed. See Evans-Wentz, *Tibetan Yoga*, pp. 125-126.

Finally, *prāṇāyāma* does not replace ordinary breathing except when the yogin desires it.

It must be added that the *prāṇāyāma* is the result of intense and sustained practices and, on account of the dangers which it presents, it must be indulged in only under the direction and control of a competent preceptor.

B. Interdependence Between the Mind and Breathing. The Effects of Prāṇāyāma

According to Bhoja the breathing processes precede the activities of the senses and of the mind and, for that reason, there exists a relation of interdependence between the mind and breathing, and thus, by blocking the activity of the senses and the flux of ideas, *prāṇāyāma*, or breath control, gives to the mind the power of concentration. The Haṭha Yoga follows the same doctrine. *Haṭhayogapradīpikā* II.2 says that when the "air" is agitated, the mind is agitated, and the mind is pacified when the "air" becomes quiet. Hemacandra, *Yogaśāstra*, V. 1 and 2, echoes the same view: "*where there is mind, there is "air"; where there is "air", there is mind; both have the same function, one is penetrated by the other...with the destruction of one, there occurs the destruction of the other; when one functions, so does the other...*" Tibetan yoga also adopts this doctrine of interdependence between the mind and breathing (Evans-Wetz, *Tibetan Yoga*, p. 185, note 3). As says Th. Brosse, *Études Instrumentales*, p. 123, "the relation—one can even say the rigorous correspondence—between the mental and the breathing activity is one of the fundamental postulates of the psycho-physiology of the Yoga."

It is not that only mental activity and emotional states exert an influence on breathing. In its turn, breathing does have an influence on mental activity and on effective life. The first aspect of this opinion is easy to verify: anger and fear, for example, accelerate and disturb breathing. The second aspect, that is, the influence of breathing on mental activity and the emotional states, does not easily lend itself to verification. But the therapeutic results obtained by western medicine, by means of control of breathing and the necessary mental concentration which it implies[82] would prompt one to think that such an influence cannot be doubted.[83]

The yogins unanimously praise the calming and positive effect that *prāṇāyāma* has on the mind. See Swami Śivānanda, *Kuṇḍalinī Yoga*, p. 108, *Practical Lessons*, p. 99, *The Science of Prāṇāyāma*, p. 99; Swami Abhedānanda, *Yoga Psychology*, pp. 82 and ff.; H. Āraṇya, p. 89; Swami Kuvalayānanda, *Prāṇāyāma*, p. 51; Dukes, *Yoga*, pp. 147 and 177; Yogi Ramacaraka, *Ciencia Hindú-Yogui de la respiración*, pp. 30, 219-221.

C. Relation Between this sūtra and the Preceding one

In our view the present *sūtra* is related to the previous one by the particle *vā* ("or") and by the fact that the words *bhāvanātas* (I.33) and *pracchardanavidhāraṇābhyām* (I. 34) are in the same case. Consequently there exist for Patañjali two means to produce mental serenity (*cittaprasādana*). The first—mentioned in I.33—consists in producing in oneself determined, specific sentiments; the other means is *prāṇāyāma* or breath control. That is the

82. Hauer, *Der Yoga*, pp. 318 and 474, note 3; Th.Brosse, *Études Instrumentales*, p. 124.

83. Cf. Schultz, *El entrenamiento*, p. 85: "*...we must admit that, in a unitary conception of the living organism, although the "body" does not exercise any influence on the "soul", both component elements fulfil a similar function in a biological process so remarkably unitary as the affectivity. It is easy to understand that a technique, which is able to allow a person, who has been trained in it, to put into rest, through a momentaneous, animic concentration, organs that are bearers of expression so essential as muscles, veins, heart and respiratory apparatus, and even allows him to diminish the tonus of the abdominal organs, may suppress an important part of the affective process*".

interpretation of Vijñānabhikṣu (*Yogavārtika*), H. Āranya, Bengali Baba, Rama Prasada. The serenity of the mind is a direct and immediate effect of *prāṇāyāma* (Vijñānabhikṣu, *Yagasārasaṃgraha*, p. 45). As in the case of the preceding *sūtra*, the serenity of the mind, produced by *prāṇāyāma*, bears with it the emotional stability of the mind.[84] The stability of the mind is an indirect and mediate effect of *prāṇāyāma*.

D. Prāṇāyāma and Mental Fixation

As we have said earlier *prāṇāyāma* is essentially the control, the regulation of breathing. But generally *prāṇāyāma* implies the fixation of the mind on the rhythmic breathing process which it generates. The rhythmic breathing process is converted into the centre of attention of the mind. See Evans-Wentz, *Tibetan Yoga*, p. 125. But this fixation is not something essential in *prāṇāyāma*. During *prāṇāyāma* the mind can be fixed on another object which is not the rhythmic breathing.

E. Abnormal Effects of Prāṇāyāma

We have said that *prāṇāyāma* produces a state of mental peace. But if the reduction of the volume of air absorbed—which is one of the aspects of *prāṇāyāma*—is intensified, then there occur a lowering of the vital tone and a weakening of consciousness, which can be compared to what takes place in cataleptic, comatic or other similar states. The lowering of the vital tone reduces the

84. Some authors as Woods, following Vyāsa and Vācaspati Miśra unite the present *sūtra* I.34 with the following one I.35; in their opinion Patañjali is attributing to *prāṇāyāma*, as an effect, the stability of mind, a concept that has been dealt with in *sūtra* I.35 and following ones. This interpretation is not sound in our opinion for the same reasons that have been indicated in our commentary and besides that because the constructions of *sūtras* I.34 and I.35 are completely different and do not allow both *sūtras* to be coordinated according to the rules of the *sūtra* style. Following this interpretation, that we do not accept, the direct and immediate effect or *prāṇāyāma* would be the stability of mind, without taking into account, as an intermediate stage, the serenity of the mind

nervous waste, the cardiac contractions, the need for oxygen and enables certain yogis to undergo such abnormal trials as remaining buried for a long time. Attained by means of *prāṇāyāma* this state has been compared to the hibernation of some animals, like the marmot, for example.[85]

85. See note 7.

35

विषयवती वा प्रवृत्तिरुत्पन्ना (मनसः) स्थितिनिबन्धनी ॥

VIṢAYAVATĪ VĀ PRAVṚTTIR UTPANNĀ (MANASAḤ) STHITINIBANDHANĪ.

Cause (s) of stability (sthiti) (of the mind) (are) either (vā) a continued process (pravṛtti) with object as soon as it arises (utpanna).

It may be recalled that in the *sūtras* I.35-39, Patañjali is concerned with the stability (*sthiti*) of the mind in its intellective-cognitive aspect. All these *sūtras* are related among themselves by means of the particle *vā* ("or"). But, in spite of these *sūtras* being related among themselves, they do not have the same grammatical construction, as is easily seen in the translations of the same *sūtras*.

A. Criterion for the interpretation of the present sūtra

The interpretation of the present *sūtra* depends on the meaning of the term *pravṛtti* and precisely it is difficult to establish with what meaning does Patañjali use it. In any case it is evident that a *pravṛtti* (with the characteristic of *viṣayavat*, with object) must signify a mental operation which produces the stability of the mind, as the *sūtra* asserts it. This must be the criterion which must be used as a guide in our attempts to establish the meaning of *pravṛtti* in the present *sūtra*.

B. Traditional interpretation of pravṛtti and of viṣayavat

Vyāsa begins his commentary of this *sūtra* by saying that *pravṛtti* is the consciousness or knowledge of sensation (*saṃvid*) of supernatural or divine (*divya*), smell, taste, colour, touch and sound, which arise in the yogin when he fixes his mind on the tip of his nose, on the tip of his tongue, on the palate, on the middle part of the tongue, on the root of the tongue, respectively (*nāsikāgre dhārayato'sya ya divyagandhasaṃvit, sa gandhapravṛttiḥ, etc.*). (It is understood that divine smell, etc. constitute the objects (*viṣaya*) of the *pravṛtti.*) Vyāsa also adds that the *pravṛtti* which arises in relation to the moon, the sun, the planets, jewels or a lamp (i.e. which has as its object the moon etc.), must be considered as a *pravṛtti* with object. The interpretation of *pravṛtti* which Vyāsa gives at the beginning of his commentary is adopted by the commentators Vācaspati Miśra, Bhoja, Śaṅkara and Kṛṣṇavallabha.

According to Vyāsa, Vācaspati Miśra, Bhoja and Vijñānabhikṣu (*Vārtika*) the word *viṣayavat* must be understood in the sense of "with object (of the senses)": smell, taste, etc. The word *viṣaya* which integrates the word indicated, would, according to them, signify only the sense objects.

The majority of the modern translators understand *pravṛtti* and *viṣayavat* according to Vyāsa's interpretation and do, in their observations, explicitly recognize their adhesion to the said interpretation : "higher objective perception called *viṣayavatī*" (H. Āranya); "higher sense-activity" (Rama Prasada). Rām Śarmā and Harikṛṣṇadās Goyandakā preserve the term *pravṛtti* in its Hindi translations, but they add the explanation that *pravṛtti* has the meaning which Vyāsa attributes to it at the beginning of his commentary. Ballantyne translates : "sensuous immediate cognition", which he explains, in his commentary, as : "mystical sense perception". Further, he explains the *sūtra* in conformity with Vyāsa.

C. The Translations of Pravṛtti and of Viṣayavat of Bengali Baba, Woods and Hauer

Bengali Baba and Woods, whose works, in addition to the translation of the *sūtras*, bear the translation of the commentary of Vyāsa, respectively translate by : "the sense-objective manifestation", and "a sense activity...connected with an object". Hauer (*Der Yoga, p.* 242) says: "Funktion, die auf ein bestimmtes Objekt gerichtet bleibt".

D. Our Interpretation of the terms pravṛtti and viṣayavat

(a) In our opinion, *pravṛtti* means a continued, sustained *vṛtti* (process). The following reasons support our translation :

1. Given Patañjali's rigorous use of the technical terms, to which we have referred on many occasions, the term *pra-vṛtti* must signify the same idea as *vṛtti* or a similar idea with a special nuance or determining element suggested by the prefix *pra.*

2. The prefix *pra-* contains the idea of "forward" and communicates to some adjectives a tone of intensity.

3. In its general sense, the word *pravṛtti* means "advance", "continued advance", "occupation", "activity", "continued effort", "perseverance", "continuity", "permanence". By translating the term *pravṛtti* by "continued or sustained *vṛtti*", we do not go beyond the semantic area covered by the prefix *pra-* and by the general acceptance of the word *pravṛtti.* What we are doing is simply to add to the word *vṛtti* a special nuance or determining component which, what is signified by *pra-* and by *pravṛtti*, authorizes us to add to them.

We may now explain what we mean by continued *vṛtti,* by taking perception (*pratyakṣa*) as an example. We recall that, in agreement with the explanation in our commentary of *sūtra* I.7, Section A, *pratyakṣa,* perception, comprises the apprehension of a material reality (sensorial perception) or of a mental reality (mental perception, *perceptio animi*), or of experiences. *Pratyakṣa* is a *vṛtti* (I.7) by means of which the mind knows an object. We are concerned here with an instantaneous act. If the mind is fixed on the perceived object and the act of perception is prolonged, the perception *vṛtti* is converted into a sustained *vṛtti*, that is, into the *pra-vṛtti*—perception. What distinguishes the *vṛtti pratyakṣa* from the *pravṛtti pratyakṣa* is this aspect of continuity.

(b) As regards *viṣayavat* we take the term *viṣaya* in this expression as designating any object of perceptual, sensorial or mental knowledge, in cenformity with what we have pointed out in Section B of our commentary on *sūtra* I.11 and *viṣaya-*

vat means, consequently, "with object", "object" being understood in the sense already indicated.

Having thus established the concept *pravṛtti*, we may now proceed to ask the following question :

E. What are the vṛttis which are able to be converted into pravṛttis ?

An analysis of the *vṛttis* dealt with by Patañjali in the *sūtra* I. 6 leads one to the conclusion that only the *vṛttis pratyakṣa* (perception), *smṛti* (attention) and *nidrā* (deep sleep) can be prolonged, continued, in such a way as they convert themselves into *pravṛttis,* that is, continued *vṛttis.*

Anumāna is, as we have pointed out in the commentary on *sūtra* I.7, a reasoning or inferential process which culminates into a conclusion. It is a discursive operation which moves from one step to the other of the inference (there is smoke on the mountain—where there is smoke there is fire—there is fire on the mountain). It is formed, composed of the constitutive elements of the reasoning activity. It is possible for each of these steps to be prolonged, for the mind to establish itself in one of the constitutive elements of the operation, in the acts of intuition, by means of which the mind grasps the different affirmations which constitute the reasoning act; but in itself, in its totality, the process cannot be prolonged precisely because of its discursive and composite nature.

Āgama (testimony), *vikalpa* and *viparyaya* (error) introduce, so to say, a mental product, into the mind of him who receives the information, into the mind of him in whom the *vikalpic* or erroneous operation is realized. The mind can detain itself in the grasping of this mental product, but *āgama, vikalpa* and *viparyaya* cannot in themselves be prolonged.

Smṛti means, according to Patañjali's definition in I. 11, the non-complete disappearance of a perceived object and, as we have shown in the corresponding commentary, comprises both attention and memory. If I perceive a sensorial or mental object and do not allow it to move out of the focus of my consciousness, that is an act of *smṛti*—attention. The *smṛti-*

attention can be prolonged, be converted from *vṛtti* into *pravṛtti*, as is the case with perception, as we have explained in Section D of the commentary of this *sūtra*.

Now let us see what is the situation regarding *smṛti*-memory. In accordance with Section D of our commentary on *sūtra* I.11, when a *saṃskāra* (latent subliminal impression) is reactivated, there reappears before consciousness the object perceived earlier, to which the said *saṃskāra* corresponds. If we do not allow this object—which reappears before consciousness—to disappear, we then have, as in the case explained in the previous paragraph, an act of *smṛti*-attention which applies to the recollected object. The act of *smṛti*-memory, by means of which the object perceived earlier reappears before consciousness, cannot be prolonged. It is instantaneous.

As regards the deep sleep (*nidrā*) *vṛtti*, it is easy to note that it can be prolonged, converting itself into a *pravṛtti*. This *vṛtti* cannot have an object (*viṣaya*).

F. The Function of the smṛti-attention in the transformation of the vṛtti pratyakṣa into the pravṛtti pratyakṣa

The *smṛti*-attention cannot occur without the perception of a material or mental object, the non-disappearance of which it produces. But the material or mental object, which does not disappear, is actually an object of perception and not of the *smṛti*-attention properly said. On being prolonged, *smṛti*-attention does prolong, in its turn, the perception of the perceived object. It is indeed the *smṛti*-attention which makes possible the conversion of the *vṛtti pratyakṣa* into the *pravṛtti pratyakṣa*. While the *smṛti*-attention lasts, the *vṛtti pratyakṣa* is prolonged. *Smṛti*-attention then always accompanies the *pravṛtti* perception; it is a concomitant element of the latter. *Smṛti*-attention exists always together with the *pravṛtti* perception.

G. To Which pravṛtti does the present sūtra refer ?

The present *sūtra* refers to the *pravṛtti* perception of material or mental objects. This derives from the explanations given in

Section E of this commentary. Actually only the *vṛttis pratyakṣa, smṛti*-attention and *nidrā* can be converted into *pravṛttis*. The *pravṛtti nidrā* cannot be taken into consideration in this *sūtra* because it is not "*viṣayavat*", it lacks an object. As regards the *pravṛtti smṛti*-attention, its position is more *sui generis* : it cannot occur of its own, without a perception to which it adheres. And this perception, in its turn, cannot, without this *pravṛtti smṛti*, convert itself into a *pravṛtti* perception.

The interpretation which we give to *pravṛtti* fully meets the requirement of the criterion established in Section A of the commentary of this present *sūtra* : a perceptive mental process, be it sensorial or mental, which prolongs itself by fixing the mind on a determined object, does of necessity stabilize the mind. See our commentary of *sūtra* I. 13, Section B.

H. Critique of the other interpretations and translations

The interpretations and translations referred in Sections B and C of the commentary of the present *sūtra* are not acceptable insofar as they do not satisfy the requirement of the criterion described in Section A. Indeed, neither the "*saṃvid* (sensation) of a super-natural smell, etc." (Vyāsa) nor a "higher objective perception" (H. Āraṇya), nor a "higher sense-activity" (Rāma Prasāda), nor a "sensuous immediate cognition" (Ballantyne), nor a "sense objective manifestation" (Bengali Baba), nor a "sense activity...connected with an object", nor a "Funktion" (Hauer), do by themselves constitute the factors which stabilize the mind.

With the purpose of introducing, in his interpretation of *pravṛtti*, an element of stabilization, which in its turn explains the stabilizing effect of the *pravṛtti* itself, Vyāsa says that the *saṃvid* of the supranatural smell, etc. arises out of the yogin's concentration on the tip of his nose, etc. Thus the stability would result from the concentration which precedes the *pravṛtti*, and not from the *pravṛtti* properly said. Moreover, at no time does Patañjali affirm that, for a *pravṛtti* to emerge, the concentration of the mind must precede it.

With the same purpose of introducing a stabilizing element in his interpretation of *pravṛtti*, Hauer translates *viṣayavat*, which simply means "with object", by "which persists directed towards a determined object"; this is an arbitrary interpretation.

I. Utpanna

Utpanna literally means "arisen", "emerged". Its presence in this *sūtra* serves simply to determine that stability starts, as soon as a *pravṛtti* with object arises, that is, in the very moment in which begins the prolongation of a sensorial or mental perception.

J. [*Manasaḥ*]

Most editions include the word *manasaḥ* in this *sūtra*; only a few—like the Kashi Sanskrit Series No. 83—do not. We exclude it from our text because we believe it must be a late interpolation, since neither Vyāsa, nor Vācaspati Miśra, nor Bhoja, nor Vijñānabhikṣu comment on it or explain it. Besides it is not necessary.

36

विशोका वा ज्योतिष्मती ॥

VIŚOKĀ VĀ JYOTIṢMATĪ.

or (*vā*) (*a continued process* : *pravṛtti*) *without pain* (*viṣoka*) *and luminous* (*jyotiṣmat*).

A. Translation of the sūtra

In conformity with the *sūtra* style, in this *sūtra*, the expressions *pravṛtti* (which we have included between brackets in the translation of the *sūtra* for the sake of clarity), *utpanna* (as soon as it arises) and *sthitinibandhanī* (cause of stability) which appear in the previous *sūtra*, must be understood as implicit.

The idea of the previous *sūtra* is that a prolonged process, with object, as soon as it arises, stabilizes the mind. The present *sūtra* indicates that another type of prolonged process—without suffering and luminous—as soon as it arises, does likewise originate the stability of the mind.

B. Viśoka (*without suffering*)

This expression signifies a characteristic of the *pravṛtti* to which the present *sūtra* refers. It concerns a *pravṛtti* from which every painful, unpleasant element (contrary to the concentration of mind) is absent. As we have said in Section A of our commentary on *sūtra* I. 16, suffering is an effect of the *rajas guṇa*. Therefore, the presence of this characteristic in the present *sūtra* indicates that the element *rajas* is absent from the *pravṛtti* referred to in this *sūtra*, which corresponds to what is said in Section C of this commentary.

C. Jyotiṣmat (*luminous*)

Our commentary on *sūtra* I. 16 (section A) refers to the Sāṃkhya theory of the three *guṇas* or elements, constitutive substances or factors of matter : *sattva, rajas* and *tamas*. In relation to *sattva* we have pointed out that its function is manifestation, that is, it is due to it that objects become manifest in consciousness. To complete these concepts we add that *sattva* is "illuminating" (*prakāśaka*), according to Kārikā 13 of the *Sāṃkhyakārikā* of Īśvarakṛṣṇa. And the commentary of Gauḍapāda *ad locum* elucidates the point by saying that when, from among the three elements, *sattva* predominates *"then the limbs (of the body) become light, and lucidity of mind and sharpness of the senses are produced"* (*Tadā laghūny aṅgāni buddhiprakāśaś ca prasannatendriyāṇāṃ bhavati*). In his commentary on the *Kārikā* 12 the same Gauḍapāda says that *"when sattva predominates, then by subduing rajas and tamas, together with their characteristics, it stands out in its own essence of joy and of illumination"* (*Yadā sattvam utkaṭaṃ bhavati tadā rajastamasī abhibhūya svaguṇaiḥ prītiprakāśātmanāvatiṣṭhate*).

We agree with Bhoja (*jyotiḥśabdena sāttvikaḥ prakāśa ucyate*) and understand *jyotis* as synonymous with *prakāśa*, which expresses the fundamental, illuminative function of *sattva*. Therefore, the expression *jyotiṣmat* ("luminous"), that qualifies the *pravṛtti* to which this *sūtra* refers, indicates that this *pravṛtti* is of a sāttvic nature. That is, it is a process by means of which something is presented, manifested before the consciousness in a lucid form. Later we shall show what is the "object" which manifests itself in front of the consciousness.

D. The pravṛtti of the Present sūtra is "without object"

The previous *sūtra* and the present *sūtra* are coordinated by means of the particles *vā...vā* ("either...or"). Both *sūtras* alternately indicate, as factors of stabilization, the *pravṛtti* "with object" (the previous *sūtra*) and the *pravṛtti* "without suffering and luminous" (the present *sūtra*). On considering the form of grammatical construction and in accordance with the *sūtra* style, we must understand that the *pravṛtti* dealt with in this *sūtra*, in contradistinction to the *pravṛtti* of the previous *sūtra*, is moreover a *pravṛtti* without object.

E. To what pravṛtti does the present sūtra refer?

In accordance with what has been explained in the previous *sūtra* there exist three possible *pravṛttis*: perception (*pratyakṣa*) in its sensorial, mental and experiential forms; the *smṛti*-attention and deep sleep (*nidrā*). We also recall that *smṛti* is a necessarily concomitant factor of the *pravṛtti* perception and that it is always present in perception.

In our opinion the present *sūtra* does not refer to *nidrā*, since the latter can never be qualified as '*jyotiṣmat*', "luminous", since the *pravṛtti nidrā* is a process in which the *guṇa tamas* predominates, while the *guṇa sattva* is absent.

Nor can the sensorial or mental *pravṛtti* perception be the subject matter of the present *sūtra*, because these *pravṛttis* are "with object" and have been examined in the previous *sūtra*.

The *pravṛtti* or prolonged process referred to in this *sūtra* can only be the third type of perception (*pratyakṣa*). (See *sūtra* I. 7, Section A) or the existential or experiential "perception" which lacks an object. See Note 1 of *sūtra* 7. The experience to which this *sūtra* refers must be lacking of suffering and is luminous in the sense in which we have already explained.

Two experiences mentioned by Patañjali, which can constitute the *pravṛtti* perception to which this *sūtra* refers, are *ānanda* (bliss) and *asmitā* (consciousness of existence) mentioned in *sūtra* I. 17. For further details we refer to the commentary on this *sūtra* (i.e. I. 17). Thus, as in the case of the previous *sūtra* the yogin fixes his attention on an external object and thus prolongs the perception of this same object, likewise in the case of the present *sūtra*, the yogin fixes his attention on an inner experience of his own, like the ones mentioned earlier, while prolonging the "perception" of the same and absorbing himself in them. In the *bhakti* mystics the preferred experience will be the love for the divinity and the yogin fixes his attention on the experience of love for the divine.[86]

86. The method of Schultz knows also the concentration on experiences. See *El entrenamiento*, pp. 95, 201-202.

37

वीतरागविषयं वा चित्तम् ॥

VĪTARĀGAVIṢAYAṂ VĀ CITTAM.

Or *(acquires stability) the mind which has for object (viṣaya) some being devoid of passion (vītarāga).*

A. Grammatical construction of this sūtra and of the two following sūtras

These three *sūtras* are interrelated by means of the particle *vā*, "or". We must moreover understand, in accordance with the commentator Vyāsa, the words *sthitipadaṃ labhate*, "acquires stability". The subject of the verb *labhate* which we have to understand, is *cittam*, expressed in this *sūtra* and implied in the two following *sūtras*. These three *sūtras* are coordinated among themselves by the particle *vā*: "or".

B. Interpretation of this sūtra

With regard to this *sūtra* it is only proper to adopt the traditional interpretation according to which, to obtain stability, the mind must concentrate itself on some Hindu saint like Nārada (Vijñānabhikṣu, *Yogasārasaṃgraha*: p. 47), who has succeeded in ridding himself completely of all passion.

C. Commentary of Vijñānabhikṣu

The commentary which Vijñānabhikṣu (*Vārtika*: *ad locum*) makes on the present *sūtra*, is interesting indeed. In this *sūtra* Patañjali limits himself to saying that the yogin can take as the object of concentration a being who is devoid of passion. Vijñānabhikṣu enhances the interpretation of the present *sūtra* by pointing out that this type of concentration performs a moral transformation of the yogin who takes as support (*ālambana*) (that is, as the object of concentration) some saint's mind purified of all passion, who absorbs (*uparakta*) himself in it and who, by means of fixation (*dhāraṇā*) on it, assumes its form (*tadākāra-tāpanna*). By freeing itself in its turn of all passion (*virakta*), this mind acquires the aptitude to stabilize itself in some other support (*sadālambanāntare 'pi sthitiyogyatāṃ labhata ity arthaḥ*).

In their commentary on this *sūtra*, H. Āraṇya, Vivekānanda, Purohit, Dvivedī, Taimni adopt points of view similar to that of Vijñānabhikṣu.

The principle of unconscious "mimetism", which is implied by the interpretation of Vijñānabhikṣu and of the other authors mentioned, is besides quite plausible.[87]

87. Schultz, *El entrenamiento*, pp. 202-203: "*Once the subjects have reached some experience about their interior life, we give to them another task that in a certain way is the opposite to the previous one: to present to their minds, being in a state of deep absorption, the image of some other person in the most concrete and plastic way that it is possible and to submit themselves to the effects of that appearance*". Unfortunately Schultz does not give more details about this matter.

We must not confound the practice, to which this *sūtra* refers and which is located in the concentration stage, with the practice of taking some person as a model to which all actions and feelings must conform. See the advice of Christian mysticism to imitate Christus. See L. de la Palma, *Camino Espiritual* 2.7.2 (p.528 Biblioteca de Autores Cristianos).

38

स्वप्ननिद्राज्ञानालम्बनं वा ॥

SVAPNANIDRĀJÑĀNĀLAMBANAṂ VĀ.

Or (the mind) that takes oniric knowledge (svapnajñāna) or nidric knowledge (nidrājñāna) as support (ālambana).

A. Construction of the sūtra

We must simply indicate that the expression *jñāna* must be taken in conjunction with both *svapna* and *nidrā*. Consequently, the *sūtra* indicates two other supports (*ālambana*) or objects of concentration: the oniric knowledge (*svapnajñāna*) and the *nidric* knowledge (*nidrājñāna*).[88]

B. The Oniric Knowledge (svapnajñāna)

It is impossible that Patañjali would, in this *sūtra*, propose that the support of the concentration be the dream, or better still, the oniric fantasy or vision (*svapna*). Such an interpretation does not take into account the observations made in the preceding Section A. Moreover it is impossible for a yogin to concentrate on a dream unless he is sleeping—a state in which it is incorrect to speak of concentration.[89]

We make ours Bhoja's interpretation which speaks of "dream" (*svapna*) when the *ātman*, or the individual spirit, "experiences" (*bhoktṛtvam ātmanaḥ*), but does so solely through the mediation

88. Oniric knowledge: dream. Nidric knowledge: knowledge that takes place during deep sleep. See section C.

89. Probably it is because of this impossibility that some interpreters like Vācaspati Miśra, Vivekananda and H. Āranya consider that the meaning of this *sūtra* is that the object of concentration can also be an oniric vision which one has had and which one remembers. It seems to us that this interpretation cannot be accepted, since it introduces an element that is not considered in Patañjali's *sūtra*—the remembrance of the oniric vision one has had.

of the mind (*manomātreṇa*) and by holding up the processes of the external senses (*pratyastamitabāhyendriyavṛtter*). Oniric knowledge, in accordance with the interpretation of Bhoja, is the knowledge of an "object" which the mind creates without the intervention of the senses—in other words, a mental image similar to a dream or an oniric vision which the yogin produces in himself in the state of wakefulness. It is on this image that the yogin concentrates.

C. The Nidric knowledge (nidrājñāna)

As we have said in Section E of our commentary of *sūtra* I. 10, deep sleep (*nidrā*) comprises the experience of the non-existence of the other mental processes, the experience of the void left by the cessation of the other mental processes. The *nidric* knowledge—to which this *sūtra* refers—is this experience of non-existence, this experience of the void.

As in the case of the oniric knowledge, Patañjali does not, in this *sūtra*, propose deep sleep (*nidrā*) as the support of the concentration, but that knowledge (*jñāna*) or experience which occurs in relation to deep sleep.

In practice, the yogin produces in himself, in the state of waking, an intellectual and emotional void, similar to what takes place in deep sleep, and labours in such a way that there arise in him no sensations, ideas, images, sentiments, so that his mind stays empty. This state of vacuity serves as an "object" of concentration for him. The yogin fixes his mind and concentrates on it. As in *sūtra* I. 36 the yogin is absorbed in a pleasurable sensation, in the same way, in the present case, the yogin absorbs himself in the *nidric* vacuity, in the characteristic emptiness of deep sleep.

39

यथाभिमतध्यानाद्वा ॥

YATHĀBHIMATADHYĀNĀD VĀ.

or with meditation (dhyāna) on what pleases him.

A. Dhyāna: meditation

In III. 1, Patañjali defines *dhāraṇā* as follows: *"Deśabandhaś cittasya dhāraṇā"*: *"dhāraṇā* is the fixing of the mind on one place". It consists in fixing the mind on one single point which can be a part of the body or some external object. In III. 2, he defines *dhyāna* thus: *tatra pratyayaikatānatā dhyānam*: *"dhyāna is the concentrated attention (ekatānatā) to a single content of consciousness (pratyaya:*[90] *idea, experience) on that place"*. Once the mind has been fixed on some point by means of *dhāraṇā*, the yogin must strive until only a single content is held in his mind. This can be either a single representation or idea, or a single experience, while he rejects any intruding alien idea or experience and, moreover, brings to a focus, so to say, this single and only content on the point selected in the *dhāraṇā*.

Dhyāna is an act of attention directed to some particular object. When it is prolonged or intensified, it gives rise to *samādhi* or concentration of the mind, the consequence of which is the cessation of all the mental processes, and to which we have referred in Section E of our commentary of the *sūtra* I. 20.

B. Freedom in the Choice of the Object

If we take this expression in its broadest sense (material object,

90. Regarding the word *pratyaya* see section C of our commentary of *sūtra* I.10.

mental reality, content of an experience), any object can be chosen for *dhyāna*. Of all these objects (in addition to those mentioned in *sūtras* I.35-38) we expressly single out the sacred syllable *AUM*, symbol of the Lord, to which the *sūtra* I. 27 and our commentary on it refer.

40

परमाणुपरममहत्त्वान्तोऽस्य वशीकारः ॥

PARAMĀṆUPARAMAMAHATTVĀNTO 'SYA VAŚĪKĀRAḤ.

Its (asya: of the mind) subduing action (vaśīkāra) has as limits extreme smallness (pramāṇu (tva)) and extreme greatness (paramamahattva).

A. Subduing Action (vaśīkāra)

Literally *vaśīkāra* means "action of subduing, of subjugating, action of putting under the yoke". For the sake of clarity we call it "subduing action".

B. Its (asya)

The pronoun *asya* refers to *citta* (mind), a concept which is central to the preceding *sūtras* I.37, 38 and 39. See Section A of the commentary on *sūtra* I.37.

C. Extreme Smallness (paramāṇu (tva)) and Extreme Greatness (paramamahattva).

The suffix-*tva* must be applied to both terms of the compound. We must, therefore, understand: *paramāṇutva* and *paramamahattva.*

D. Idea of the sūtra

In the preceding *sūtras* Patañjali has mentioned the different objects on which the mind can concentrate itself. All that Patañjali does in the present *sūtra* is that he is clarifying the notion that the mind has the ability to concentrate itself on an extremely small (*aṇu*) "object", like the atom, as on an extremely large (*mahat*) "object", like the universe. The mind can conceive the infinitely small as well as the infinitely great and then concentrate itself on it.

E. Taimni's Interpretation

Taimni translates *vaśīkāra* by "mastery", and refers *asya* to the yogin. According to him Patañjali, in this *sūtra*, would be saying "there is no limit to the powers of the yogi"—an idea which one frequently encounters among the exponents of Yoga. These powers are studied by Patañjali in Book III.

In connection with these powers, it is to be noted, I. *vaśīkāra* does not signify "mastery" in the sense of power; 2. that *asya* cannot mean "of him": "of the yogin", because the concept of yogin has not appeared in the preceding *sūtras*, which refer—as we have already pointed out—to the mind; and 3. that a reference to the magic powers of the yogin is out of place at this moment of the exposition which is analysing the process of trance[91].

91. Purohit, Dvivedī, Rama Prasada, Hauer (*Der Yoga* p. 243) seem to adopt an interpretation similar to that of Taimni; Vivekananda, H. Āranya, Ballantyne, R. Sharmā, Harikṛṣṇadās Goyandakā adopt an interpretation similar to ours, as expressed in the sections of this *sūtra's* commentary.

41

क्षीणवृत्तेरभिजातस्येव मणेर्ग्रहीतृग्रहणग्राह्येषु तत्स्थतदञ्जनता समापत्तिः ॥

KṢĪṆAVṚTTER ABHIJĀTASYEVA MAṆER GRAHĪTṚGRAHAṆAGRĀHYEṢU TATSTHATADAÑJANATĀ SAMĀPATTIḤ.

The establishment (tatstha (tā)) (of the mind)) with its mental processes destroyed (kṣīṇavṛtti) in the subject (grahītṛ) or in an act of perception (grahaṇa) or in an object (grāhya) and (as the consequence of this establishment) the coloration (tadañjanatā) (of the mind) by them—like a transparent crystal—constitutes samāpatti.

A. Translation of the term samāpatti

The term *samāpatti* has been translated in the following ways: "balanced-state" (Woods), "engrossment" H. Āranya), "transformation" (B. Baba), thought-transformation" (Rama Prasada), "illumination" (Purohit), "complete identity" (Dvivedī), "consummation" (Taimni), "Zusammenfallen' (Hauer, *Der Yoga*, p.243).

According to Monier-Williams' Dictionary, *samāpatti* normally means "coming together", "meeting", that is, "encounter", "reunion". Of the versions mentioned above, that of Hauer best preserves the current meaning of the expression. We choose not to translate the expression *samāpatti*, because there is not in English a word which corresponds to the complex process described by Patañjali in this *sūtra*, and because we believe that words like "reunion", "encounter" or similar ones do not suggest anything related to that process, and can lend themselves to confusion.

B. The Concept of samāpatti

With the aim of facilitating the understanding of the following explanations, we may offer an idea of what is a *samāpatti* (of the mind) on an object.

The mind "stabilizes" itself : that is, it concentrates and fixes itself on a single object. As this fixation becomes increasingly intense, it carries with it the gradual elimination of all the mental processes. What remains is only the mental process corresponding to the perception of the object on which the yogin has been concentrating. And as the fixation becomes more and more intense, and as the gradual elimination of all the mental processes is taking place, the mind correspondingly becomes "coloured" by this object.

By the "coloration of the mind by the object" (*tadañjanatā*) we must only understand the fact that the consciousness—on account of this act of intense attention which is in the course of being realized at the moment of fixation—is, so to say, absorbed in the object or, in other words, that the object invades, and takes possession of, the entire field of consciousness.

C. "With its mental processes destroyed" (*kṣīṇavṛtti*)

The adjective *kṣīṇavṛtti*, "with its mental processes destroyed", refers to the mind, *citta*, a concept which we must understand as implicit in this *sūtra*, and which is to be taken from the preceding *sūtras*.

Vyāsa and Vijñānabhikṣu explain *vṛtti* by *pratyaya*, which actually designates anything which presents itself to consciousness (see Section C of our commentary on *sūtra* I.10). Though *vṛtti* and *pratyaya* do not strictly refer to the same thing, as *vṛtti* indicates a mental process and *pratyaya* the product which, by means of this mental process, arrives at consciousness, however, for the purpose of the explanation which follows, this identification of both terms is acceptable. Vyāsa and Vijñānabhikṣu pointedly observe that, when the *samāpatti* is produced, the *pratyayas* have not all been destroyed or eliminated, since there subsists one *pratyaya*—the *samāpatti* itself which constitutes in itself a *pratyaya* (Vyāsa : *kṣīṇavṛtter iti pratyastamitapratyaya-*

syety arthaḥ. Vijñānabhikṣu : *pratyayasya pratyayāntarasyeti arthaḥ samāpatter api pratyayatvāt*).

It is evident that in *samāpatti* there occurs an act of perception (*sui generis* by the intensity) in which something becomes present to consciousness. Moreover, during the *samāpatti* the mental process *smṛti*-attention persists, since, on account of it, the "object" on which the mind concentrates itself, does not disappear from the consciousness (see *sūtra* I.11 and our commentary, Section D).

Further it must be said that the elimination or the destruction of the *vṛttis*, to which this *sūtra* refers, is the result of the *ekatattvābhyāsa*, "the effort for stability in a single entity"; this has been dealt with in *sūtras* I.30-39 and referred to in this *sūtra* by means of the term *tatstha* (*tā*).

D. *"Establishment of the Mind in"* (*tatstha* (*tā*)); *"coloration of the mind by"* (*tadañjanatā*)

In the preceding Section B of this commentary we have shown what it must be understood by means of these two expressions : "absorption" of the mind in the "object" on which it has concentrated itself (*tadañjanatā*), as a consequence of the act of intense attention which this concentration implies (*tatstha* (*tā*)).[92]

As can be seen in the preceding paragraph and in the explanation given of *samāpatti* in Section B of this commentary, we have—in the compound *tatsthatadañjanatā*—assumed that the first part of the same *tatstha* (*tā*) gives the reason or the cause of the *tadañjanatā*, the second part of the compound. Vijñānabhikṣu interprets this compound in the same way (*tatsthitatayā tadañjanatā*).

E. *"Like a Transparent Crystal"*

The comparison which Patañjali has made in the present *sūtra* does not constitute a mere literary embellishment. As is

92. *Tatstha*(*tā*) designates the stabilization (*sthiti*) of the mind on an object. Bhoja interprets this term by *ekāgratā* (one-pointedness, mental fixation).

well known, the *sūtra* style constantly strives to achieve the greatest economy of words. Consequently the comparison introduced in this *sūtra* must express an important element of the process which this *sūtra* describes.

Above all we may point out that the comparison is elliptically expressed : on being placed on a coloured object, a piece of crystal appears to be tinged with the colour of that object. This image appears in other Sanskrit philosophical texts like *Ātmabodha* 15 and *Hastāmalaka* 12. See also Vijñānabhikṣu (*Vārtika*, commentary on this *sūtra*).

This comparison shows that "the establishment of the mind in" and the "colouring of the mind by" the "object" in which the concentration is verified, are accompanied by a state of absolute *passivity* of the mind. As the transparent crystal remains totally passive in front of the coloured object which lends it its colour, in like manner does the mind not accomplish any activity at all, once it has been established or fixed in the "object". The "colouring" of the mind by the "object" is brought about without the active intervention of the mind. The mind stands passively in front of the "object" and the latter "colours" it.

This "*colouring*" *is total.* As the crystal is totally invaded by the colour of the object on which it has been placed, in like manner the "object", which is facing the mind, invades the field of consciousness, and completely fills it. This "object" is the only one which exists for the mind, it is the only one which is reflected in the mind, the only one which reaches it.

In the case of the comparison both the transparent crystal and the coloured object—although they persist in actually remaining two separate and different entities—appear, from the moment in which the transparent crystal is placed on the coloured object, as a single thing: a coloured crystal. What has taken place is an amalgamation, an *identification*, a *uni*-fication of both. Similarly, although the mind and the "object" of concentration are two separate and different realities which, at the moment of the *samāpatti*, appear, in the experience of the mystic yogī, as if they are amalgamated, identified, *uni*-fied, on account of the total absorption of the mind in the "object".

Again, as the transparent crystal does not undergo any *modification* by the fact of "taking" the colour of the object on which it is placed, likewise the mind is not modified on being absorbed in the "object".

In his commentary of the present *sūtra* (*Vārtika*), Vijñānabhikṣu explains the expression *tadañjanatā* thus : *samyak tadākāratā:*[93] *"the complete adoption on the part of the mind of its (of the object) form"*. Without any doubt this explanation is offered in accordance with the Sāṃkhya theory of the *vṛttis* (mental processes), though in this case it is applied to perception, according to which the mind, in the act of perception, transforms and modifies itself, by adopting the form of the object it perceives. See our commentary of *sūtra* I.2, Section B.

To us, Vijñānabhikṣu's interpretation seems erroneous, as it is not congruent with the image used by Patañjali, who expressly says that the mind does not undergo any modification in the act of absorbing itself in the "object", just as the crystal is not in the least modified on taking the coloration of the object. In the philosophical texts of Vedānta mentioned in Section E of this commentary, the same image is used to indicate that neither the *Ātman* nor Viṣṇu, to which these texts refer, undergo any modification in their contact with matter. Further, had Patañjali wished to express this idea, he would have, instead of *tadañjanatā*, used the expression *tadākāratā* and, instead of the image of the transparent crystal, some other more appropriate image to express this Sāṃkhya conception—like that of water which takes the form of the vessels which contain it—a comparison often used to this effect.

F. "Objects" of Concentration

Patañjali says that *samāpatti* is realized in relation : (1) to the perceiver (*grahītr*); (2) to the perceiving (*grahaṇa*), and (3) to what is perceived (*grāhya*), that is, the yogin concentrates on one or the other.

93. Bhoja gives an interpretation similar to that of Vijñānabhikṣu: tataś ca sthūlasūkṣmagrāhyoparaktaṃ cittaṃ tatra samāpannaṃ bhavati evaṃ grahaṇe grahītari ca samāpannaṃ tadrūpapariṇāmatvaṃ boddhavyam.

What is to be perceived (*grāhya*). By this we must understand the material objects and the mental realities or, in other words, the "gross" and the "subtle" objects. (See *sūtras* I.7, Section A; I.11, Section B; I.17, Sections B and C; I.35, Section D.)

Of course, of the material or mental objects, not all are fit or appropriate (*yogya*) for concentration. It is obvious that a loud noise, however rhythmic it can be, or a fluttering bird, could never be used as a support for concentration. The objects which are appropriate for the practice of concentration are a place in the body (such as the tip of the nose, the space between the eyebrows, or the navel), a luminous point, a sound (like the ticking of a clock), the image of a divinity, a religious symbol, the sacred symbol *AUM* repeated orally or mentally, etc. See C. Dragonetti, "El método yóguico", in F. Tola and C. Dragonetti's *Yoga y Mística de la India*, pp. 170 and 172.

Perception (*grahaṇa*). This expression designates the *act* of knowledge, the process of the perception (*pratyakṣa*) in its three aspects—sensorial, mental and experiential. (See *sūtras* I.7, Section A and I.35, Section D.) But, just as not every object (*grāhya*) is fit for concentration, in the same way not any act of perception (*grahaṇa*) can be used as the support for mental fixation or stability. Of the perceptive acts, it is the experiential perception which is the most appropriate for concentration and it is understood that even from among the experiential perceptions only a few are appropriate to this effect, as, for example, the experience "without pain and luminous" to which *sūtra* I.36 refers, or the "sensation of bliss" (*ānanda*) (see *sūtra* I.17, Section D), or the emptiness of deep sleep (see *sūtra* I.38). See note 1 of our commentary of *sūtra* I.7 on the perceptive nature of experience.

The Perceiver (*grahītṛ*). The *grahītṛ* is the seer (*draṣṭṛ*) (see *sūtra* I.3 and note 2 of *sūtra* I.16), the subject of knowledge. The concentration on the perceiver is actually the concentration on *asmitā*, the "I-am-ness", "the consciousness of (I) am", "the consciousness of (I) exist", since the *asmitā* is the consciousness of himself that the seer has (see our commentary of *sūtra* I.17, Section E).

42

तत्र शब्दार्थज्ञानविकल्पैः संकीर्णा सवितर्का समापत्तिः ॥

TATRA ŚABDĀRTHAJÑĀNAVIKALPAIḤ SAṂKĪRṆĀ SAVITARKĀ SAMĀPATTIḤ.

There (tatra) (exist) the samāpatti with analysis of gross object (sa-vitarka), mixed with words (śabda), object (artha), knowledge (jñāna) and vikalpas.

A. There (tatra)

That is, among the *samāpattis*. The previous *sūtra* has defined the *samāpatti*. The *sūtras* I.42-44 indicate four classes of *samāpatti*: *samāpatti* with or without *vitarka*, *samāpatti* with or without *vicāra*.

B. The Terms samāpatti, vitarka, artha and vikalpa

In relation to the terms *samāpatti*, *vitarka*, *artha* and *vikalpa*, which appear in this *sūtra*, see Section D of this commentary and *sūtras* I.41; I. 17; I.28 and I.9 (respectively) together with our commentaries *ad locum*.

C. Interpretation of the present sūtra and its criticism

The majority of the translators like H. Āranya, Taimni, Ballantyne, Vivekananda, Dvivedī, Rama Prasada, Purohit, Hauer, follow Vyāsa and take the compound *śabda-artha-jñāna-vikalpaiḥ* as governing *saṃkīrṇa* and both words as the *predicate* of *savitarkā samāpattiḥ*. According to them Patañjali is, in this *sūtra*, defining *samāpatti* with *vitarka* and is defining it as a *samāpatti* mixed with "words" (*śabda*), etc.[94]

94. Woods takes *saṃkīrṇa*, in the sense of "confused", as a predicate of *savitarkā samāpattiḥ* and he considers that the composed word of the

First of all we have to recall that, as we have earlier pointed out it is not admissible that a technical expression like *vitarka* can, in the same Book First, be given two different meanings, one in *sūtra* I. 17 and the other in this *sūtra*. We must, therefore, understand *vitarka* in both *sūtras* with the same meaning. The commentators offer two meanings for the word *vitarka*, one in relation to *sūtra* I. 17 and the other in relation to the present *sūtra*. We believe that of these two meanings only one can be adopted, both for *sūtra* I. 17 and for the present *sūtra*, and that is the meaning given by the commentators in relation to *sūtra* I. 17 (analysis of the gross object) which we have explained in our commentary of the said *sūtra*, because : 1. it is not possible to accept that this *sūtra* contains a definition of *samāpatti* with *vitarka*; and 2. the second meaning which the commentators give to *vitarka*, in the context of this *sūtra*, is not admissible.

1. Patañjali uses the term *vitarka* in *sūtra* I.17. It is not possible to think that he will define it now, twentyfive *sūtras* later. The fact that he has used it in *sūtra* I.17 without defining it, indicates that, as in other cases, its meaning is clear for him and for his environment.

In *sūtra* I. 44 Patañjali compares *vicāra* with *vitarka*, indicating that the only difference between both of them is that of *vicāra* referring to subtle objects (the idea being implicit that *vitarka* refers to gross objects—both categories of objects are maintained by the Sāṃkhya). This difference is, therefore, *essential* for the distinction between *vitarka* and *vicāra*, according to the same Patañjali. Now, if Patañjali, in this *sūtra* I. 42—as the traditional interpretation has it—be *defining vitarka*, then there would result that what is specifically essential to

sūtra is *a* complement of cause that explains why this *samāpatti* is "confused". According to Woods' translation this *sūtra* does not define the *samāpatti* with *vitarka*, but it indicates only one of its characteristics: confusion and its cause. This interpretation of Woods cannot be accepted because it cannot be admitted that Patañjali would dedicate a *sūtra* to a secondary characteristic of the *savitarkā samāpattiḥ*: its being confused owing to the presence of *śabda* etc.

vitarka, its fundamental characteristic, would be absent from this definition : that is, its reference to the gross; and that only two *sūtras* later, in I. 44, this essential characteristic would be mentioned. This cannot be accepted especially as we are dealing with an exponent as careful and precise as is Patañjali. We do not then have, in this *sūtra*, a definition of *samāpatti* with *vitarka*.

2. If this *sūtra* gave a definition of *samāpatti* with *vitarka*, *vitarka* would be the assemblage of the four elements mentioned in the *sūtra*, that is, *śabda*, *artha*, *jñāna*, *vikalpa*. *Samāpatti* with *vitarka* would be the *samāpatti* with these four elements and, consequently, *samāpatti* without *vitarka* (*nirvitarka*) would have to be the *samāpatti* without these four elements. But, as Patañjali points out in the following *sūtra*, *samāpatti* without *vitarka* is a *samāpatti* in which there are neither *śabda*, nor *jñāna*, nor *vikalpa*, but in which there is indeed *artha*. Therefore, as *sa*- (with) affirms in *savitarka* the presence of something which *nir*- (without) negates in *nirvitarka*, this something cannot be the four elements mentioned, all of which occur in *sa-vitarka* and one of which persists in remaining in *nir-vitarka*. It must be something different from these four elements, something which becomes present in *sa-vitarka* and which is absent in *nir-vitarka*. In our opinion, this something is the analytical mental operation, *vitarka*, as we have described it in Section B of our commentary on *sūtra* I.17, the presence or absence of which determines the *savitarkic* or *nirvitarkic* characteristic of *samāpatti*.

According to what has been said earlier and as our translation shows, we consider that Patañjali in this *sūtra* is not defining *samāpatti* with *vitarka*. The concept of *samāpatti* has already been defined in the *sūtra* I. 41 and the concept *vitarka* is, as we have already indicated, a concept which being already known, is not defined by Patañjali. What Patañjali does in the present *sūtra* is simply to indicate a series of elements which are to be found in the *samāpatti* with *vitarka*, which accompany the analytical operation which constitutes *vitarka* (and which are not to be found in the *samāpatti* without *vitarka*, with the exception of one of them : *artha*).

D. The samāpatti with vitarka

The mind has concentrated itself on a "gross" object. Its processes have been destroyed with the exception of the intense perceptive process and of the *smṛti*-attention which the concentration implies. The mind is absorbed in the object of its concentration, the object invades the entire field of consciousness.

In this stage of concentration the mind is performing an analytical and particularizing activity which puts in evidence all the constitutive parts and all the gross particularities and attributes of the gross object; they acquire a presence.

In the course of this concentration, which is accompanied by this analysing and particularizing activity on a gross object, the mind operates with the help of words (*śabda*) which refer to the object (*artha*) and its specific particularities. That the mind operates with words obviously implies that, in the *samāpatti* with analysis of gross objects, the *smṛti*-memory is functioning, because the latter is the *sine qua non* condition of the utilization of the word.

Besides that the *artha*- what the word designates, its "object" is still present in this concentration with *vitarka*.

Moreover there occurs in the mind a knowledge (*jñāna*) and finally a *vikalpic* activity takes place.

By "knowledge" we mean a normal cognitive process, by means of which the subject seizes, apprehends an object (*artha*) *as what it is*. The object has a meaning for the subject, the latter "understands" it, knows what it is, while having a more or less precise consciousness of its properties, uses, finality, possibilities, etc., in which process occur words whose meaning is understood.

As regards the *vikalpic* activity, present in the *samāpatti* with *vitarka*, it is not easy to determine which *vikalpas* are being dealt with, especially as Patañjali does not mention it and the concept of *vikalpa* is very extensive.

Following Vyāsa, Vācaspati Miśra and Vijñānabhikṣu and the traditional interpretation founded in them (Rama Prasada, H. Āranya, Taimni, etc.) the *vikalpa* to which this *sūtra* refers would consist in the apprehension—as if they were a single entity —of three entities, that is: the word, its object, and the knowledge of the object designated by the word—distinctive entities in terms of their nature and their qualities (*dharma*). It would be a matter of the identity, of the con-fusion of the word, its object and the knowledge. Vijñānabhikṣu calls this *vikalpa* by the name of '*abhedavikalpa*', the *vikalpa* of identity. This type of *vikalpa* would occur in every normal cognitive process and would even be maintained in this *samāpatti* : the yogin has not freed himself from the mechanisms of normal knowledge.

This interpretation compels anyone who adopts it to understand the compound *śabdārthajñānavikalpaiḥ* as one in which the first three terms determine the last one : "with the *vikalpas* of word, object and knowledge". On the contrary, we consider that the four expressions are coordinated among themselves and we translate accordingly.

But Vijñānabhikṣu, *Vārtika ad locum*, allows one to understand that, along with the *vikalpa* mentioned earlier, other *vikalpas* are possible : "*śabdādivikalpair yathāsambhavam anye'pi vikalpā upalakṣaṇīyāḥ*".

We believe that one of the *vikalpas* most adequate to the type of *samāpatti* dealt with in this *sūtra* is the mental process which necessarily occurs with the analytic operation of a gross object (*vitarka*) which constitutes the essence of this *samāpatti*, the mental process which consists in attributing the several parts—the "presentation" (*sākṣātkāra*) of which is being made by the mind—to the whole that constitutes the object; as if these parts were separate things which "belong" to the whole; as if these parts were not actually the whole partially and successively "presented" *whole*. See Section D, I and II, of our commentary of *sūtra* I. 9. For example, if the yogin concentrates on a flower, during the analysis which takes place, the mind individualizes "the petals of the flower", "the corolla of the flower", "the stamens of the flower", etc., as if the petals, the corolla, the stamens, etc. were the "property" of the flower and as if they were not in reality *the flower*. This is the *vikalpa* which, in our opinion, accompanies the *samāpatti* with *vitarka*. This *vikalpa* is not the only one that accompanies the *savitarka-samāpatti*. It is also accompanied by the *vikalpas* that normally accompany all *savikalpa* perception.

D. The savitarka samāpatti and the savikalpaka perception

Because of the presence (in the special kind of concentration referred to in this *sūtra*) of the analytical and particularizing activity (*vitarka*) of the mind, of the words (*śabda*), of the cognitive process (*jñāna*), and of the *vikalpic* activity, it can be said that in the yogin's mind is still taking place a perceptive process which has to do with what the Indian epistemological theories call a "*savikalpaka* perception". Other *vikalpas* that can accompany the *samāpatti* dealt with in this Sūtra would be all the *vikalpas* that usually accompany any *savikalpa* perception as the *vikalpas* of class, name, identity with oneself, difference from others.

43

स्मृतिपरिशुद्धौ स्वरूपशून्येवार्थमात्रनिर्भासा निर्वितर्का ॥

SMṚTIPARIŚUDDHAU SVARŪPAŚŪNYEVĀRTHA-MĀTRANIRBHĀSĀ NIRVITARKĀ.

(and) the (samāpatti) without analysis of gross object (nirvitarka), which (presents itself), once the purification (pariśuddhi) of smṛti has been produced, as devoid (śūnya) of its own nature (svarūpa) and in which only the object (artha) shines (nirbhāsa).

A. Purification (pariśuddhi) of smṛti

In Section D of the commentary of the previous *sūtra* we have indicated that, in the *samāpatti* with analysis of gross object, the mental process *smṛti* functions in its double aspect of attention and memory. As attention it impedes the disappearance of the object of concentration of the field of consciousness and, as memory, it makes possible the use of words.

The present *sūtra* says that, in the *samāpatti* without analysis of gross object, a "purification" (or "cleansing") of *smṛti* takes place, which implies that the *smṛti* still persists, although in a purified state. This "purification" consists in the fact that the words (*śabda*) disappear, words with the help of which the mind still functioned in the stage of *samāpatti* with *vitarka* and, as a consequence of this disappearance, there also disappear normal knowledge (*jñāna*) and the *vikalpas* which need words in order to exist, but not *artha*, since Patañjali tells us in the same *sūtra* that the *artha* subsists. In other words : the purification of the *smṛti* consists in the fact that the memory aspect of the *smṛti* has stopped functioning.

That this is the meaning of the term "purification" is evident for the following consideration. The *samāpatti* with analysis of gross object, dealt with in the preceding *sūtra*, is accompanied by words (*śabda*), object (*artha*), knowledge (*jñāna*) and *vikalpas*. In the present *sūtra* Patañjali says that only the object (*artha*) occurs when the "purification" of *smṛti* has been produced. It is therefore clear that the result of "purification" of *smṛti* consists, as we have just said, in the elimination of the words and, as its consequence, in the elimination of (normal) knowledge (*jñāna*) and of the *vikalpas*.

This interpretation does not essentially differ from that given by the traditional commentators.

B. "As devoid of its own nature" (*svarūpaśūnyā-iva*)

The *samāpatti* has been defined in *sūtra* I. 41. Its constitutive elements are : (1) the stability of the mind in the "object" chosen for the concentration; (2) the coloration of the mind by the said "object". These two characteristics are mentioned in the *sūtra* quoted.

Moreover, according to what has been said in our commentary on the same *sūtra*, the *samāpatti* constitutes a perception (*sui generis* because of its intensification).

We may also note that in *samāpatti* with or without *vitarka*, the gross object chosen for the concentration stays all the time before the consciousness of the yogin who concentrates on it (*smṛti*), considering that the fixation in and the coloration by the said object, being the essential elements of the *samāpatti* mentioned by the *sūtra* which defines it, cannot be absent while the *samāpatti* subsists.

In the expression which we are commenting in this section the word *iva* ("as if") is supremely important. It indicates that depriving the *samāpatti* of its own nature is only apparent : the *samāpatti* is as if deprived of its nature, but in fact it is not. What the latter is saying is that, *although it does not seem to be so*, the stability of the mind in, and its coloration by, the object (*main signs of the samāpatti*) continue to occur. See the reason for this false appearance in Section C of this commentary, last paragraph.

C. "In which only the object (artha) shines (nirbhāsa)"

Anyhow, of the elements which, according to the previous *sūtra*, accompany the *samāpatti* with analysis of the gross object (*vitarka*) (words, object, knowledge and *vikalpas*), at the moment of the *samāpatti* without *vitarka*, which is a more advanced stage of concentration, there only (*mātra*) subsists the object (*artha*) on which the mind is fixed and which colors it. In Section A of this commentary we have already indicated that the "purification" of the *smṛti* carries with it the disappearance of the words and, consequently, of knowledge and of the *vikalpas*, but not of the *artha*. Patañjali leaves no doubt with regard to the expression *arthamātranirbhāsa*.

The extraordinary presence of the *artha*—extraordinary for being the only one which subsists in this stage of the process and for the enrichment acquired thanks to the analytical work which has been developed in the preceding stage—monopolizing the consciousness of the yogin, and—as a consequence of it—the disappearance of the word (*śabda*), of the normal knowledge (*jñāna*), and of the *vikalpas* create the false appearance that the stability of the mind in the object and its coloration by it have also disappeared. The yogin is no more aware of the process of stabilization and coloring of his mind that has taken place in him; this stabilization and coloring do not exist for him, as it were. For this reason Patañjali can say that the *samāpatti* at this moment of the process appears *as if* deprived of its own nature.

D. Phenomenon to which this sūtra refers

The phenomenon described in the present *sūtra* is the following: the mind of the yogin persists in the state of being stabilized in the object chosen for the concentration and this object invades it totally—the object with all its "gross" particularities rendered present by virtue of the process of analysis which has been verified in the preceding stage. There occur, in the yogin's mind, neither words nor, *consequently*, the *vikalpas* nor the normal knowledge (*jñāna*) which require, the ones and the other, words to manifest themselves. The *artha* subsists, and it reaches the mind of the yogin, without any word, or concept, or normal act of *jñāna*, or *vikalpas*, completely alone and nude. There only remains the object *in se* and the yogin in front of it. Anything else has disappeared. In the commentary of the *sūtras* I.47 and I.48, we shall show that in this moment there occurs the *prajñā*, which is not an act of normal knowledge, but an extra-ordinary act of intuition.

E. The nirvitarka samāpatti and the nirvikalpaka perception

Because of the disappearance of the *vitarka* activity of the mind and of all the elements which accompany normal knowledge (*śabda*, *vikalpa*), it can be said that in the yogin's mind is taking place a perceptive process which has to do with what the Indian epistemological theories call a "*nirvikalpaka perception.*"

44

एतयैव सविचारा निर्विचारा च सूक्ष्मविषया व्याख्याता ॥

ETAYAIVA SAVICĀRĀ NIRVICĀRĀ CA SŪKṢMAVIṢAYĀ VYĀKHYĀTĀ.

By means of this (samāpatti) has been explained the (samāpatti) of the subtle (sūkṣma) object with analysis (savicāra) and without analysis (nirvicāra).

A. Homologation of the samāpattis with and without vitarka with the samāpattis with and without vicāra, respectively.

The meaning of this *sūtra* is that with the explanation given in regard to the *samāpatti* with and without *vitarka* (analysis of gross object), the *samāpatti* with and without *vicārā* (analysis of subtle object) also has been clarified. See our commentary of the *sūtra* I.17, Sections B and C. Consequently, in this *sūtra* Patañjali is fully homologating the *samāpatti* with *vitarka* to the *samāpatti* with *vicāra* and the *samāpatti* without *vitarka* to the *samāpatti* without *vicāra*, the only difference, between the *samāpattis* with and without *vitarka* and the *samāpattis* with and without *vicāra*, being that in the first two the object of concentration is a gross object and, in the last two, a subtle object. From this homologation one draws the conclusion that all that has been said with regard to the *samāpattis* with and without *vitarka* also applies to the *samāpattis* with and without *vicāra* and *vice versa.* See in particular *sūtras* I. 42 and 43; I.47-48, with their respective commentaries.

B. Position of the diverse samāpattis in the yogic process

A very important consequence of the complete homologation of the *samāpattis* with and without *vitarka* with the *samāpattis* with and without *vicāra*—with the exception of the object—is that it cannot be assumed that there exists between them a hierarchical difference. The *samāpatti* with *vitarka* and the *samāpatti* with *vicāra* represent the same stage, the same level of the concentration process. Likewise with the *samāpatti* without *vitarka* and the *samāpatti* without *vicāra*. It must not be thought that the two *samāpattis* with *vicāra* and without *vicāra* represent more advanced stages of concentration, those which are attained only after overcoming the stages which represent the *samāpattis* with and without *vitarka*. One may only speak of a hierarchical superiority of the *samāpatti* without *vitarka* in face of the *samāpatti* with *vitarka* and of the *samāpatti* without *vicāra* in face of the *samāpatti* with *vicāra*. The *samāpattis* without *vitarka* and without *vicāra* actually represent more advanced stages of concentration. It may be averred that there exist two parallel paths of concentration : one which is supported by a gross object and the other which has a subtle object for support. The final goal can be reached by following one or the other path : the total and absolute restraint of the mental processes, without it being necessary to pass from one to the other at a determined moment of the process.

45

सूक्ष्मविषयत्वं चालिङ्गपर्यवसानम् ॥

SŪKṢMAVIṢAYATVAM CĀLIṄGAPARYAVASĀNAM.

The condition of subtle object (sūkṣmaviṣayatva) has the undetermined (aliṅga) as limit.

A. Gross elements and subtle elements in accordance with the Sāṃkhya doctrine

As we have shown in the introduction, this is one of the *sūtras* which, to be understood, require to be referred to the doctrines of the Sāṃkhya philosophical system. As we have explained in Section B of our commentary of *sūtra* I.17, the elements of material reality can be classified in two groups : (1) gross elements which are the *mahābhūta* (space, air, fire or light, water and land) and (2) the subtle elements which are in a growing degree of subtlety : the *indriyas* (organs of senses and of activity), the *manas* (mind), and the five *tanmātras* (essences of sound, touch, colour, taste, smell); the *ahaṃkāra* (cosmic consciousness); the *mahat* or *buddhi* (cosmic intellect) and, finally, the *prakṛti*, primordial matter of that from which derive the other subtle elements mentioned and the gross elements. *Prakṛti* thus is the highest stage of subtlety. *Puruṣa* or spirit—completely separate from the *prakṛti* and its derivatives—does not fall under the category of subtle element and it cannot be said of it that it constitutes a more advanced stage of subtlety than *prakṛti*. *Aliṅga* in the present *sūtra* designates *prakṛti*.

B. Meaning of the present sūtra

It must not be thought that Patañjali has included this aphorism in this first Book for the purpose only of recalling a principle of the Sāṃkhya doctrine. His intention must be more profound and more in relation to the process he is describing. We understand that what this *sūtra* purports to say is that the *samāpatti* with or without *vicāra*, referred in both cases to a subtle object, however subtle may the object be, cannot take us further than the primordial matter or *prakṛti*, of which any subtle object is, in a more or less remote grade, a transformation. Consequently the *samāpatti* with or without *vicāra* will never be able to take us to the *puruṣa*. The way of the *samāpatti* ends in the *prakṛti*, that is, in the realm of the material reality; the *puruṣa* dwells outside its range.

The warning contained in this *sūtra* comes at an opportune moment, since in the following *sūtras* Patañjali will refer to the last stage of the *samāpattis*, which ends immediately in that stage of the yogic process which comes after and well beyond the *samāpattis* (stage which indeed leads to the isolation of the *puruṣa*, which is centered in the restraint or cessation of all the mental processes, and in which is realized the passage from empirical material reality to the spiritual or transcendental reality). In this *sūtra* Patañjali fixes in advance, as if with the intention to avoid misunderstandings, the terminal possibilities of the *samāpattis*.

This *sūtra* enables us to appreciate in its true dimension the *prajñā* or intuitive knowledge which emerges, as we shall see later, in the transparence of the *samāpatti* without *vicāra:* the *prajñā* is a knowledge which, however superior it may be to normal discursive knowledge, and different from it, notwithstanding it operates in the material realm; its object can never be the *puruṣa*; it is incapable of leading one to transcendence.

This *sūtra* states once more a theme which is dear to the philosophical speculation of India: the inability of human reason, understood in its broadest sense, to arrive at the Absolute, and the resulting necessity to have recourse to another means for that purpose. And that is Yoga.

46

ता एव सबीजः समाधिः ॥

TĀ EVA SABĪJAḤ SAMĀDHIḤ.

These (samāpattis) are concentration (samādhi) with seed (bīja).

A. The samāpattis are forms of samādhi

The four *samāpattis* dealt with in the preceding *sūtras* I. 42, I. 43, I. 44 constitute forms of mental concentration—concentration with seed. As the definition of *samāpatti* in *sūtra* I. 41 states it, the mind has, in the four *samāpattis*, stabilized itself in an "object" which colours it or completely absorbs it. But, in addition to the forms of *samādhi* constituted by the *samāpattis*, there exists another form of concentration dealt with by Patañjali in the *sūtra* I.51—concentration without seed. In other terms, any *samāpatti* is concentration, but not any concentration is *samāpatti*.[95]

B. The Expression bīja ("Seed")

Literally *bīja* means "seed". See Section B of our commentary of the *sūtra* I. 25.

There are two interpretations of the term *bīja* in the present *sūtra* and, as a result, two interpretations of the same *sūtra*:

(a) Bhoja, in his commentary *ad locum*, explains *bīja* by "*ālam-*

95. *Sūtra* 3 of the Third Book utilizes terms of *sūtra* I.43 (which defines or describes *samāpatti* without analysis of a gross object) in order to define *samādhi*. This definition is defective since it identifies *samādhi* only with two of its forms, *samāpatti* without *vitarka* and *samāpatti* without *vicāra*, while actually *samādhi* comprehends not only these two forms of *samāpatti* but all *samāpattis*, and moreover there exists a kind of *samādhi* which is not constituted by any *samāpatti*.

bana", "point of support".[96] The meaning of the *sūtra* in the context of this interpretation is that the forms of concentration constituted by the *samāpattis* do metaphorically have a "point of support" in the object on which the mind has been concentrated. "Supported" in a determined "object", the mind succeeds in eliminating all the rest.

This is also the interpretation of Vyāsa, Śaṅkara, Harikṛṣṇadās Goyandakā, Ballantyne, Taimni, H. Āranya, although they do not affirm—as explicity as Bhoja does—the equivalence *bīja*=*ālambana.*

(b) Other interpreters maintain for *bīja* its literal meaning of "seed". Rāmānanda Sarasvatī, Dvivedī, Vivekānanda, Hauer, (*Der Yoga*, pp. 243 and 466, note 11) follow this interpretation. According to it, the forms of *samādhi* constituted by the *samāpattis* have in themselves the seed or potentialities (*saṃskāras*) of new mental activities (*vṛttis*), which necessarily have to actualize themselves and, as a result, constitute factors of bondage. (See Section G of our commentary of *sūtra* I. 18). Hauer and Dvivedī think that *bīja* stands for the seed of new *vṛttis*. Rāmānanda Sarasvatī understands *bīja* in the sense of "seed of bondage" (*vivekakhyātyabhāvena bandhabījasattvāt sabījatvaṃ draṣṭavyam*).

Vijñānabhikṣu (*Yogasārasaṃgraha*, p. 26) considers that the forms of *samādhi* constituted by the *samāpattis* are "with seed" both because they have a "point of support" (*ālambana*) and because they give rise to new mental activities (*dhyeyarūpālambanayogāt tadāpi vṛttibījasaṃskārotpatteś ceti*).

We abide by the second interpretation. In the preceding *sūtras* Patañjali has already said that any *samāpatti* is with reference to a gross or subtle object. If this *sūtra* affirmed that the *samāpattis* have a point of support, that is, they are related to an object which serves them as such, it would be explaining something which has already been explained. Consequently, the *sūtra* would be unnecessary, if we take into account that the *sūtra* style aims at, more than anything else, conciseness and economy of words.

96. On the "point of support" in the Christian mystic practices see Underhill, *Mysticism*, p. 364.

Besides that, it is far-fetched to take *bīja*, which basically signifies "seed" (and metaphorically "origin") in the sense of "point of support", since there exists no relation whatsoever between both senses. On the other hand, the adoption of the literal meaning of *bīja*, "seed", adds an element necessary for the description, which begins in the following *sūtra*, of the last stage of the yogic process. The reference to the notion of *saṃskāra* (subliminal impression) by means of its synonym *bīja*[97] is opportune at this moment, since Patañjali, in the description of this final stage will operate with the help of two notions: the notion of *prajñā* (intuitive knowledge) and that of *saṃskāra*. Finally it is by means of the expression *bīja* that Patañjali shall oppose the non-final forms of concentration constituted by the *samāpattis* to the final forms of concentration. Taken in the sense of "*seed*" the word *bīja* characterizes more effectively the final concentration, than the same term, taken in the sense of "point of support", since the essential feature of the final concentration is such that in it are not produced *saṃskāras* or potentialities which require to be actualized.

97. The word *bīja* can be considered as a synonym of *saṃskāra* since the image of a seed is adequate to indicate the function which corresponds to a *saṃskāra*. See section G of our commentary to *sūtra* I.18 and section D of our commentary to *sūtra* I.24, and L.de la Vallée Poussin, "Le Bouddhisme et le Yoga de Patañjali" p. 231.

47

निर्विचारवैशारद्येऽध्यात्मप्रसादः ॥

NIRVICĀRAVAIŚĀRADYE 'DHYĀTMAPRASĀDAḤ.

In the transparence (vaiśāradya) of (samāpatti) without analysis of subtle object (nirvicāra) (there is) inner (adhyātma) quietude (prasāda).

A. Transparence (vaiśāradya)

We translate *vaiśāradya* by "transparence". Woods does so by "clearness". According to the interpretation of the commentators Vyāsa, Bhoja,[98] Vācaspati Miśra, Vijñānabhikṣu, this word could be translated by "purity", as Taimni and Dvivedī actually do.

This word refers to that state of the mind which occurs in the *samāpatti* without *vicāra*, state in which the mind, in an act of intuitive knowledge (to which Patañjali refers in the following *sūtra*), integrally and simultaneously grasps the object in all its truth, without the words and the *vikalpas* intervening between the object and the mind and, accordingly, without the mind bringing forth any act of normal, necessarily partial, superficial and impure knowledge, by the intrusion of the words and *vikalpas*.

B. Quietude (Prasāda)

This word refers also to quietude, calmness, inactivity in that the mind becomes immersed, once it has been seized by the *samāpatti* without *vicāra*. The mind is stabilized in one and only "object", "coloured" by it, that is, absorbed in it. Only the representation of the said object is present in it, for all the other *vṛttis* have ceased. There is no discursive activity of any

98. Vaiśāradyaṃ nairmalyam.

sort. The mind does not accomplish any work outside the unitary and integral apprehension of the object in which it has fixed itself.

In addition to the aspect of intellectual quietude referred to earlier there does likewise occur in the transparence of the *samāpatti* without *vicāra* a quietude of an emotional nature. The stopping of the *vṛttis* simultaneously bears with it the cessation of all emotional activity.[99] That is why serenity becomes a characteristic of the yogin immersed in an intense meditation.

99. Vijñānabhikṣu, *Yogasārasaṃgraha*, p. 4, rightly observes that in the restraint of the *vṛttis* that Patañjali enumerates in *sūtra* I.6, takes place also the restraint of the *vṛttis* such as desire, action etc. (icchākriyādirūpavṛttīnāṃ caitannirodhenaiva nirodho bhavati).

48

ऋतम्भरा तत्र प्रज्ञा ॥

ṚTAMBHARĀ TATRA PRAJÑĀ

There (tatra) (occurs) the intuitive knowledge (prajñā) which bears in itself the truth (ṛtambhara).

A. There (tatra)

The expression *tatra* can refer either to the transparence (*vaiśāradya*) of the *samāpatti nirvicāra* (without analysis of a subtle object), or to the inner quietude (*adhyātmaprasāda*) of the preceding *sūtra*.

Most of the commentators and translators do not say anything thereon. Śaṅkara, Kṛṣṇavallabha, Woods, adopt the second alternative. We understand that *tatra* refers to the transparence of the *samāpatti nirvicāra*, because the latter is the more important concept of the *sūtra* mentioned and because the image of transparence or purity has more to do with the notion of truth implicit in the concept of *prajñā* than that of inner quietude: it is thanks to this transparence or purity that in *prajñā* the object becomes present to the mind in all its truth. This interpretation is adopted also by Rāmānanda Sarasvatī.

B. Prajñā (intuitive knowledge)

Vyāsa, Vācaspati Miśra, Vijñānabhikṣu, Rāmānanda Sarasvatī and Kṛṣṇavallabha (*ad* I.47) describe the *prajñā* which arises in the transparence of the *samāpatti* without analysis of subtle object[100] as a vision (*āloka*), by means of which the pure (*aśuddhyāvaraṇamalāpeta*, *svaccha*) and attentive (*sthitipravāha*, *ekāgra*-

100. We must have present that the *prajñā* dealt with in this *sūtra* is only a kind of *prajñā*. Next *sūtra* will refer to the *prajña* of what has been heard, i.e. which originates in the act of hearing, and to the *prajñā* of inference.

tādhārā) mind grasps the object in its totality (*dhyeyagatāśeṣa-viśeṣa-pratibimbodgrāhin*, *sarvārthagrāhin*) in a non-discursive form (*kramānanurodhin*) and simultaneously (*yugapad*). The characteristics, referred to by the commentators mentioned as being specific to *prajñā*, and alluded to by the present *sūtra*,[101] correspond to the characteristics of the intuitive knowledge in the western tradition.[102]

Moreover, of the two types of knowledge, the "intuitive knowledge" is the only type of knowledge which can arise in the stage of the yogic process in which we find ourselves, when, according to the preceding *sūtras* and their respective commentaries, all the specific elements and factors of discursive knowledge have disappeared.

We may then translate the expression *prajñā* by "intuitive knowledge", "intuition".

C. *Ṛtaṃbharā* (*which bears truth in or with itself*)

Literally *ṛtaṃbharā* means: "which bears truth in or with it-

101. Even if commentators do not indicate it, we must think that, as a consequence of the disappearance of words, *vikalpas* and normal knowledge, the *prajñā* puts the mind, in a direct and immediate way, in contact with the object in its integrity, presenting it without the interposition of any element extraneous to the object which is grasped and to the mind which grasps it.

102. Cf. Leibnitz, "Meditationes de cognitione", in *Opuscula*, p.11: "Et certe cum notio valde composita est, non possumus omnes ingredientes eam notiones simul cogitare: ubi tamen hoc licet, vel saltem in quantum licet, cognitionem voco intuitivam": "*When the notion is very complex, we cannot grasp simultaneously all the notions that compose it; when that is possible, or at least to the extent to which that is possible, I call it an intuitive cognition*"; Descartes, *Regulae ad directionem ingenii* III (p. 20): "Per intuitum intelligo. . mentis purae et attentae...non dubium conceptum" :"*I understand by inuition. . a concept devoid of doubt and formed by a mind that is pure and attentive*" and XI (p. 98): "ad mentis intuitum duo requirimus: nempe ut propositio clare et distincte, deinde etiam ut tota simul et non successive intellegatur": "*We require two things for the intuition of the mind: 1- that the proposition be undestood in a clear and distinctive way and 2- that it be understood in its integrity, simultaneously* and not gradually"; Saint Thomas, *Summa Theologiae*, 2.2 g. 180 art , 3: "*simplicem intuitum veritatis:*" "*the simple intuition of truth*"; J. Bernhart, *Die philosophische Mystik*, p. 82, and W. Völker, *Kontemplation und Ekstase*, pp. 200 and ff.

self". Vyāsa, Bhoja, Rāmānaṇda Sarasvatī, explain the term by *satyaṃ bibharti*; Woods, Taimni, Dvivedī translate it by "truth-bearing".

The *prajñā* which occurs in the transparence of the *samāpatti* without analysis (of subtle object) and the main characteristics of which were described in the preceding section, bears the truth in itself or with itself.

It is necessary to keep in mind that for Patañjali, in agreement with the present *sūtra*, not any intuitive knowledge bears the truth in or with itself, since the *sūtra* we are commenting very clearly stipulates that the *prajñā* which bears the truth in or with itself is that which emerges *there*, that is, in the transparence of the *samāpatti* without analysis (of subtle object), or that which occurs in the stage of the yogic process which immediately precedes the total and absolute restraint of all the activities of the mind. Accordingly, not every *prajñā* has the exceptional status of being the means to know the truth. Only that *prajñā* which occurs at this moment of yoga has such an exceptional status. A cognitive act can be intuitive, but if it does not take place in the course of the *samāpatti* mentioned, it cannot be *ṛtaṃbharā*.[103]

It is not difficult to understand why the *prajñā* which occurs in the *samāpatti* without analysis (of subtle object) is the bearer of truth in or with itself. By a sustained activity of analysis the mind has been particularizing all the details and constitutive elements of the object, which it afterwards, simultaneously and in its totality, grasps in an act of intuitive knowledge. It is this arduous analytical and particularizing task which enables the mind to know *yugapad* the object as it really is, with the integrity of all the

103. We can designate this *prajñā* with the name of yogic *prajñā*. Some authors like Vyāsa, Rāmānanda Sarasvatī, Kṛṣṇavallabha, H. Āranya, etc., interpreting this *sūtra* in a very particular and erroneous way, consider that the word *ṛtaṃbhara* is not a predicate of *prajña*, to which this *sūtra* refers, but only its name: "there (takes place) the *prajñā* (that is called) 'bearer of truth' ".

elements which compose it, in all the richness of its reality, in its unconfoundable individuality.[104]

104. The *sūtra* that follows will indicate another circumstance which can be taken as another reason whereby this *prajñā* is true. It puts the mind in contact not with a universal but with a particular, with a reality in itself. That same *sūtra* will indicate two kinds of *prajñā*, that of the act of hearing and that of the inference, to which it is not possible to apply the attribute of "true", and which are different from the yogic *prajñā*.

49

श्रुतानुमानप्रज्ञाभ्यामन्यविषया विशेषार्थत्वात् ॥

ŚRUTĀNUMĀNAPRAJÑĀBHYĀM ANYAVIṢAYĀ VIŚEṢĀRTHATVĀT.

(Prajñā: intuitive knowledge) has an object (viṣaya) different from (that of) the intuitive knowledges (prajñā) of the act of hearing (śruta) and of inference (anumāna) for the reason that the particular (viśeṣa) is (in this case) the artha.

A. Other characteristic of the yogic prajñā

The present *sūtra* indicates a characteristic of the yogic *prajñā* dealt with in the preceding *sūtra*, which distinguishes it from the *prajñā* which occurs in the act of hearing and from the *prajñā* which occurs in inference. This characteristic consists in the fact that the particular (*viśeṣa*) constitutes the *artha* (object) of the yogic *prajñā*. In this moment of the yogic process, i.e. in the *samāpatti* without analysis (of subtle object), "only the object (*artha*) shines (*nirbhāsa*)", as *sūtra* I.43 says. But this object (*artha*) which is the only one which shines at this moment is something particular. In other words, with the yogic *prajñā* is known the particular, the individual, the singular, a subtle object *in itself*.

B. Viṣaya and artha

As we have explained in section B of our commentary on *sūtra* I.11, and in section C. of our commentary on *sūtra* I.28, *viṣaya* means the "object" as related to an act of knowledge, and *artha* means also the "object" not in relation to an act of knowledge, but considered in itself. We have also said that any *artha* can become the *viṣaya* of a cognitive act.

Sūtra I.43 has said that, from the elements enumerated in I.42, only the element *artha*, i.e. the "object" considered in itself, remains. *Sūtra* I.49 makes clear that that remaining element, that *artha*, is the particular (*viśeṣārthatvāt*), which becomes the *viṣaya*, i.e. the "object" of the cognitive act that is the *prajñā* (*anyaviṣayā*).

C. The prajñā of the act of hearing and the prajñā of inference

According to Patañjali's thought, the information which one receives orally and the premises, as well as the conclusion of an inference, are grasped by means of intuition. If someone told me: 'It is raining on the mountain', a direct and immediate comprehension of the content of this information occurs in my mind, a unique and simple act of my mind by means of which I make mine this information. Likewise, the premises of the *locus classicus* of Indian inference: 'Where there is smoke, there is fire', and 'on the mountain there is smoke', and the conclusion, which derives from them: 'therefore, there is fire on the mountain', are understood by me in a direct and immediate form, in three unique, simple acts of the mind.

By the application of what has been exposed in the preceding *sūtra*, the *prajñās* which occur in the act of hearing and in inference are not *ṛtaṃbharā*, do not bear in or with themselves the truth, in the sense in which it has been explained in Section C of the commentary of the preceding *sūtra*. The reasons for this are obvious. These two types of *prajñā* do not refer to anything particular, individual, singular, to an object *in itself*. They refer—as the commentators indicate, in accordance with the meaning of the *sūtra*—to the general, to the universal. With these *prajñās* the mind does not come in direct or immediate contact with a reality constituted by a determined subtle object. Moreover both *prajñās* do not arise from the analytical and particularizing process which precedes the *samāpatti* without *vicāra* and by means of which the object has become present in all the richness of its constitutive elements and thus remains fixed before the mind.

D. Do transparence (vaiśāradya), quietude (prasāda) and the prajñā Ṛtaṃbharā Occur in the Samāpatti Without Analysis of Gross Object?

With good reason it could be thought that the transparence

(*vaiśāradya*), the quietude (*prasāda*) and the *ṛtaṃbharā prajñā* can occur only with the *samāpatti* without *vicāra*, in accordance with the *sūtras* I. 47 and 48 which place these three phenomena in the said *samāpatti*.

However we believe that the three mentioned phenomena occur also in the *samāpatti* without *vitarka* or without analysis of gross object, by taking into account the fact that in the *sūtra* I. 44 Patañjali has completely homologized the *samāpatti* without *vitarka* with the *samāpatti* without *vicāra*. Moreover there is no reason for the three phenomena mentioned not to be produced in the *samāpatti* without *vitarka*. In fact, in this *samāpatti*—and likewise in the *samāpatti* without *vicāra*—the mind has been fixed on a gross object; only one representation dominates in it—that of the gross object chosen for the concentration. The object presents itself before the mind with all its characteristics that have been individualized and brought to the field of consciousness by means of the analytical and particularizing activity which has been performed in the previous stage of the *samāpatti* with *vitarka*. The words, the normal knowledge, and the *vikalpas* have been eliminated and the gross object, chosen for the fixation of the mind, shines alone in consciousness. The process is thus analogue to that which takes place in the *samāpatti* without *vicāra*. It is logical to suppose that, as a result, the same effects are produced in both: transparence of vision, without the intervention of any element foreign to the object, mental quietude and immobility and the intuitive knowledge which carries to the yogin's mind the truth and reality of the gross object on which it has concentrated itself.

Once the opinion which we are suggesting has been accepted, we must also admit that the two following *sūtras*, which describe the last stage of the yogic process, apply to the *samāpatti* without *vicāra* as well as to the *samāpatti* without *vitarka*.[105]

105. We have treated in this *sūtra*, the theme to which section C refers, because it is only in this *sūtra* that Patañjali ends his study of *prajñā*.

50

तज्जः संस्कारोऽन्यसंस्कारप्रतिबन्धी ॥

TAJJAḤ SAṂSKĀRO 'NYASAṂSKĀRAPRATIBANDHĪ

The saṃskāra (subliminal impression) born from this (tat = prajñā) hinders the other saṃskāras.

A. Sāṃkhya explanation of this sūtra

For the explanation of the present *sūtra* it is necessary to have recourse to the concepts of the Sāṃkhya which we have studied earlier. See Section D.II of our commentary of the *sūtra* I. 11; the Section G of our commentary of the *sūtra* I.18 and Section B.(b) of our commentary of the *sūtra* I.46.

Like any mental activity, *prajñā* leaves a subliminal impression (*saṃskāra*) which must actualize itself in new mental activities and which constitutes a factor of bondage to the cycle of transmigration and hinders freedom. As the commentators Vyāsa and Rāmānanda Sarasvatī and Kṛṣṇavallabha point out, the *saṃskāra* of *prajñā* gives rise to new acts of *prajñā*.

Neither Patañjali nor the commentators elucidate why the *saṃskāra* produced by intuitive knowledge hinders the appearance of other *saṃskāras*. Bhoja explains this ability of the *saṃskāra* of the *prajñā* in virtue of the strength given to this *saṃskāra* by the fact that the *prajñā*, which engenders it, is in contact with reality, something which does not happen with the other *saṃskāras* (*...tattvarūpatayā'nayā janitāḥ saṃskārā balavattvād atattvarūpaprajñājanitān saṃskārān bādhituṃ śaknuvanti...*). For his part Rāmānanda Sarasvatī offers an explanation similar to that of Bhoja (*anādir api vyutthānasaṃskāras tattvāsparśitvāt tattvasparśiprajñāsaṃskāreṇa bādhyate*).

These explanations are based on the principle that the *saṃskāras* produced by mental acts "which enter into contact with the reality" have greater strength than those produced by acts "which do not enter into contact with the reality" and can, for this reason, impede their emergence. This could be considered as a principle of the Sāṃkhya doctrine although the impression is that it is a principle that has been conceived *ad hoc*.

We think it is possible to explain the present *sūtra*, always in the context of the Sāṃkhya and with the concepts referred to by Patañjali, but leaving aside at the same time the indicated principle utilized by the commentators Bhoja and Rāmānanda Sarasvatī. In this stage of concentration the *prajñā* is being produced; it is the only activity of the mind that remains; the *prajñā* necessarily produces a *saṃskāra*, that at its own turn will produce a new act of *prajñā* and nothing else; and so on in an alternative process; this *saṃskāra* of the *prajñā* is the sole *saṃskāra* that can be produced, since there is not another mental activity that could leave also *saṃskāras* of another kind. In this moment of the yogic process the *saṃskāra* of the *prajñā* is the only dynamic, active factor, which keeps the *prajñā* act going on, since the normal consciousness and the will of the yogin have already ceased functioning.

Why does Patañjali say that it is the *saṃskāra* of the *prajñā* that hinders the production of other *saṃskāras*, and not that it is the *prajñā* itself that does so ? We think that Patañjali expresses himself in this way because of the importance that the *saṃskāra* has in this moment of the yogic process. The *saṃskāra*, at this stage of concentration, produces the *prajña* and the existence of the *prajñā* implies that any other mental process must be absent and there cannot be production of any other kind of *saṃskāras*. Patañjali is right in saying that it is the *saṃskāra* of the *prajñā* (as the cause of this situation) that hinders the appearance of other *saṃskāras*, instead of saying that it is the *prajñā* (as the effect) which does so.

B. Explanation of the process described in this sūtra in general terms

As can be seen, at this moment of the yogic process we only have an act of intuitive knowledge which supposes a total absorption in only one idea, a total monoideism, that is, the attention is fixed, with extraordinary intensity, on one single, determined object, and cannot, on that account, have any other mental activity.

As the consciousness and the will of the yogin at this stage of the process do not function anymore, we must understand (as we shall see in the commentary of the next *sūtra*) that the yogic process including the *prajñā* goes on intensifying itself only by unconscious forces. The *saṃskāra* notion, to which we have referred in the previous section, alludes to the unconscious activity of the mind.

51

तस्यापि निरोधे सर्वनिरोधान्निर्बीजः समाधिः ॥

TASYĀPI NIRODHE SARVANIRODHĀN NIRBĪJAḤ SAMĀDHIḤ

In the restraint (nirodha) also (api) of this (saṃskāra), by virtue of the restraint of all (sarvanirodha), (there occurs) the concentration (samādhi) without seed (nirbīja).

A. Meaning of the present sūtra according to the Sāṃkhya doctrine

The present *sūtra* describes the final moment of the yogic process. It is constituted by the restraint of the *saṃskāra* of the *prajñā* (*tasyāpi nirodhe*)[106], which is the ultimate *saṃskāra* which has remained active. The restraint of this *saṃskāra* means also the total restraint (*sarvanirodhāt*). What has occurred then is the total and absolute restraint of all the mental processes and of all the *saṃskāra* produced by them, which in their turn, as in a vicious circle, are the cause of new processes. It is the mental concentration "without seed" (*nirbīja*)[107], the highest stage of concentration. At this moment the *puruṣa* dwells established in its own nature (*sūtra* I.3); it recovers its primal, true and authentic nature of an absolute, "*pure, isolated,*

106. What is important is not the restraint of the *prajñā* in itself, because this restraint will leave alive the *saṃskāra* produced by the *prajñā*, and this *saṃskāra* necessarily would produce a new *prajñic* act. The restraint of the *saṃskāra* on the contrary means that the "seed" of any new prajñic activity is destroyed, whereby the total restraint takes place. It is due to this mechanism that Patañjali describes the *nirbīja samādhi* in function of the restraint of the *saṃskāra* and not in function of the restraint of the *prajñā*.

107. Regarding the word "seed", see point B of our commentary of *sūtra* I.46.

free" (Vyāsa) entity, and becomes again what it had always been : the Absolute—that is, a compact mass of pure consciousness, without limitations of space and time, without any inner or external object in which it can be reflected, reduced to motionlessness and to the silence of a quietude raised to its highest level.

B. How the restraint of the saṃskāra of prajñā is produced, according to the Sāṃkhya doctrine

The commentators evince a principle of explanation according to the doctrine of the Sāṃkhya, regarding the way in which the *saṃskāra* of the *prajña* is restrainted. According to Vyāsa "the *saṃskāra* born from *nirodha* destroys the *saṃskāras* born from *samādhi*" (*nirodhajaḥ saṃskāraḥ samādhijān saṃskārān bādhata iti*) and, according to Bhoja *ad* I. 18 "the *saṃskāras* born from *nirodha* burn the *saṃskāras* born from the *ekāgratā* (concentration) and also burn themselves" (*evam ekāgratājanitān saṃskārān nirodhajāḥ svātmānañ ca nirdahanti*). What we must retain from these explanations is the fact that the destruction of the *saṃskāra* of the *prajñā* is accomplished by another *saṃskāra*, in this case the *saṃskāra* of *nirodha*, in the same way as the *saṃskāra* of the *prajñā* destroys the other *saṃskāras*, as we have seen in the preceding *sūtra*.

One may object to this explanation of the phenomenon described by this *sūtra* on the basis of Sāṃkhyan concepts, that, insofar as it means the cessation of all mental process, the total *nirodha* does not actually produce any *saṃskāra*.

C. Explanation of the suppression of prajñā in general terms

In general terms we can explain the restraint of the *prajñā*, the last residue of conscious life, in the general perspective of the progress in the yogic process.

Once he has started the yogic process which must take him to the *samādhi* without "seed", the yogin moves from one stage of this process to the other : from the *nirodha* mentioned in the *sūtra* I.17 to the *nirodha* mentioned in I.18; from the *samā-*

pattis with analysis (*savitarka, savicāra*) to the *samāpattis* without analysis (*nirvitarka, nirvicāra*) (*sūtras* I.42,43,44); from the functioning of the *prajñā* to its suppression (*sūtras* I. 48-51). The passage from one to another of these stages means a restraint of the mental processes, which is each time greater, a concentration each time more intense and, as a consequence of all this, an approximation to the goal for which strives the yogin—the absolute restraint, the *samādhi* without "seed". But, to the measure in which this process is being realized, the area covered by consciousness diminishes accordingly. If, by a conscious exercise of his will during the first moments of the yogic process, the yogin rejects the external and internal stimuli which disturb him from the concentration on a single object and maintains his attention fixed on this object, little by little, simultaneously with the reduction of the area covered by consciousness, his will will begin to stop functioning and, as a result, will have each time less and less participation, less influence in the progess which, in the course of the yogic process, fulfils itself in its march to the predetermined goal. We must then seek in the realm of the unconscious the explanation of the progress towards the total and absolute restraint, once the consciousness and the will do not allow their presence to be felt any more in the yogic process. This process has become an unconscious, automatic, and autonomous process, similar to the processes of the deepening of normal sleep and of self-hypnotic sleep, with which, as we have indicated earlier, Yoga has many points in common.[108] The conviction that, by means of the yogic practice, the absolute and total suppression of the mental processes can be attained, the expectation of arriving at this state, the will to reach it, and an adequate training under the direction of an experienced master, are without doubt the factors, which, acting in the unconscious level, explain the

108. According to Bonaventura's mystic doctrine, the divine grace is the dynamic factor which makes that the soul go beyond the different stages which constitute the mystic path. Cf. Gilson, *La philosophie de Saint Bonaventure*, pp. 369-370.

suppression of the *prajñā* and the beginning of total and absolute *nirodha*.

Once the total restraint is produced with the disappearance of the intuitive knowledge, absolute voidness reigns in the mind; it is the deep calm, the profound silence, the "*cesó todo*"[109] of San Juan de la Cruz, the yogic or mystic trance.

109. This expression appears in the last stanza of the mystic poem: "Noche Oscura del alma."

"*Quedéme y olvidéme,*
el rostro recliné sobre el Amado,
ceśo todo *y dejéme,*
dejando mi cuidado
entre las azucenas olvidado."

REFERENCES

Editions, commentaries, translations

Hariharānanda Āraṇya, *Yoga Philosophy of Patañjali*, Calcutta, University of Calcutta, 1963. It contains the aphorisms of Patañjali, the commentary of Vyāsa, an English translation of both, and a commentary in English by the author.

J. R. Ballantyne and Govind Sastri Deva, *Yoga-sūtra of Patañjali*, Calcutta, Suśil Gupta (India) Private Ltd., 1960. It contains an English translation of the aphorisms of Patañjali and a commentary in English by the authors.

Bengali Baba, *The Pātañjala Yogasūtra*, Poona, N. R. Bhargawa, 1949. It contains the aphorisms of Patañjali, the commentary of Vyāsa, an English translations of both, and notes by the author. Rept. 1980, Motilal Banarsidass, Delhi.

M. N. Dvivedī, *The Yoga-sūtras of Patañjali*, Adyar, Madras, India, The Theosophical Publishing House, 1947. It contains the aphorisms of Patañjali together with an English translation and notes by the author.

G. Feuerstein, *The Yoga-Sutra of Patañjali, A new Translation and Commentary*, Folkestone, Kent (England), Dawson, 1979. It contains the aphorisms of Patañjali together with an English translation and notes by the author.

Harikṛṣṇadās Goyandakā, *Pātañjalayogadarśana*, Gorakhpur, Gītā Press, saṃvat 2023. It contains the aphorisms of Patañjali, and a Hindi translation and commentary.

Gangānātha Jhā, *The Yoga-Darśana. The Sutras of Patañjali with the Bhāṣya of Vyāsa*, Bombay, Bombay Theosophical Publication Fund, 1907. It contains an English translation of the aphorisms of Patañjali and of the commentary of Vyāsa, and notes by the author.

Ch. Johnston, *The Yoga Sutras of Patañjali*, London, J. M. Watkins, 1952. It contains the English translation of the aphorisms of Patañjali and a commentary by the author.

J. León Herrera, *El Yoga Sutra de Patañjali*, Lima, Ed. Ignacio Prado Pastor, 1977. It contains the aphorisms of Patañjali and their Spanish translation together with the Spanish translation of Bhoja's commentary.

Nāgojī Bhaṭṭa or Nāgeśa Bhaṭṭa, *Vṛtti*, Vārāṇasī, Chowkhamba, 1930. It contains the aphorisms of Patañjali together with the indicated commentary.

Nārāyaṇa Tīrtha, *Yogasiddhāntacandrikā and Sūtrārthabodhinī*, Vārāṇasī, Chowkhamba, 1911. It contains the aphorisms of Patañjali together with the two indicated commentaries.

References

Patañjali, Die Wurzeln des Yoga. Die Yoga-Sūtren des Patañjali mit einem Kommentar von P. Y. Deshpande. Mit einer neuen Übertragung der Sūtren aus dem Sanskrit herausgegeben von Bettina Bäumer, Bern-München-Wien, Otto W. Barth Verlag, 1979. It contains the German translation by B. Bäumer and a commentary by P. Y. Deshpande of the aphorisms of Patañjali.

Pātañjalayogadarśanam, ed. Rāmaśaṅkarabhaṭṭācārya, Vārāṇasī, Bhāratīya Vidyā Prakāśan, *s.d.*. It contains the aphorisms of Patañjali, the commentary of Vyāsa, the sub-commentary of Vācaspati Miśra, and a scholarly introduction in Sanskrit.

Pātañjalayogasūtrabhāṣyavivaraṇam of Śaṅkara-bhagavatpāda, ed. Rama Sastri and Krishnamurthi Sastri, Madras, Government Oriental Manuscripts Library, Madras Government Oriental Series No. XCIV, 1952. It contains the aphorisms of Patañjali, the commentary of Vyāsa, and the sub-commentary attributed to Shaṅkara.

Pātañjalayogadarśanam, with The Commentary of Vyāsa and a Hindi gloss by Svāmī Śrī Brahmalīna Muni, Varanasi, Chowkhamba Sanskrit Series Office, The Kashi Sanskrit Series 201, 1970.

Purohit Swāmi, *Aphorisms of Yoga by Bhagwān Shree Patanjali*, London, Faber and Faber Limited, 1937. It contains an English translation of the aphorisms of Patañjali with some notes.

Rāmānanda Sarasvatī (or Yati), *Pātañjaladarśanam, with a gloss called Maṇiprabhā*, Benares, Vidya vilas Press, Benares Sanskrit Series—No. 75, 1903. It contains the aphorisms of Patañjali together with the commentary *Maṇiprabhā.*

Rāma Prasāda, *The Yoga Sūtras of Patañjali*, Allahabad, Sacred Books of the Hindus, 1924. It contains the aphorisms of Patañjali, the commentary of Vyāsa, the sub-commentary of Vācaspati Miśra and a complete English translation.

Rām Śarmā, *Yoga-darśana*, Barelī, Uttar Pradesh, Saṃskṛti Saṃsthān, 1967. It contains the aphorisms of Patañjali, and a Hindi translation and commentary.

Svāmī Vijñānāśrama, *Pātañjala Yogadarśanam*, Ajmer, Madanlāl Lakṣmīnivās Caṃḍak, 1961. It contains the aphorisms of Patañjali, the commentaries of Vyāsa and Bhoja and a translation into Hindi of the aphorisms and of both commentaries.

I. K. Taimni, *The Science of Yoga. A Commentary on the Yoga-sūtras of Patañjali in the light of modern thought*, Adyar, Madras, India, The Theosophical Publishing House, 1965. It contains the aphorisms of Patañjali, together with an English translation and commentary.

Vijñānabhikṣu, *Yogasārasaṃgraha*, ed. Svāmī Sanātanadeva, Delhi-Vārāṇasī-Paṭna, Motīlāl Banārsīdāss, *s. d.*. It contains its Sanskrit text together with a Hindi translation.

Vijñānabhikṣu, *Yoga-sāra-saṅgraha*, Adyar, Madras, India, Theosophical Publishing House, T.P.H. Oriental Series No. 10, 1933. It contains the Sanskrit text,together with an English translation by Gaṅgānātha Jhā.

Vijñānabhikṣu, *Yogavārtikam*, ed. Rāmakṛṣṇaśāstrī and Keśavaśāstrī, in *The Pandit* Vol. V (1883) and Vol. VI (1884), Benares.

Vijñānabhikṣu, *Yogavārttika*, Text with English translation and critical notes along with the text and English translation of the Pātañjala Yogasūtras and Vyāsabhāṣya, by T. S. Rukmani. Vol. 1 *Samādhipāda*, Delhi, Munshiram Manoharlal Publishers, 1981.

Swami Vivekānanda, *Raja-Yoga or conquering the internal nature*, Calcutta, Advaita Ashrama, 1966. It contains the aphorisms of Patañjali with an English translation and commentary.

M. R. Yardi, *The Yoga of Patañjali*, Poona, India, Bhandarkar Oriental Research Institute, Bhandarkar Oriental Series No. 12, 1979. It contains an Introduction, the Sanskrit text of the *Yogasūtras*, an English translation and Notes.

Yogadarśanam, Banāras, B. K. Śāstrī, 1939. It contains the aphorisms of Patañjali, the Sanskrit commentary of Kṛṣṇavallabha; the commentary of Bhoja together with a Sanskrit sub-commentary on it.

The Yogasūtram by Maharṣī Patañjali with the Yogapradīpika Commentary by Pandit Baladewa Miśra, ed. by Dhundhiraj Śastri, Benares, Chowkhamba, 1931. It contains the aphorisms of Patañjali together with the commentary *Yogapradīpika.*

J. H. Woods, "The Yoga-sūtras of Patañjali as illustrated by the Commentary entitled The Jewel's Lustre or Maṇiprabhā", in *Journal of the American Oriental Society*, 39, 1915, pp. 1-114. It contains the English translation of the commentary *Maṇiprabhā*.

J. H. Woods, *The Yoga-System of Patañjali or the Ancient Hindu Doctrine of Concentration of Mind*, Delhi-Varanasi-Patna, Motilal Banarsidass, 1966. It contains the translation into English of the aphorisms of Patañjali, the commentary of Vyāsa, and the sub-commentary of Vācaspati Miśra.

Studies

Swami Abhedānanda, *How to be a Yogi*, Calcutta, Ramakrishna Vedanta Math, 1962.

Swami Abhedānanda, *Yoga Psychology*, Calcutta, Ramakrishna Vedanta Math, 1960.

R. Sh. Bhattacharya, *An Introduction to the Yogasūtra*, Delhi, Bharatiya Vidya Prakasana, 1985.

S. Bhattacharya, "The Concept of Videha and Prakṛti-laya in the Sāṃkhya-Yoga System", in *Annals of the Bhandarkar Oriental Research Institute*, 48 and 49, 1968, pp. 305-312.

References

Altered States of Consciousness, edited by Ch. T. Tart, New York, Anchor Books, 1972.

Altered States of Awareness, with introductions by T. J. Teyler, San Francisco, W. E. Freeman and Company (*Scientific American*), 1972.

B. K. Anand, G. S. Chhina and Baldev Singh, "Studies on Shri Ramanand Yogi during His Stay in an Air-Tight Box", in *The Indian Journal of Medical Research*, Vol. 49, No. 1, pp. 82-89, January, 19761.

B. K. Anand, G. S. Chhina, and Baldev Singh, "Some Aspects of Electroencephalographic Studies in yogis", in *Altered States of Consciousness*, pp. 515-518.

J. G. Arintero, *La evoluciôn mística en el desenvolvimiento y vitalidad de la Iglesia*, Madrid, Biblioteca de Autores Cristianos, 1959.

Atemschulung als Element der Psychotherapie, herausgegeben von L. Heyer-Grote, Darmstadt, Wissenschaftliche Buchgesellschaft, 1970.

Th. Aufrecht, *Catalogus Catalogorum, An alphabetical register of Sanskrit works and authors*, Wiesbaden, F. Steiner, 1962.

B. Bagchi and M. Wenger, "Electrophysiological correlates of some Yogi exercises", in *Electroencephalogram Clinic Neurophysiology*, 1957, Suppl. No. 7, pp. 132-149.

H. Beckh, *Buddhismus* (*Buddha und seine Lehre*), Berlin und Leipzig, W. de Gruyter, 1928.

K. T. Behanan, *Yoga a Scientific Evaluation*, New York, Dover Publications, 1937.

Th. Bernard, *Hatha Yoga, Una técnica de liberaciôn*, Buenos Aires, Ediciones Siglo Veinte, 1966.

J. Bernhart, *Die Philosophische Mystik des Mittelalters von ihren antiken Ursprüngen bis zur Renaissance*, Darmstadt, Wissenschaftliche Buchgesellschaft, 1967.

J. Bronkhorst, "God in Sāṃkhya", in *Wiener Zeitschrift für die Kunde Südasiens und Archiv für indische Philosophie*, Band XXVII, 1983, pp. 149-164.

Th. Brosse, *Etudes Instrumentales des Techniques du Yoga, Expérimentation psychosomatique*, Précédé de *La nature du Yoga dans sa tradition* par J. Filliozat, Paris, Ecole Francaise d'Extreme-Orient-A. Maisonneuve, 1963.

G. Bugault, *La notion de "prajñā" ou de sapience selon les perspectives du "Mahāyāna"*, Paris, Editions E.de Broccard, 1968.

S. Chatterjee, *The Nyāya Theory of Knowledge*, Calcutta, University of Calcutta, 1965.

L. Chertok, *L' Hypnose*, Paris, Payot, 1972.

C. M. Codd, *Introduction to Patañjali's Yoga*, Adyar, Madras, India, The Theosophical Publishing House, 1966.

G. Coster, *Yoga and Western Psychology. A comparison*, London, Oxford University Press, 1957.

A. Cuvillier, *Essai sur la mystique de Malebranche*, Paris, J. Vrin, 1954.
A. Daniélou, *Yoga. The Method of Re-Integration*, London, Christopher Johnson, 1954.
N. Das and H. Gastaut, "Variations de l'activité éléctrique du cerveau, de coeur et des muscles squelettiques au cours de la méditation et de l'extase yoguique", in *Electroencephalogram Clinic Neurophysiology*, 1955, Suppl. 6, pp. 211-219.
S. N. Dasgupta, *Yoga As Philosophy and Religion*, Delhi, Motilal Banarsidass, 1973.
S. N. Dasgupta, *Yoga Philosophy in relation to other Systems of Indian Thought*, Delhi, Motilal Banarsidass, 1974.
S. N. Dasgupta, *A History of Indian Philosophy*, Cambridge, At the University Press, 1961-1966. Reprint, Motilal Banarsidass, Delhi.
J. M. Dechanet, *Yoga cristiano en diez lecciones*, Bilbao, Desclée de Brouwer, 1970.
Der Weg des autogenen Trainings, Herausgegeben von D. Langen, Darmstadt, Wissenschaftliche Buchgesellschaft, 1968.
P. Deussen, *Allgemeine Geschichte der Philosophie*, Leipzig, 1894 ff.
P. Dukes, *Yoga*, Barcelona, Brughera, 1966.
M. Eliade, *Patañjali et le Yoga*, Paris, Editions du Seuil, 1962.
M. Eliade, *Techniques du Yoga*, Paris, Gallimard, 1948.
M. Eliade, *Yoga, Immortality and Freedom*, New York, Pantheon Books-Bollingen Series LVI, 1958.
Entretiens 1955 par J. Monchanin, J. Filliozat, A. Bareau, Pondichéry, Institut Français d'Indologie, 1956.
W. Y. Evans-Wentz, *Tibetan Yoga and Secret Doctrines*, Oxford, Oxford University Press, 1967.
G. Feuerstein, *The Yoga-Sūtra of Patañjali. An exercise in the Methodology of Textual Analysis*, New Delhi, Arnold-Heinemann, 1979.
E. Frauwallner, *Geschichte der indischen Philosophie*, I. Band, Salzburg, Otto Müller, 1953.
R. Garbe, "Sāṅkhya", in *Encycolopaedia of Religion and Ethics*, ed. by J. Hastings, Vol. XI, Edinburgh, T. & T. Clark, 1962, pp. 189-192.
R. Garbe, *Sāṃkhya und Yoga*, Strassburg, Karl J. Trübner, 1896.
R. Garbe, *Die Sāṃkhya-Philosophie*, Leipzig, H. Haessel, 1917.
E. Gilson, *La philosophie de Saint Bonaventure*, Paris, Vrin, 1953.
E. Gilson, *La Théologie Mystique de Saint Bernard*, Paris, J. Vrin, 1969.
B. Gindes, *Nuevos conceptos sobre el hipnotismo*, Buenos Aires, Editorial Psique, 1965.
H. von Glasenapp, *Die Philosophie der Inder. Eine Einführung in ihre Geschichte und ihre Lehren*, Stuttgart, Alfred Kröner, 1958.
B. Gupta, "Savikalpa pratyakṣa (judgemental perception) as Viśiṣṭa jñāna," in *Our Heritage*, 4, Calcutta, 1956, pp. 107, 114.

H. Hatzfeld, *Estudios Literarios sobre mística española*, Madrid, España, Gredos, 1968.

J. W. Hauer, *Der Yoga, ein indischer Weg zum Selbst*, Stuttgart, Kohlhammer, 1958. It also contains the aphorisms of Patañjali and a German translation by the author.

F. Heiler, *Die buddhistische Versenkung, Eine Religionsgeschichtliche Untersuchung*, München, Ernst Reinhardt, 1922.

P. Humbertclaude, *La Doctrine Ascétique de Saint Basile de Césarée*, Paris, G. Beauchesne, 1932.

H. Jacobi, "Über das ursprüngliche Yogasystem", in *Sitzungsberichte der Preussischen Akademie der Wissenschaften. Phil-hist.Kl.* 1929, pp. 581-624 (—*Kleine Schriften*, Herausgegeben von B. Kölver, Wiesbaden, Franz Steiner, 1970, pp. 682-725, Teil 2).

H. Jacobi, "Über das ursprüngliche Yogasystem. Nachträge und Indices", in *Sitzungsberichte der Preussischen Akademie der Wissenschaften. Phil.-hist.Kl.* 1930, pp. 322-332 (=*Kleine Schriften*, pp. 726-736, Teil 2).

H. Jacobi, "The dates of the philosophical Sūtras of the Brahmans", in *Journal of the American Oriental Society*, 31, 1911, pp. 1-29 (=*Kleine Schriften* herausgegeben von B. Kölver, Wiesbaden, Franz Steiner, 1970, pp. 559-587.

F.—D. Joret, *La Contemplation Mystique d'après Saint Thomas d'Aquin*, Lille-Bruges-Bruxelles, Société Saint Augustin-Desclée de Brouwer, 1923.

Y. Jovananda, *Prácticas de concentración y meditación*, Buenos Aires, 1971.

A. Kasamatsu and T. Hirai, "Science of zazen", in *Psychologia*, 1963, 6, pp. 86-91.

A. Kasamatsu and T. Hirai, "An Electroencephalographic Study on the Zen Meditation (Zazen)", in *Altered States of Consciousness*, pp. 501-514.

A. Kasamatsu, T. Okuma, S. Takenaka, E. Koga, K. Ikeda, and H. Sugiyama, "The EEG of "Zen" and "Yoga" Practitioners", in *EEG Clinic Neurophysiology*, 1957, 9, pp. 51-52.

A. B. Keith, *Sāṁkhya System, A History of the Samkhya Philosophy*, Calcutta, Y.M.C.A. Publishing House, 1949.

G. M. Koelman, *Pātañjala Yoga, From related Ego to Absolute Self*, Poona, Papal Athenaeum, 1970.

W. S. Kroger, *Clinical and Experimental Hypnosis.* In *Medicine, Dentistry and Psychology*, Philadelphia and Montreal, J. P. Lippincott Company 1963.

S. Kuvalayānanda, *Āsanas*, Bombay, Popular Prakashan, 1964.

S. Kuvalayānanda, *Prāṇāyāma*, Bombay, Popular Prakashan, 1966.

G. J. Larson, *Classical Sāṃkhya. An Interpretation of its History and its Meaning*, Delhi, Motilal Banarsidass, 1969.

Ch. Laubry et Th. Brosse, "Documents recueillis aux Indes sur les "Yoguis" par l'enregistrement simultané du pouls, de la respiration et de l'éléctro-cardiogramme", in *Presse Médicale*, No. 83, 14 oct. 1936.

A. H, Maslow, *Religions, values and peak-experiences*, U.S.A., Penguin Books, 1978.

P. Masson-Oursel, *Esquisse d'une Histoire de la Philosophie Indienne*, Paris, Paul Geuthner, 1923.

P. Masson-Oursel, *El Yoga*, Buenos Aires, Editorial Universitaria de Buenos Aires, 1966.

R. de Maumigny, *La práctica de la oración mental, Oración Ordinaria, Oración Extraordinaria*, Madrid, Editorial Razón y Fe, 1962.

A.-M. Meynard, *Théologie Ascêtique et Mystique*, Paris, P.Lethielleux, 1923.

Max Müller, *The Six Systems of Indian Philosophy*, Varanasi, Chowkhamba Sanskrit Series Office—The Cowkhamba Sanskrit Studies Vol.XVI,1199.

W. Michel, *La respiration volontaire. Recherches sur ses bases physiologiques*, Paris, Librairie Maloine, 1951.

R. Mishra, *Fundamentos de Yoga. Manual de Teoría, Práctica y Aplicación*, Buenos Aires, Editorial Dédalo, 1973.

K. K. Mittal, "Problem of Perception", in *Buddhist Studies*, University of Delhi, No. 6, May, 1979, pp. 36-38.

C. Naranjo and R. Orstein, *On the Psychology of Meditation*, Dallas, Pennsylvania, Penguin Books, 1977.

G. Oberhammer, "Meditation und Mystik im Yoga des Patañjali", in *Wiener Zeitschrift für die Kunde Süd- und Ostasiens und Archiv für indische Philosophie* IX, 1965, pp. 98-118.

G. Oberhammer, *Strukturen yogischer Meditation*, Wien, Verlag der österreichischen Akademie der Wissenschaften, 1977.

G. Oberhammer, "Die Gotteserfahrung in der yogischen Meditation", in *Offenbarung als Heilserfahrung im Christentum, Hinduismus und Buddhismus*, Freiburg, Herder, 1982, pp. 145-166.

M. P. Pandit, *Kuṇḍalinī Yoga, A brief Study of Sir John Woodroffe's "The Serpent Power"*, Madras, Ganesh & Co., 1962.

F. Poli, *Yoga ed esicasmo*, Bologna, Editrice Missionaria Italiana, 1981.

K. H. Potter, *Encyclopedia of Indian Philosophies. Bibliography*, Delhi, Motilal Banarsidass, 1983.

Problemas actuales de la Hipnosis, Comp. por G. H. Estabrooks, México, Fondo de Cultura Económica, 1967.

Radhakrishnan, *Indian Philosophy*, London, G. Allen & Unwin Ltd., 1962.

Rai Bahadur Srisa Chandra Vasa, *An Introduction to the Yoga Philosophy*, New Delhi, Oriental Books Reprint Corporation, 1975.

Y. Ramacharaka, *Ciencia Hindú-Yogi de la Respiración*, Barcelona, España, Antonio Roch, *s.d.*

References

V. G. Rele, *The Mysterious Kundalini*, Bombay, Taraporevala, 1960.

L. Renou, "On the Identity of the two Patañjalis", in *The Indian Historical Quarterly*, XVI, 1940, pp. 586-591.

T. S. Rukmani, "Vikalpa as Defined by Vijñānabhikṣu in the Yogavārttika", in *Journal of Indian Philosophy*, ed. Bimal Matilal, Vol. 8, No. 4, Dec. 1980, pp. 385-392.

R. Schmidt, *Fakire und Kakirtum im alten und modernen Indien*, Berlin, Verlag von H. Barsdorf, 1921.

J. H. Schultz, *El entrenamiento autógeno. Autorrelajacion concentrativa. Exposición Clínicopráctica*, Madrid, España, Editorial Cientifico Médica, 1969.

E. Sénart, "Origines Bouddhiques", en *Conférences faites au Musée Guimet*, Paris, Ernest Leroux, 1907, pp. 115-158.

E. Sénart, "Bouddhisme et Yoga", in *Revue de l'Histoire des Religions*, Paris, Vol. 42, nov. 1900, pp. 345-364.

Ch. Sharma, *A Critical Survey of Indian Philosophy*, London, Rider & Company, 1960.

D. N. Shastri, "The Distinction between Nirvikalpaka and Savikalpaka Perception in Indian Philosophy", in *Proceedings of the All-India Oriental Conference*, 16, 1955, pp. 310-321.

J. Sinha, *A History of Indian Philosophy*, Calcutta, Sinha Publishing House, Central Book Agency, 1956 (vol.I), 1952 (vol.II).

J. Sinha, *Indian Psychology*, Calcutta, Sinha Publishing House, 1958 (vol.I), 1961 (vol.II).

S. Siddheswarananda, *El Raja Yoga de San Juan de la Cruz*, México, Editorial Orion, 1959.

S. Sivananda, *Concentration and Meditation*, Sivanandanagar, India, The Divine Life Society, 1969.

S. S. Sivananda, *Kundalini Yoga*, Buenos Aires, Editorial Kier, 1968.

S. Sivananda, *The Science of Pranayama*, Sivanandanagar, India, The Divine Life Society, 1967.

S. Sivananda, *Practical Lessons in Yoga*, Sivanandanagar, India, The Divine Life Society, 1963.

S. Shivapremananda, *Aspectos Filosóficos y Sicológicos del Yoga*. Santiago, Chile, Centro Sivananda de Yoga, 1972.

Ch. Solley and G. Murphy, *Development of the perceptual World*, Chapter 14, New York, 1960, pp. 288-317.

L. Sparks, *Autohipnosis. Una técnica de respuestas condicionadas*, Buenos Aires, Ediciones Troquel, 1962.

Th. Stcherbatsky, *The Conception of Buddhist nirvāṇa*, London—The Hague-Paris, Mouton & Co, 1965.

R. Thibaut, *La Unión con Dios,según las Cartas de Dirección Espiritual de Dom Columba Marmion*, Buenos Aires, Editorial Difusión, 1939.

F. Tola and C. Dragonetti, *Yoga y Miśtica de la India*, Buenos Aires, Editorial Kier, 1978.

E. Underhill, *Mysticism. A Study in the Nature and Development of Man's Spiritual Consciousness*, London, Methuen, 1960.

L. de la Vallée Poussin, *Nirvāṇa*, Paris, Gabriel Beauchesne, 1925.

L.de la Vallée Poussin, "Le Bouddhisme et le Yoga de Patañjali", in *Mélanges Chinois et Bouddhiques* 5, 1936-1937, pp. 223-242. Bruxelles.

S. Vijoyananda, *El Eterno Compañero Brahmananda. Biografía y Enseñanzas Espirituales*, Buenos Aires, Editorial Kier, 1961.

W. Völker, *Kontemplation und Ekstase bei Pseudo-Dionysus Areopagita*, Wiesbaden, F. Steiner, 1958.

R. K. Wallace and H. Benson, "The Physiology of Meditation", in *Altered States of Awareness* (Readings from *Scientific American*), pp. 125-131.

R. K. Wallace, "Physiological Effects of Transcendental Meditation", in *Science*, Vol. 167, No. 3926, pp. 1751-1754, March 27, 1970.

R. K. Wallace, H. Benson and A. F. Wilson, "A Wakeful Hypometabolic Physiologic State", in *American Journal of Physiology*, Vol. 221, No. 3, pp. 795-799, September, 1971.

M. Wenger, B. Bagchi and B. Anand, "Experiments in India on "voluntary" control of the heart and pulse", in *Circulation*, 1961, 24, pp. 1319-1325.

K. Werner, *Yoga and Indian Philosophy*, Delhi, Motilal Banarsidass, 1977.

M. Winternitz, *History of Indian Literature*, Vol. III, Part II (Scientific Literature), Delhi, Motilal Banarsidass, 1967.

E. Wood, *Yoga*, Harmondsworth, England, Penguin Books, 1962.

E. Wood, *Yoga Prcático. Antiguo y moderno*, México, Editorial Orion, 1956.

E. Wood, *Curso Práctico de Concentración Mental*, Beuenos Aires, Editorial Kier, 1969.

P. Yogananda, *Autobiography of a Yogi*, Los Angeles, California, Self-Realization Fellowship Publishers, 1959.

S. Yogendra, *Yoga in Modern Life*, Bombay, The Yoga Institute, 1966.

Other Texts

Amarasinha, *Amarakocha*, ed. Loiseleur Deslongchamps, Paris, Imprimerie Royale, 1839-1845.

Bonaventura, *Itinerarium mentis in Deum*, Münche, Kösel, 1961.

L.de la Palma, *Obras*, Madrid, Biblioteca de Autores Cristianos, 1967.

R. Descartes, *Regulae ad directionem ingenii*, ed. G. Le Roy, Paris, Boivin, 1933.

Dharmarāja Adhvarīndra, *Vedānta-paribhāṣā*, Calcutta, Ramakrishna Mission, 1963. It contains, besides the Sanskrit text, the translation by S. Mādhavānanda.

Dionysius, "De Mystica Theologia", in Mígne, *Patrologia Graeca*, Vol.III, 997-1064, Paris, 1889.

References

Dionisio, "Sobre la Teología Mística", texto griego, traducción y notas de C. M. Herrán y M. Riani, in *Cuadernos de Filosofía* de la Universidad de Buenos Aires (Argentina), No. 9, 1968.

Meister Eckhart, *Deutsche Predigten und Traktate,* ed. J. Quint, München, Goldmann Verlag, 1955.

Saint François de Sales, *Traité de l'amour de Dieu,* Bruxelles, A. Dewit, 1923.

Gauḍapāda ,*The Sāṃkhyakārikā of Īśvarakṛṣṇa,* ed. T. G. Mainkar, Poona, Oriental Book Agency, 1964.

Jamblique, *Les mysterès d'Egipte,* ed. des Places, Paris, Lex Belles Letters, 1966.

San Juan de la Cruz, *Obras,* Burgos, Tipogragia de "El Monte Carmelo", 1943.

G. W. Leibniz, *Opuscula philosophica selecta,* ed. P. Schrecker, Paris, J. Vrin, 1959.

M. de Molinos, *Guía Espiritual,* Barcelona, Barral Editores, 1974.

Sāṃkhyasūtram, ed. Rāma Shaṅkara Bhaṭṭācārya, Vārāṇasī, Prācyabhāratīprakāśanam, 1964. It contains the *Sāṃkhyasūtras* and the commentary of Aniruddha.

Sāṃkhya-pravacana-bhāṣya or Commentary on the Exposition of the Sāṅkhya Philosophy by Vijñānabhikṣu, ed. R. Garbe, Cambridge Mass., The Harvard University Press, 1943. It contains the *Sāṃkhyasūtras* and the commentary of Vijñānabhikṣu.

Śaṅkara, *Brahmasūtra Bhāṣya, with the Commentaries Bhāmatī, Kalpataru and Parimala,* ed. M. A. Śāstrī, Bombay, Nirṇaya Sāgar Press, 1938.

Santa Teresa de Jesús, *Obras Completas,* Madrid, Biblioteca de Autores Cristianos, 1947.

S. Thomae Aquinatis, *In librum Beati Dionysii de divinis nominibus expositio,* ed. C. Pera, Roma, Marietti, 1950.

S. Thomae Aquinatis, *Summa Theologiae* II, 2, ed. P. Caramello, Roma, Marietti, 1962.

F. Tola, *Doctrinas Secretas de la India. Las Upanishads,* Barcelona, España, Barral Editores, 1973.

Bibliography

H. R. Jarrell, *International Yoga Bibliography,* 1950 *to* 1980, Metuchen, N. J. and London, The Scaregrow Press, 1981.

P. Schreiner, *Yoga. Grundlagen, Methoden Ziele. Eine bibliographischer Uberblick,* Köln, E. J. Brill, 1979.

INDEX OF SANSKRIT TERMS

Abhāva	I·10, 29 : non-existence
Abhyāsa	I·12, 13, 18, 32 : effort for stability
Adhyātma	I·47 : inner
Āgama	I·7 : testimony
Alabdhabhūmikatva	I·30 : lake of initiative
Ālambana	I·10, 38 : foundation, support
Ālasya	I·30 : indolence
Aliṅga	I·45 : undetermined
Ānanda	I·17 : bliss
Anavasthitatva	I·30 : inconstancy
Aṅgamejayatva	I·31 : corporal agitation
Antarāya	I·29, 30 : obstacle
Anubhūta	I·11 : perceived
Anumāna	I·7, 49 : inference
Añjanatā	I·41 : coloration
Apuṇya	I·33 : demerit
Artha	I·28, 32, 42, 43, 49 : meaning, object
Asaṃpramoṣa	I·11 : non-complete disappearance
Āśaya	I·24 : accumulation
Asmitā	I·17 : consciousness of existence
Avirati	I·30 : non-cessation
Bhava	I·19 : condition
Bhāvana	I·28 : evocation
Bhrāntidarśana	I·30 : erratic perception
Bīja	I·25 : seed
Citta	I·2, 30, 33, 37 : mind
Daurmanasya	I·31 : mental unease
Dhyāna	I·39 : meditation

Prasāda	I·47 : quietude
Prasādana	I·33 : serenity
Praśvāsa	I·31 : expiration
Pratyakcetanā	I·29 : introverted consciousness
Pratyakṣa	I·7 : perception
Pratyaya	I·10, 18, 19 : experience
Pravṛtti	I·35 : continued process
Puṇya	I·33 : merit
Puruṣa	I·16, 24 : spirit
Ṛtaṃbhara	I·48 : which bears the truth
Sabīja	I·46 : with seed
Samādhi	I·20, 46, 51 : concentration
Samāpatti	I·41
Saṃprajñāta	I·17 : with knowledge
Saṃśaya	I·30 : indecision
Saṃskāra	I·18, 50 : subliminal impression
Saṃvega	I·21 : fervour
Sārūpya	I·4 : identification
Sarvajña	I·25 : omniscient
Savicāra	I·44 : with analysis (of subtle object)
Savitarka	I·42 : with analysis (of gross object)
Śabda	I·9, 42 : word
Śraddhā	I·20 : faith
Śvāsa	I·31 : inspiration
Smṛti	I.6, 11, 20, 43 : attention-memory
Stha (tā)	I·41 : establishment
Sthiti	I·13, 35 : stability
Styāna	I·30 : apathy
Sukha	I·33 : happiness
Sūkṣma	I·44, 45 : subtle
Svapna	I·38 : dream, oniric fantasy

Tattva, see Ekatattva

Upekṣā	I·33 : indifference

Vairāgya I·12, 15 : detachment
Vaiśāradya I·47 : transparence
Vaitṛṣṇya I·16 : indifference
Vastu I·9 : thing
Vicāra I·17 : analysis (of subtle object)
Videha I·19: disembodied
Vikalpa I·6, 9, 42
Vikṣepa I·30, 31 : dispersion
Vipāka I·24 : consequence
Viparyaya I·6, 8 : error
Virāma I·18 : cessation
Vīrya I·20 : energy
Viṣaya I·11, 15, 33, 37, 44, 49 : object
Viṣayavat I·45 : with object
Viśoka I·36 : without pain
Vītarāga I·37 : a being devoid of passion
Vitarka I·17 : analysis (of gross object)
Vṛtti I·2, 4, 5, 10, 41 : process
Vyādhi I·30 : sickness

Yoga I·1, 2